T0006485

'Ranges elegantly over a range of literary figures . . . a very readable account of the thrill of discovering literature . . . It is a touchingly reticent and romantic book'

Literary Review

'The nation's most prominent Shakespeare scholar tells us about his schooldays, his lifelong passion for the theatre and the key steps of his academic career . . . Bate's recollection . . . is touching . . . Where Bate deals with his mother's depression, personal experience casts light on Shakespeare's treatment of mental illness . . . At the end of the book we feel we have been on a journey'

Spectator

'Enjoyable . . . The book emphasises Shakespeare's work as a source of company and consolation, and explores its effect on other writers he discovered along the way, all of whom suffered from mental health problems, among them Sylvia Plath, Virginia Woolf, Mary Lamb and Samuel Johnson'

New Statesman

'Admirably, Bate resists the now jaundiced temptations of the literary self-help tome, though you can see where he could've succumbed and produced a softer, pastel-hued book, with title to match – How Shakespeare Saved My Life, or something similarly hideous. We get wisdom here, not rules. Shakespeare doesn't save Bate's life: Shakespeare helps him live it'

The Tablet

'Bate weaves his readings of Shakespeare – as of Johns Donne and Clare, and Samuel Johnson – into the dramatist's lightly sketched career, engaging informatively with his life and theatrical history . . . The book's central achievement is to affirm the value of enthusiastic and knowledgeable literature teaching at school as formative, not only in shaping a career, but also in creating the inner resources that can be drawn on in a crisis; Shakespeare as a lifelong and enriching alternative to religious faith'

TLS

'Jonathan Bate's book is an encouraging and welcome reminder of the importance of reading and talking about reading with young people, and proof of the layers of (to paraphrase Samuel Johnson) enjoyment and endurance strengthened by doing so. I hope lots of English teachers will read it and take heart'

**Dr Katy Ricks,
Chief Master of King Edward's School**

Also by Jonathan Bate

Bright Star, Green Light
Radical Wordsworth
How the Classics Made Shakespeare
Ted Hughes
Shakespeare Staging the World (with Dora Thornton)
English Literature
Soul of the Age
John Clare
The Song of the Earth
The Cure for Love
The Genius of Shakespeare
Shakespeare and Ovid

As editor

Stressed Unstressed: Classic Poems to Ease the Mind (co-editor)
The RSC Shakespeare: Complete Works (with Eric Rasmussen)
John Clare: Selected Poems
The Arden Shakespeare: Titus Andronicus

Mad About Shakespeare

Life Lessons from the Bard

JONATHAN BATE

WILLIAM COLLINS

William Collins
An imprint of HarperCollins*Publishers*
1 London Bridge Street
London SE1 9GF

WilliamCollinsBooks.com

HarperCollins*Publishers*
Macken House, 39/40 Mayor Street Upper,
Dublin 1, D01 C9W8, Ireland

First published in Great Britain in 2022 by William Collins
This William Collins paperback edition published in 2023

1

ISBN 978-0-00-816749-3

Typeset in Bembo by Palimpsest Book Production Ltd, Falkirk, Stirlingshire
Printed and bound in the UK using 100% renewable electricity
at CPI Group (UK) Ltd

MIX
Paper | Supporting
responsible forestry
FSC™ C007454

This book is produced from independently certified FSC™ paper
to ensure responsible forest management.

For more information visit: www.harpercollins.co.uk/green

For Stanley Wells –
and all teachers who are mad about Shakespeare

Contents

Are all the people mad?
(*Twelfth Night*)

I felt rather lonely this morning so I went and unbox'd a Shakespeare – 'There's my Comfort'.
(John Keats)

INTERVIEWER: *Which are your favorite contemporary writers?*
NABOKOV: Shakespeare.
INTERVIEWER: *We said 'contemporary'.*
NABOKOV: Always Shakespeare.

My offering is a period piece. I hope you may enjoy looking back over my shoulder.
(David Niven, *The Moon's a Balloon*)

1.

My Father's Shakespeare

My father's Shakespeare was the New Temple Edition. Pocket-sized, with bright-red boards, they sat in a row on their own little shelf above the mahogany wireless around which we gathered as a family to listen to the plummy voice of Roy Plomley's weekly presentation of *Desert Island Discs* on the BBC Home Service. 'And what book would you take, apart from the Bible and the Complete Works of Shakespeare, which are already there?' I wish I had asked my mother and father what book they would have chosen, but the presence of the Bible by their bed and the New Temple Shakespeares in the living room readied the house for the castaways who were regularly invited into our home.

My mother believed that hospitality was a duty; her mother had taken in evacuees during the war. Once a month on a Sunday afternoon we entertained a boy from the local school for the blind, a reminder to me and my brother how privileged we were to have our sight. And every Christmas we welcomed a lonely Australian or Malaysian student via a scheme organized by the Commonwealth Institute in London. That was the only time of year when another wartime rule – a frugal table – was broken.

We didn't have a television at the time of Winston Churchill's funeral, so we watched it at a neighbour's home. I laid out an imitation of the procession through the streets of London with my toy soldiers on the dining-room table. Even at the age of six and a half, I sensed that it was the end of the era that had shaped my parents.

Four years later, in 1969, we were propelled into the future, watching the moon landing on our first black and white television. It had taken the place of the big old radio with its visible valves, white knobs and the red line on the dial that moved across the names of stations near and far. The incomplete set of the New Temple Shakespeares remained on the shelf above all through my teens, as if in a shrine. I didn't open them until it was too late.

Much Ado About Nothing has never been my favourite Shakespearean comedy. Over the years, my personal number-one comedy spot has flipped between *A Midsummer Night's Dream*, *The Winter's Tale* and *Twelfth Night*. But there is one speech in *Much Ado* that I can never get out of my head. Claudio has been tricked into believing that his fiancée Hero has been unfaithful to him on the eve of their marriage. His gullibility in this regard is a black mark against his character, so he is forced to pay a heavy price. A Friar assists in a cunning plan to make him believe that Hero has died of shock and shame because of the way in which he has denounced her as a whore in the middle of their wedding ceremony. The Friar then delivers a homily that includes the lines

　　for it so falls out
That what we have we prize not to the worth
Whiles we enjoy it; but, being lacked and lost,
Why, then we rack the value, then we find
The virtue that possession would not show us
Whiles it was ours.

You never really value what you have until you have lost it.
Until it is too late. Or who you have, and what their virtues
were. This is especially true if you are a teenager, hormonally
programmed *not* to value the virtues espoused by your parents.

★

It was the summer holidays in early August 1978, the long vaca-
tion after my first year at university. I was running a show called
Magic Circus. We were a small company of student actors who
toured around the village primary schools of Kent, taking the
children off their parents' hands for an afternoon. Things always
went best when the weather was good, allowing the children
to run around and the theatre games to fill the playground while
artwork could be created inside. The afternoon in the village of
Weald was a tough one because it never stopped raining. In the
evening, I flopped in front of the television and chatted to my
mother and father. For some reason, we found ourselves looking
through albums of old black and white photographs of their
wedding and my childhood. I told myself that it was time to
ask my father to tell me about his life before getting married.
Something of which I only had the sketchiest outline: childhood
in Frinton-on-Sea, Classical Studies at Cambridge in the late
1920s with the alcoholic novelist Malcolm Lowry as his friend,

3

schoolteaching in Eastbourne and Warwickshire, then the war. But it was late by then, and I was tired. We could pick up the conversation tomorrow or tomorrow or tomorrow.

I wasn't paid for directing the Magic Circus, so I also had a morning job, teaching English language to a class of Greek schoolchildren who had taken up summer residence in Walthamstow Hall, the local girls' school. That next day, in the middle of second period, a wasp appeared. I got up to chase it and knocked a book off the table. At that moment Costi Dardoufas, the teacher who organized the summer school, came through the door. I thought he was going to tell me off for horsing around. But he just said, 'There's someone to see you.' He led me up the passage, in silence. It was Tom Mason, one of the teachers at my school and also our next-door neighbour. He told me it was my father's heart.

'How bad is he?' I asked. I knew in my heart that he was dead. Besides, that would be better than a long illness – there had been enough of those in the family. Better death than a half-life of confinement. Uncle Tom, as we used to call him when we were children, said briefly what had happened as he drove me home, after Costi had put his arm round my shoulders and told me I needn't work again.

The drive up the town had never seemed longer. I remembered the previous weekend: Dad had played his last game of cricket on a beautiful village ground nestling below the Downs. He had made twelve runs and was delighted to hear in the evening that I had scored a fifty on the same day. It was my parents' twenty-fourth anniversary, so we had gone out to dinner – a very rare treat in the 1970s. That must have been why the wedding album was still on the coffee table a few nights later.

At home, there was the family doctor and a policeman. Dad had been dead on the doctor's arrival. He had been tutoring a boy in the dining room and had apparently called Mum to come quickly. The boy was sent home. Typical Dad, teaching till the last minute. He had said that there was a terrible pain above his heart and he couldn't breathe, so he went and lay down while Mum phoned for the doctor and ran next door to Beryl Mason, who had been a nurse. She was with him when he died, while Mum was waiting at the window for the doctor.

I didn't go straight in to see Mum. First, I answered the policeman's questions and talked a little to Dr Harrison. Twenty years earlier, he had delivered me to life in the very bed on which my father had just died.

I failed in my attempt to leave a message for my brother, who was living away from home, but succeeded in telling my friends that I wouldn't be able to do Magic Circus that afternoon. I put my father's watch and wedding ring in a drawer, then went in to see my mother. She wept but was never hysterical. 'But why so soon?' she asked. I remembered a friend of hers saying, just a few weeks before, 'Enjoy him while you have him.' I began to wonder whether I had failed to heed that advice myself.

The policeman asked me to identify the body for the coroner's case, because it was a heart attack and Dad had no previous cardiac history. Then I realized that he had seemed tired the last few days, and apparently he had told Beryl that he felt a bit off on his bike one day, which made me feel guilty that through the summer I had too often hogged the family Mini.

The room was cold and dark with a musty smell. He was

wrapped in the counterpane, more like a thing than a person. Dr Harrison removed the cover and I saw the head. Mouth open as in sleep, face thin and blue. At least there was no sign of pain. Later, Mum talked of him 'lying on that bed, sweating' – but he had said nothing.

I made the first phone calls to the wider family, then sat with Mum, who was in her chair staring at the blank television screen and the New Temple Shakespeares, until the policeman came to say that the body had been taken away. I put his clothes and shoes in the wardrobe, went downstairs to tidy away the books with which he had been teaching. His typewriter was on his desk, a piece of writing half finished. What would we do with all his books?

That night I wrote out two quotations from *King Lear*:

> But his flawed heart –
> Alack, too weak the conflict to support –
> 'Twixt two extremes of passion, joy and grief,
> Burst smilingly.

And

> Vex not his ghost: O, let him pass! He hates him
> That would upon the rack of this tough world
> Stretch him out longer

If you're patient enough to persevere with him, Shakespeare will give you the words.

★

When I got round to sorting his books, I opened the New Temple Shakespeares for the first time. They were beautiful little things, each adorned with an Eric Gill woodcut on the title page. Then I made my discovery: always a methodical man, my father had written on the endpapers of each volume a note of the productions he had seen.

At random, I picked out his *Romeo and Juliet*: '27 Oct '34 Devonshire Park Theatre, Eastbourne (Touring Company).' There wouldn't have been much culture in Eastbourne during the dour years of the early 1930s. That 'touring company' bringing Shakespeare to the seaside resort's Victorian theatre, which had been given a makeover by the prolific theatre and music hall architect Frank Matcham, would have offered a rare treat. I suspected that it would not have been a distinguished version. So what must it have been like for my father to see the play again two years later in the West End? '7 Jan '36 New Theatre, London.' The legendary production in which, halfway through the run, John Gielgud and Laurence Olivier switched between the roles of Romeo and Mercutio. The young Peggy Ashcroft was Juliet and *grande dame* Edith Evans perfectly cast as the Nurse. I cursed myself for never having had the curiosity to discover that my father had seen it. Now it was too late to ask him which way round Olivier and Gielgud had played it on the night he was there.

As for the film with Leslie Howard and Norma Shearer, next on his list, I didn't even know that it existed. All I knew about Leslie Howard was that when my mother was a girl she had a crush on him in *'Pimpernel' Smith*. That was one of our favourites when she and I used to while away rainy Saturday afternoons watching old black and white movies on the television. Another was, naturally, *Brief Encounter*, romanticized by steam trains and

Rachmaninov, her favourite composer. But that was with Trevor Howard, not Leslie.

I did recall my father once saying that after he moved from Eastbourne to a school in Warwickshire, he and a girlfriend used to bicycle over to the Memorial Theatre in Stratford-upon-Avon. *Romeo* on 4 June '38 must have been one such excursion. I had never asked for stories of these expeditions, but in a rare moment of revelation about that distant past my father did once say that the relationship petered out when he went off to war. I imagine the girl as the school matron, with dark curly hair, jolly voice and floral dress, bicycling gamely to keep up with him as they whirled along lanes verged by tall grass and Queen Anne's lace.

His life was punctuated by war. 'What's your earliest memory, Dad?' my brother Michael had asked. 'Going out on to the sand dunes at Frinton, when I was six, and hearing the guns of the Somme booming across the sea.' I still find it a cause for wonder that, because my father only married in his forties, I am the grandchild of four Victorians, all born in the 1880s. My father was forty-eight when I was born; I was forty-eight when Harry, my youngest child, was born. If he and the planet stay well enough, he might live into the twenty-second century, and in that sense I will have touched four centuries. Which makes the four centuries since Shakespeare's death seem not such a long time after all.

When the second war came, my father had no hesitation in joining up. Loyal to his county, he was commissioned in the 85th (Essex) Medium Battery of the Royal Artillery, under the command of Major J. D. R. T. Tilney. If you were in the Artillery and you weren't sent to join Monty's Desert Rats in the North African theatre, you would have spent most of the war hanging around. Training, and waiting for the opening of the Second Front. While sorting through my father's books in that grieving summer of 1978, I discovered that the Battery had kept a diary in the Officers' Mess and that my father had been delegated to write it up after the war.

Several officers from his band of brothers had come to his funeral, including Major, now Sir John, Tilney. My brother's godfather, he was Member of Parliament for Liverpool Wavertree and an intimate of his recently elected party leader, Margaret Thatcher, something for which, in the circumstances, I forgave him. Over tea following the service, during which I had honoured my father's classical credentials by reading an elegiac ode of Horace in my own translation, his army friends invited me and my mother to their next annual regimental reunion, where they would toast his memory. 'Your father was the bravest man I served with,' one of them told me. 'He was mentioned in dispatches three times and really should have got the Military Cross, but he was too modest and self-effacing to let them write about what he did in that Forward Observation Post.' In the early days of the Normandy campaign he had climbed on to the roof of a church, binoculars strapped round his neck and headphones over his ears in order to radio the position of the enemy. This meant that he didn't hear the sound of the snipers firing at him, so a Canadian officer had to pull him down by the ankles. Later, as they advanced towards the Rhine, he took over the controls of a tank while under heavy fire. Finally, just as everyone was preparing for victory and being demobbed, he volunteered to join the still-unfinished war in the Far East. This earned him a medical check to establish that he was in his right mind.

The stories were all news to me. The only thing I could

remember my father ever saying about the war was that he would never forget the smell of the bloated carcasses of dead horses and the sight of refugees on bicycles or pushing their possessions in carts as he and his men trundled their howitzers and field guns through France and Belgium. So I opened the Battery Diary with genuine curiosity.

Unexpectedly, it was peppered with literary references. As on 16 August 1943:

> A peacetime Saturday afternoon at Stratford with an Avon punt sandwiched between 'Othello' and 'Winter's Tale', and this evening there are great sports v the RAF, whom we soundly defeated at football. While Rome was being declared an open city, Dvr. Scrimshaw was leaving the NAAFI manager a heap of rubble on the NAAFI floor.

I think it was Evelyn Waugh who said that the saddest words in the English language were 'too late'. It was now too late to ask my father what the officers of the Battery made of these two plays. One of them is about a general brought down by an NCO jealous of the granting of a commission to his rival. Both of them are about accusations of marital infidelity – a fear to which many a soldier in the field has been subject.

Back at university some time later, with access to a library, I dug out an old review in order to get the feel of the productions. *Othello* had opened on Shakespeare's birthday that April. The *Observer*'s critic, J. C. Trewin, concluded:

> Mr Baliol Holloway's Moor remains in the middle distance. It is hardly enough to be sonorous and direct: one misses the surge and swell of the Othello music. Mr Abraham Sofaer's

Iago is beautifully spoken, but this demi-devil of the Renaissance, his mind as swift to villainy as his hand to the sword-hilt, could hardly have been mistaken for Othello's 'man . . . of honesty and trust'. It would be happier, perhaps, if the parts were exchanged.

And exchanged they were on subsequent nights: like Olivier and Gielgud in the famous *Romeo and Juliet*, Holloway and Sofaer shared the roles of Othello and Iago. Turning to the little red New Temple Edition, I discovered that my father had in fact seen the production twice. The Battery was still stationed in Stratford in early September. He must have gone a second time in order to see what it was like with the roles reversed.

Baliol Holloway was something of an old ham, who had played the Shakespeare Memorial Theatre in Stratford-upon-Avon for decades. His best turns were comic: Malvolio in *Twelfth Night*, Parolles in *All's Well That Ends Well* (a very disreputable soldier, the antithesis of Othello), and Autolycus in *The Winter's Tale*, a role he took that wartime summer night in a production directed by Dorothy Green, another company regular, who had played Hermione back in the 1920s and Cleopatra before the Great War. Leontes was Sofaer, one of the most interesting actors of the age. Born in Rangoon to Burmese-Jewish parents, he established his reputation playing outsiders, notably Jewish-born Prime Minister Benjamin Disraeli in a Broadway production of a play called *Victoria Regina*. We think of Paul Robeson as the twentieth century's pioneering non-white Othello – he was electrifying and scandalizing New York in the role that very summer – but Abraham Sofaer also deserves to be remembered. His voice and visage were the perfect embodiment of the noble Moor.

★

By the end of 1943, the Battery had moved from their Cotswold training camp to Hove on the south coast, in preparation for what was coming soon. The officers took it in turns to make entries in the diary. Thus on 8 December:

> Should imagine that Capt. Bate is sleeping with one eye sort of half-cocked on 'Signal Training, All Arms'. But dear Lieutenant Bonnick is thinking rather on the lines 'Whenas in silks my Julia goes, / that liquefaction in her clothes – ' always of course with one eye on next week-end. To spare his bluster I'll withhold the rest of the ditty.

The lines are from an exquisite erotic lyric by the seventeenth-century Cavalier poet Robert Herrick, writing in the time of England's Civil War. The rest of the poem, in which Herrick imagines his girl's body free from the constraint of any clothes, must have been available in the Mess because it was included in *The Oxford Book of English Verse*, a copy of which travelled with the Battery.

In June 1944 they moved to Milford-on-Sea near Southampton in readiness for embarkation. One of the officers wrote in the diary: *We arrived to take our place in the stalls, just as the curtain went up on the eve of the famous 6th of June.* I appreciated the metaphor: the curtain going up as they entered the *theatre* of war. They played *one game of tennis in a peace-time club while our bombers and fighters roared over to Normandy.* And they received General Montgomery's pep talk, distributed in writing to the entire army. It included a poetic quotation:

> He either fears his fate too much,
>   Or his deserts are small,

Who dare not put it to the touch,
  To win or lose it all.

Some of the chaps wondered who the author was. They soon got their answer. Those were the days when poetry was in the blood of the officer class. The Battery Commander was able to go straight to page 364 of *The Oxford Book of English Verse* and identify the (slightly misquoted) quatrain by James Graham, 1st Marquis of Montrose, accomplished poet, tactically brilliant soldier, Covenanter turned Royalist, executed in Edinburgh in 1650 during the Civil War.

They were held back from the first wave and then diverted to the mudflats of the Thames Estuary. My father would have looked northwards and seen the sand dunes of the Essex coast from which he had heard the guns of the Somme nearly thirty years earlier when he was a boy. They rounded the Thanet shoreline, where we would spend our seaside summer holidays twenty years later when I was a boy. They hugged the English coast, witnessing doodlebugs flying overhead towards London, then crossed the roiling Channel and, dodging depth charges, disembarked on Juno Beach, which had initially been taken by the Canadian Allies.

A small envelope had dropped out when I opened the Battery Diary. It contained two letters, written in a shaky hand on wafer-thin paper, from the mother of a lance-bombardier – the artillery equivalent of lance-corporal. His name was Fisher. The first letter was a request for the details of his death. 'Don't trouble to spare me one bit as I would like to know just how he met his death and where he was buried.' She added, 'He was all that I had left.'

I had been studying for the Shakespeare paper of my English

degree all through the summer term in the months before my father's death. I had focused especially on some of the lesser-known plays such as the *Henry VI* trilogy, the historical dramas about the Wars of the Roses that he wrote early in his career. Mrs Fisher's request brought to my mind an exchange between brothers. A messenger comes on with news that the courageous Richard Plantagenet, Duke of York, has been slain on the battle-field. His eldest son, Edward, wants to be spared the details: *O, speak no more, for I have heard too much*. His youngest son, Richard, has the opposite reaction: *Say how he died, for I will hear it all*. My brother and I were like that when my father died: for him it was more than enough to hear the news, whereas I wanted to know every last detail. Mrs Fisher, all alone, wanted to hear it all.

My father must have written with an account of the circumstances, because the second letter was her response. 'I cannot really believe it to be true,' she began, 'but as he would say "Be Brave", as I have told you he was all I had, but I must now face the lonely years alone. He was such a lovely boy.' The letter went on with a request for advice about how to dispose of her boy's beloved motorcycle and the hope that there would be a little army pension. It was clear that something about the nature of his death had shocked her deeply. Leafing through the diary, I found the explanation. It had happened on their very first day in France, as they unloaded the big guns on Juno Beach:

First casualty: Lbdr. Fisher killed by a gun running over him.

Killed in an accident before the Battery had fired a shot in anger. There was nothing heroic about that. I thought of the words of the common soldier Michael Williams, when he and

John Bates argue with the disguised King Henry V in Sir Thomas Erpingham's camp on the night before Agincourt: *I am afeard there are few die well that die in a battle*. War and again war; the poetry of war. Western poetry began with war: Homer's *Iliad*. At school, our study of poetry had begun with war, with

> Gas! GAS! Quick, boys! . . .
> And each slow dusk a drawing-down of blinds.

Wilfred Owen raging against

> The old Lie: *Dulce et decorum est*
> *Pro patria mori*.

The sentiment made my father uncomfortable. He didn't believe it was a lie. He believed in duty. He was a Classics teacher; the odes of Horace were his favourite poems, along with the verse of A. E. Housman. His desert island book would probably have been either *A Shropshire Lad* or his pocket edition of Horace. Once, in the quiet voice which meant that he often lost authority in the classroom, he schooled me in the context of the phrase quoted by Owen. Horace's poem was about honour, which meant integrity. The line about it being a sweet and decorous thing to die for your country was followed by a line about cowardice, running away from battle. And the lines after that were about not bowing to the changeable wind of popular opinion. It didn't matter whether your party won or lost at the polls, the important thing was to stay true to your own principles.

An opinionated teenager, I fought back, armed with Shakespeare. One of our A-Level set texts was *Henry IV Part 1*.

I had been preparing for the exam by learning quotations. Conveniently forgetting that Sir John Falstaff is a coward and a liar who commits an atrocity on the battlefield, and that his friends run away from battle immediately after King Harry says *Once more unto the breach, dear friends*, I launched into his assault on my father's cherished value:

> Can honour set to a leg? No. Or an arm? No. Or take away the grief of a wound? No. Honour hath no skill in surgery, then? No. What is honour? A word. What is that word 'honour'? Air. A trim reckoning! Who hath it? He that died o' Wednesday. Doth he feel it? No. Doth he hear it? No. Is it insensible, then? Yea, to the dead. But will it not live with the living? No. Why? detraction will not suffer it. Therefore I'll none of it.

My father deflected. *Henry IV Part 1* was absent from the red row of his New Temple Shakespeares and the flyleaf at the back of *Part 2* was a blank, suggesting that he had not seen either of the Falstaff plays. He simply replied that *Henry V* was a play that had always meant a lot to him.

Now I knew why.

★

The evening of VE Day, Tuesday, 8 May 1945. Eighty-five (Essex) Medium Battery Royal Artillery are on one side of the Rhine, the Russians on the other. The regiment has fought for nearly a year. Their heavy guns have helped to liberate Boulogne and Calais, to clear the south bank of the River Scheldt and capture Walcheren Island, to cross the Roer, to advance through the

Reichswald Forest and reach the Rhine. They have travelled 1,285 miles and spent 211 days in action, participating in Operations Totalize, Tallulah, Wellhit, Undergo, Switchback, Infatuate, Mallard, Blackcock, Veritable, Plunder, Torchlight and Varsity. Between them, their vehicles have run up mileage in excess of three hundred thousand, using over forty thousand gallons of fuel at a cost of two shillings per gallon. They have fired over fifty thousand rounds, the shells weighing more than two thousand tons.

Captain Bate, Officer Commanding B Troop, has done the deed of bravery at the Forward Observation Post that should have won him a Military Cross. He has also had to write letters to the families of young gunners killed in action, though none could have been as hard as that first one, to the mother of Lance-Bombardier Fisher. The Battery have seen things that no one should be forced to see. In the battle to clear the River Scheldt of the enemy so that the Allies could bring in supplies from the port of Antwerp, they have suffered heavy losses as the result of a huge explosion caused by an accident involving the Royal Engineers, a modified Bren gun and a tank of nitro-glycerine. In the words of the Battery Diary, *a pleasant farmhouse with its apple covered orchard* had within two minutes been transformed into *a blasted heath, all the trees stripped of their leaves and every apple on the ground.* Shakespearean resonances again. A scene of peace echoing Justice Shallow's mellow Gloucestershire orchard in the deep England of *Henry IV Part 2* had become the battle-scarred landscape where Macbeth encounters first the Weird Sisters and then the bloodstained sergeant: *upon this blasted heath.*

Since then, they have watched with approval as photographs of Buchenwald are pinned on noticeboards in churchyards for the edification of the German people. And today they have tuned their radio to the BBC frequency and heard the King's speech proclaiming Victory in Europe. Now there are *bonfires, effigies, song, rum and beer* to see out the day in the Sergeants' Mess, officers and men together, divisions of class and rank forgotten. And then Major Tilney, who for some reason bears the nickname Mary, recites a poem in iambic pentameter with laconic feminine endings, in which he commemorates their battles and their route march:

> Ten months ago we left that English haven,
> Leaving, for Wanstead, Milford-by-the-Sea.
> Little we knew then what the future covered;
> Would it have helped had we known what it would be?
> Friends to be lost and laurels to be garnered

On it goes, until a climax is reached with a nod to Churchill's *broad sunlit uplands* of victory and a voicing of the hope that everyone who is sharing that night will remember how they had fought to build a future worth the having, *Giving to those unborn a fuller life*. Major Tilney then launches into full Crispin Day mode, straight out of *Henry V*:

> Then looking back we'll justly bore our children,
> Telling again the names of bygone strife.

How very English to use the self-deprecating oxymoron *justly bore* in the context of war stories. In a clever variation on the original, the poem lists the names not of the soldiers in the company, but of the towns they had liberated:

Norrey and Mondeville, Roquancourt, Cramesnil . . .
Boulogne's La Vignette, bomb bespattered Blacourt . . .
Gennep and Boeckelt and the Siegfried Line . . .
Xanten and Wardt, then on across the Rhine . . .

Of course this *jeu d'esprit*, dashed off on the day of victory after
five and a half years of war's attrition, was not Shakespeare. But
it was wholly inspired by Shakespeare:

Old men forget; yet all shall be forgot,
But he'll remember with advantages
What feats he did that day. Then shall our names,
Familiar in his mouth as household words –
Harry the king, Bedford and Exeter,
Warwick and Talbot, Salisbury and Gloucester –
Be in their flowing cups freshly rememberèd.
This story shall the good man teach his son,
And Crispin Crispian shall ne'er go by,
From this day to the ending of the world,
But we in it shall be rememberèd;
We few, we happy few, we band of brothers.
For he today that sheds his blood with me
Shall be my brother.

Shakespeare gave those men on VE night, as he has given soldiers
for generations, the words in which they could express their
fraternal bond in arms and remember their fellows who had
given their lives for friend and country. That incomparable,
oft-quoted phrase: *we band of brothers*.

Looking up the original speech in *Henry V*, and remembering
my mother telling me how she had gone to see Olivier's film

when it was released just a few months after D-Day, I was struck by the line *This story shall the good man teach his son*. My father was a good man, who believed in duty and that code of honour which King Harry articulates so memorably, but he was also a quiet, modest man. I had learned from his comrades-in-arms that in editing the Battery Diary for print, he had again and again omitted accounts of his own deeds of daring. Like so many of his generation, he did not think it right to boast and he probably found it painful to remember, except during those annual regimental reunions. So he did not heed Shakespeare's advice to *teach his son* the story of his service in time of war. And now it was too late. Which made the Battery Diary and the red pocket New Temple Shakespeare, with its handwritten record of playgoing, all the more precious.

★

I had my own take on *Henry V* by then. And my own view of Olivier's film.

My lucky generation still finds it hard to grasp the experience of war. As we grew up in the 1960s, we watched movies featuring cartoon villainous Nazis and plucky stiff-upper-lipped Brits escaping from a prisoner of war camp by burrowing a tunnel beneath a vaulting horse in the exercise yard. Or eccentric boffins designing bouncing bombs to burst a dam. But that was entertainment, not the real thing. Vietnam was too far away for little Englanders to understand, and even though the civil war on the streets of Belfast and Derry sometimes reached the mainland in the form of horrific bombings, that was called terrorism and was regarded as something distinct from a proper war in which the very future of the nation, even the world, was at stake.

The nearest I came to an understanding of the experience my parents had been through in the summer of 1939 was in August 1968. Every morning my mother would come into the bedroom I shared with my brother and open the curtains. That day, my father came too. Something's up, I thought. They told me the morning's news: Russian tanks had rolled into Prague. The spring thaw was over. They did not say it, but I knew what they were thinking: this might mean another war. I saw the fear in their eyes: my father was hitting the Normandy beach a second time, my mother back in a Kentish field, a teenage girl picking hops as Hurricane and Heinkel wove their dance of death above.

It didn't happen, of course, and as I went through my teens and grew my hair I rebelled against my parents' values, as every teenager should. For duty, I read deference; for patriotism, militarism. Shakespeare helped me in this. As we studied *Henry IV Part 1*, we laughed at the old chivalric code of Harry Hotspur. He may have been brave, but he was vain and hot-headed. He charges into a council of war, only to say, *A plague upon it, I have forgot the map!* I felt I was living life to the full when drinking in the pub with my mates: just like Prince Hal in Eastcheap, in flight from his father's stuffy court. We even had our own Sir John Falstaff: Bob Taylor the drama teacher, who would buy us pints and tell tall tales.

I couldn't forgive Hal for disowning Falstaff when he becomes king at the end of *Henry IV Part 2*. So when I read *Henry V*, my favourite scene was not the rousing rhetoric of St Crispin's Day and the *band of brothers*, but Mistress Quickly telling of old Falstaff's death, broken-hearted at his rejection. Besides, King Harry's claim to France was shown to be very dubious, justified only in that ridiculously convoluted speech by the Archbishop. This was no just war. And my problem with Olivier's film was that it glossed over the mess of war, the moral ambiguity. It cut out the traitors, Cambridge, Scroop and Grey – allegedly at the behest of Winston Churchill, who thought that it would be bad for morale to include any fifth columnists in a wartime film. Olivier also omitted the King's threat to allow his soldiers to rape the daughters and kill the babies of the people of Harfleur. And the admission in the Epilogue that winning the war was fruitless since England soon dissolved into bloody civil war. I wanted to see a much darker *Henry V*, a film that showed the real price of war.

A decade after my father died, I was living in Los Angeles and was invited to an advance screening of a forthcoming version. There hadn't been a successful Shakespeare on the Hollywood screen for many years, so there was a real buzz about this new *Henry V* – especially as it was by the rising star Kenneth Branagh. I had admired his acting when he played the part in Stratford. My hope was that the film would prick the bubble of honour. To my surprise, when the music swelled and Branagh mounted a cart to deliver the *band of brothers* speech a tear came to my eye and for the first time in my life I felt . . . *patriotic*. Maybe it was simply because I was in west LA, six thousand miles from home, but Shakespeare had pulled off his special trick of upending your expectations, making you see the opposite point of view from the one you started with. Now I understood the sense of duty, of sacrifice, of purpose, above all of brotherhood, that had made the war years in their way the most fulfilling time of my father's life.

This time, there was no glossing over the treachery of Cambridge, Scroop and Grey. And this time, the dubious justification for the war, played for comedy in the Olivier, was all intrigue in flickering light. But there was one notable omission shared with Olivier: Branagh's film cut the scene in which King

Harry orders the killing of the prisoners of war, an action – to use the phrasing of Captain Fluellen, the moral conscience of the army – *expressly against the law of arms*. Fluellen is referring to the French killing the boys and the baggage-carriers, and King Harry's action is sometimes justified as revenge for this, but the text makes it clear that he orders the killing of the French prisoners *before* the attack on the non-combatants.

After the screening, Branagh talked about his desire to create something very different from the old Olivier film. He had been inspired by the historian John Keegan's *The Face of Battle*, which told the story of Agincourt, Waterloo and the Somme from the point of view not of the generals and strategists, as in traditional military history, but from that of the common soldiers, who know nothing of what is going on beyond the fear and the noise, the mud and the blood, of their immediate surroundings. And at the end of the battle, he had wanted to show the full price of war, which it seemed to me he had done consummately well by way of the long tracking shot in which the King bears the body of Falstaff's pageboy (a young Christian Bale) through the leavings of the carnage.

When questions were invited, I challenged Branagh about the omission of the killing of the captured French. He said that it would have slowed the pace at the climax of the battle scene and that it wasn't necessary to include it because he had added a scene earlier in which the King does not merely order the hanging of his old friend Bardolph for robbing a church, but witnesses the noose being put round his neck. This, Branagh alleged, was sufficient to show that the King had a ruthless streak. But in the film this is the cue for a flashback to the tavern scenes when he was Prince Hal, one of the boys out on the lash, back in *Henry IV Part 1*. Recalling their larks in his mind's eye, King Harry wells up with personal remorse for the loss of Falstaff and Co. That is hardly to be compared with the chilling order to kill the prisoners. Besides, another cut was the scene in which Pistol, the braggart from the days of the King's wild youth, also acts *expressly against the law of arms* by threatening to cut the throat of his French prisoner unless he is given a stack of money. The mess of war.

I was not angry since I came to France, says King Harry when the boys and baggage-carriers are killed. Shakespeare knew that anger on the battlefield can unleash the bloodiest of revenge. In the early 1970s, we knew that too. We knew about revenge killings in Northern Ireland. And we knew about the My Lai massacre. But Shakespeare also knew of humankind's extraordinary capacity for resilience and restraint. After hearing of the miraculous disproportion in the numbers of the dead on the field of Agincourt, King Harry says:

And be it death proclaimèd through our host
To boast of this.

That was the thing about my father's generation: they neither boasted nor complained. Even if I had asked him, my father would have played down his brave deed in the Forward Observation Post. And then there was our next-door neighbour, Tom Mason, who came to find me on the morning my father died: one would never have known from his words and his demeanour that during the months when 85th Battery were grinding their way through France and Germany, he was in a camp in the Far East, enduring unimaginable brutality and deprivation as, in the euphemism of a colleague, 'a guest of his Imperial Majesty the Emperor of Japan'.

My Father's Shakespeare

One sentence in the Battery Diary especially disquieted me:

It is an odd war, the night the BC saw a grave of eight people (four children) at Cormelles – pushed into a cellar by the Germans, hand grenaded and finished off with a tommy gun – RHQ Officers' Mess with visiting BCs had brandy and cigars.*

Only an Englishman, I think, could have used the understatement 'odd' in that context. Shakespeare was there first. Once Cleopatra has lost her battle and her beloved Antony, all she wants is death. A simple countryman brings her a snake and she asks for confirmation that its bite will be mortal. To which the countryman says: *The worm's an odd worm.*

'Write about what you know': that's what they teach you in creative-writing classes. Undeniably, much of the best war literature is written by men and women who knew the experience of war. My friend Chris, who seemed to have read everything, persuaded me that *The Spanish Farm Trilogy* of R. H. Mottram was a gem of Great War literature because it was such an accurate record of the author's experiences on the Western Front. The same could be said of Vera Brittain's *Testament of Youth*. My father had huge admiration for *Alamein to Zem Zem*, the memoir of tank-driving war poet Keith Douglas, who kept a copy of Shakespeare's sonnets in his battledress pocket throughout the desert campaign. He was killed by a German mortar at the age of twenty-four, three days after D-Day. And nothing brings you closer to the American experience of Vietnam than *The Things They Carried* by Sergeant Tim O'Brien of 3rd Platoon, A Company, 5th Battalion, 46th Infantry Regiment of the 23rd

---

* BC = Battery Commander; RHQ = Regimental Headquarters.

Division: *They carried all they could bear, and then some, including a silent awe for the terrible power of the things they carried.*

Shakespeare shared their *awe* – a combination of woe and wonder, he called it – in the face of extremity, of battle, of death. But he was never a soldier. He didn't fight in the Low Countries like his friend and rival Ben Jonson, just as he didn't murder a king like Macbeth or go mad like Lady Macbeth. He wrote about what he didn't know: Cleopatra and the asp, a prince slumming it in a tavern, the Battle of Agincourt. He gives us the best education because he takes us not only through the cycles of birth and copulation and death that we all know, but also on journeys to places such as battlefields and broken minds where we hope we will never have to go. So that if we do have to confront the worst, we can learn his lesson that people come out on the other side of it.

I happened to host the poet Joseph Brodsky at a time of personal anguish. He recognized that something was not right. He did not pry, but simply said, 'Whatever it is, if it is not organic, you will survive.' This was the testimony of an expert witness, a man who had endured a show trial, forcible confinement in a mental hospital and exile to the Gulag. His empathy for my petty sorrows was a mark of his great soul. But Shakespeare's art seems to me greater, because his own life was for the most part comfortable and rather boring. It was only in imagination that he entered into the spirit of those who have lost everything and still endure. Edgar in *King Lear*, for example, driven from home, stripped naked, on the run, reduced to feigned madness, then confronting his tortured and blinded father, but still able to say:

> The worst is not,
> So long as we can say 'This is the worst'.

THE LIFE OF
KING HENRY V
by William Shakespeare

London: J. M. DENT & SONS LTD.
New York: E. P. DUTTON & CO. INC.

My father's Shakespeare

2.

Erecting a Grammar School

In one of my earliest memories, my brother and I are in our beds and our mother is reading a chapter of *The World of Pooh*, the two Winnie-the-Pooh books gathered in a single volume, published in 1958, the year of my birth. This was the first edition to have full-colour illustrations by E. H. Shepard. The jacket showed Pooh, Piglet, Rabbit and Roo leaning out over the white bars of the Poohsticks bridge as Eeyore floats on his back along the meandering blue stream. After the story was finished and before my star-patterned bedside light was switched off for the night, Mum let me examine the map of the Hundred Acre Wood on the endpapers.

It showed a variety of inviting homes. There was Pooh, sitting comfortably on a long log in front of where he lived *Under the name of Sanders*. Piglet very small in front of the very grand beech-tree house that had, according to the broken board beside it, once belonged to Trespassers W, short for Trespassers Will, short for Trespassers William. Owl's tree, the one that, I would discover, had two signs, reading respectively *Plez ring if an rnser is reqird* and *Plez cnoke if an rnsr is not reqid*. These were written by Christopher Robin, who was the only one in the forest who could spell. Then there was Rabbit's burrow-hole; Kanga's house, adjacent to the sandy pit that was Roo's playground; Eeyore's gloomy place; and Christopher Robin's own home. It was a world that felt safe, as mine did. My mother was a Kanga. I didn't know then that she also had Eeyore in her genes. My father, always the schoolmaster, was one-part Owl and one-part Rabbit – he was entirely without the bossiness, but liked to be very organized, which he had needed to be when playing a captain's part in the siege of Caen in 1944. My brother wasn't really a character in the book: he was always busy in another world with his trains and his model-making. I bounced around like Tigger and as a slightly spoilt younger child shared Pooh's taste for both honey and condensed milk with my snack at elevenses – though, so as not to seem greedy, I could happily have done without the bread.

The words at the top were what I liked most about the map. On the left was a copse marked *NICE FOR PICNICKS*. We lived near A. A. Milne's inspiration for the *100 AKER WOOD*, the Ashdown Forest. We went there ourselves for gorsey picnics and Poohsticks thrown from a bridge alleged to be the original. And on the right, in the very top corner of the map, was the widening stream beyond the bee tree, where my eye went past *BIG STONES AND ROX* to the words *TO NORTH POLE*. Much as I loved my cosy childhood world, I wanted to get out. To go on *expotitions* to other worlds, new worlds.

We could not, however, afford to travel. In those days, only the very well-to-do went on holiday abroad. At the beginning of each school year, I was quietly humiliated by the tales of more prosperous schoolmates who had flown to such exotic locations as Spain and even the fabled Riviera. I had never been on a plane. The best that my family could manage was a bucket-and-spade week beside the sea in Broadstairs, where my grandmother lived at the magical address of 55 West Cliff Road. She was cared for by my maiden aunt and each summer we formed a relief party, looking after Granny while Auntie Joan went hiking in the Alps. The closest I got to abroad was the slideshows of her travels, with which we were regaled at some length when we paid a brief return visit to West Cliff Road each freezing January.

I must have realized that the only way I was going to discover other worlds would be by reading. The first book that I can remember reading on my own was a little oblong hardback called *Around the World with Ant and Bee*. It took me to Paris, New York, Moscow, even Sydney and Tokyo. Later, I miniaturized myself with the Borrowers, messed about on the river with Ratty and Mole, followed Mijbil the otter to the west coast of Scotland in *Ring of Bright Water*.

When I was nine, my older cousin Diana moved to a school much nearer to our home than hers. She suffered from severe motion sickness, so in order to shorten her journey on the school bus she came to stay in our tiny guest room during the week in term time. One evening we talked about books and she asked me if I had read *The Lion, the Witch and the Wardrobe*. I had not. The next week, she came back with her family's well-thumbed hardback copy. And then *Prince Caspian* and *The Voyage of the Dawn Treader*, all the way through to *The Last Battle*. I could not get enough of this other world. I rejoiced in the exploits of Reepicheep the mouse. Lucy felt like the little sister I longed for, and I developed an especial fondness for the old professor. O, to have a rambling house like his, with a library and proper opportunities for hide and seek. I wrote my own stories in imitation, giving my world of talking animals the astonishingly original name of Animalia. Although we went to church each week, my parents taking their religious duties very seriously, I didn't twig that Narnia housed a Christian allegory and I felt rather cheated when I discovered that it did.

I started reading Sherlock Holmes stories instead. I still have the volume of *Collected Short Stories* that my parents gave me for Christmas when I was eleven – my brother and I were allowed to choose our main present, maximum price £2. The Conan Doyle was just a little more, but an exception was made because it was a book. Once again, I revelled in worlds so different from my own staid suburbia: the hansom cabs clattering past 221B on foggy Baker Street, all those granges and lodges in the country, holding their secrets and dark deeds. What I liked about Holmes himself was the mixture of forensic rationality and romantic energy – the violin sonatas, the restless, angular passion for new adventures, to stave off the boredom, the endless boredom, the melancholy that came with it.

Then I turned thirteen and stopped reading books.

★

Our town of Sevenoaks claimed an – albeit tenuous – connection with Shakespeare. Each day as I strode, not crept, willingly to school, satchel in hand, I passed Cade Lane at the bottom of our road and then skirted the cricket ground called Solefields that would become my summer domain of triumph and disaster. At the junction with the road that led to Tonbridge, our cricketing rivals, there was a plaque on the stone wall explaining that this was the site of the Battle of Solefields, fought in the year 1450 between men of Kent led by Jack Cade and the king's troops under the command of Sir Humphrey Stafford.

Rebel leader Jack Cade had compiled a 'Complaint of the Poor Commons of Kent' and assembled a ragtag army on Blackheath. Forced to retreat, they ambushed the pursuing royal forces near Sevenoaks. During the skirmish, Stafford and his brother were killed. Commoner Cade presumptuously donned Sir Humphrey's armoured velvet jacket and his spurs. Emboldened, he and his followers marched to London, where they became more interested in looting than revolution. The rebels were defeated in a battle on London Bridge. Cade fled, only to be captured by a Kentishman called Alexander Iden. He was injured in the fray and died of his wounds as he was being taken back to London, where he was given a posthumous mock trial before his body was dragged through the streets and quartered, the pieces being sent as a salutary warning to various locations in Kent where rebellion had been fomented.

Shakespeare dramatized this story in one of the 'Wars of the Roses' plays that I studied in the summer term before my father's death. It was published in 1594 under the catchy title *The First Part of the Contention betwixt the two famous Houses of Yorke and Lancaster, with the death of the good Duke Humphrey: And the banishment and death of the Duke of Suffolke, and the Tragicall end of the proud Cardinall of Winchester, with the notable Rebellion of Jacke Cade: And the Duke of Yorkes first claime unto the Crowne.* In the First Folio, it would be rebranded as *Henry VI Part 2*. (*Part 1*, it seems, was what we would now call a 'prequel'.) The Battle of Solefields takes place on stage, though the location is not specified beyond the fact that it is in Kent.

Neither side comes off well. Stafford would not have endeared himself to Shakespeare's groundlings by calling the commoners *filth and scum*, while Cade, despite proclaiming that *all things shall be in common*, is a vain upstart and rabble-rouser rather than a proto-socialist revolutionary who genuinely believes in liberty. He puts on Stafford's armour as a sign of his victory – in an age when dress was a mark of status and gender, Shakespeare always loved a subversive swap of clothing – but then announces with savage relish that the bodies of the dead brothers will be dragged to London, where he intends to release all the prisoners from the jails and cause general havoc. He also proclaims that when he is king, no young woman will be allowed to marry until he has taken her virginity for himself.

Being illiterate, Shakespeare's Cade has a particular hatred of learning. When the rebels capture the Lord Saye, Cade turns that word *filth* on to him:

I am the besom that must sweep the court clean of such filth as thou art: thou hast most traitorously corrupted the youth of the realm in erecting a grammar school: and whereas before, our forefathers had no other books but the score and the tally, thou hast caused printing to be used, and contrary to the king, his crown, and dignity, thou hast built a paper-mill.

As punishment for these crimes, the rebels behead the Lord Saye and his son-in-law, Sir James Cromer. Their heads are brought on to the stage on poles and made to kiss.

Shakespeare owed his education to a recently erected grammar school in Stratford-upon-Avon; he found the sources for his plays in books; the printing of his poem *Venus and Adonis* made his name; and he could not have written *Henry VI Part 2* without paper. So on the matter of grammar schools, books, printing and paper, he could hardly have been in sympathy with Cade. The mob on the rampage has no care for literature. In this respect, the scene anticipates the chilling moment in *Julius Caesar* when Cinna the Poet is torn to pieces by the crowd because they have mistaken him for Cinna the Conspirator.

James Fiennes, 1st Baron Saye and Sele, was indeed executed as a gesture to placate the rebels, because his abuse of his great power in Kent was one of their chief complaints. (Ralph Fiennes, whom I first saw as a dazzling Dauphin in *King John* and then as Troilus in the Swan Theatre in Stratford-upon-Avon, and his brother Joseph, who so wittily played *Shakespeare in Love*, are descendants through a cadet branch of the family.) The latter part of the Saye and Sele title was acknowledgement of the Baron's ownership of the manor of Seal, a village on the edge of Sevenoaks. Given this association and the location of the Battle of Solefields, it is plausible that the grammar school Shakespeare had in mind when he wrote this speech for Cade was indeed Sevenoaks, founded in the early fifteenth century to give a secular classical education to the boys of the town.

The school was unusual. Because it was a lay foundation, it was unaffected by the upheaval of the Reformation. Because it was in a backwater, it escaped the Victorian reforms whereby many grammar schools became 'public' (i.e. private) schools, which had the effect of excluding local boys. It also bypassed the Education Act of 1944 in which grammar schools lost some of their autonomy and resources through the exclusion of fee-paying pupils. When a reforming headmaster called Kim Taylor arrived in the late 1950s, he described the school as 'medieval-modern': it was, he said, 'as though a clock had got so far behind the time that it seemed ahead of it'. About a third of the boys had their fees paid by the Kent County Council, the others by their parents. There were fee-paying boarders, but in a minority, in contrast to the historic public schools that were dominated by the ethos of boarding.

The distinctive nature of the school gave Taylor the opportunity to experiment. Old customs were mingled with innovations. Uniform was capped with an Edwardian-style straw boater known as a biff, even as one of the boarding houses became an 'International Centre' self-governed by pupils from all around the world. Mathematics was taught in a new way, sparking the imagination of my contemporary Simon Donaldson, who went on to win a Fields Medal for his breakthrough in four-dimensional geometry. There was an after-school Technical Activities Centre, where my brother spent all his time building computers and miniature steam locomotives. Music lessons began with jazz improvisation. An exchange scheme gave the option of spending a term at a school in France. The Art Room was open all day, inviting boys to come in – lured by a gramophone backing-track of Jimi Hendrix, Bob Dylan or the Velvet Underground – and do their own thing with coffee pots, guitars, plaster casts, disembowelled lawnmowers, barbed wire and, as visionary art master Bob White put it, 'piles of machinery decomposing like Cézanne's apples'. It attracted the creative rebels – out of the Art Room crowd of my generation came punk-rock bands The Gang of Four and the Mekons, the award-winning films of Paul Greengrass, and the highly distinctive documentary collages of Adam Curtis.

Taylor had moved on by the time I was at the school in the 1970s, but his spirit remained. Public-school traditions were called into question. There was no place for muscular Christianity: in morning assembly, in place of hymns and prayers, there were talks by staff or pupils on ethics, politics, the arts, even existentialism. Militaristic CCF (Combined Cadet Force) was optional, not compulsory, with community service or environmental projects offered instead. The latter was known as Digweed, not because it involved digging weeds (though it did), but because it had been proposed by a boy of that name who was a conscientious objector. I opted for VSU (the Voluntary Service Unit) and still have vivid memories of performing conjuring tricks in care homes for the elderly, leading drama workshops with severely autistic children, and going to afternoon discos at Leybourne Grange, a self-contained 'colony' in a crumbling mansion that had been established in the 1930s as a home for more than a thousand so-called 'Mentally Defective Persons' (most of whom had Down's Syndrome and were among the warmest people I had ever met).

Political debate was encouraged. Jim Guyatt, our history teacher, took an unashamedly Marxian approach to the discipline, choosing the Russian Revolution as our special topic. And we were encouraged to engage with contemporary politics. Mock elections took place and senior figures from every party, along with trade union leaders and captains of industry, were invited to address the entire sixth form during 'Wednesday Period Eight'. Even the leader of the ultra-right-wing National Front was given a platform. He said that immigrants should be repatriated because the races were genetically different from each other, so should not mix. His prime piece of evidence was that 'Black people can't swim'. When it came to questions at the end, a Black student in the back row put his hand up and said, 'I'm the captain of the school swimming team.' Cheers, laughter and applause raised the roof and sank the speaker.

The hybridity of the school, with its combination of freedom from regulation, resources made possible by the fee-payers, and social diversity created by the free places, was only possible in the 1960s and 1970s, before the free places were abolished with the introduction of 'comprehensive' state education. The problem with the system was that there were not enough free places for everybody, so selection was made on the basis of the dreaded 11-plus exam.

'What will happen if I don't pass, Dad?'

'Well, we couldn't possibly afford to send you to Tonbridge, so you'd have to go to the Wildernesse.'

This was not a metaphor: it really was the name of the secondary modern school at the other end of town, which offered none of the opportunities that those who passed the test were privileged to receive. Taylor himself recognized both the social injustice of the public-school system and the inhumanity and waste of the 11-plus. It would have been Utopian to suppose that his educational experiments might one day be made available for all. Sevenoaks could only be a crucible for innovation because it was financially independent, academically selective, and answerable only to its governors, not the government. If Shakespeare was most fortunate in his time and place of birth, as the Tudor educational revolution was creating new grammar schools in small towns such as Stratford-upon-Avon, opening up unprecedented opportunities for middle-class boys, then so was I, born into a generation where Kent County Council paid not only for my place at school but also for three fully subsidized years at university. There was no such thing as student debt.

*

I wasn't aware of the privilege at the time. I have only the vaguest memory of my parents' relief that the 11-plus had been a success for me, as it had for my brother two years before. And I didn't really take advantage of the opportunities in my first few years at the school. I lived for football and cricket. Is it because some combination of testosterone and peer pressure turns so many boys off reading between the ages of thirteen and fifteen that – to judge from the gender balance of English courses, library usage and fiction-buying – a love of literature is more common among women than men?

The Sevenoaks way of addressing this problem was to abandon grammar and précis, the traditional stuff of school English classes, in favour of creative writing and analysis of the work that language does in many different contexts. As headmaster Taylor explained,

> Classes will be spent on, say, advertising, or TV or film and other forms of pop culture and mass communication; or on the quality of life in cities, and town planning; or, perilously, on the work and influence of Freud, Adler and Jung. What were once red herrings become a main dish.

By linking personal passions to creative projects, the English department gave boys far more interest in writing than they would have had if lessons had involved grammatical drilling and morally improving texts. My first project, channelling the love of birdwatching that I had learned from my mother, was a polemic against a government proposal to build a third London airport on the mudflats of the Maplin Sands off the Essex coast, a haven for migratory birds including rare avocets. This sowed the seed of a lifelong interest in the uses of literature as a means of addressing ecological questions.

As for reading, Taylor continued, books that had once been studied because they were acknowledged masterpieces in the history of English literature were abandoned in favour of *works that deal with situations of concern to boys, by writers who are themselves concerned, or 'committed'*:

> Gone, at school level, are Addison and Steele, so much favoured a generation ago: in have come not only George Eliot and D. H. Lawrence but books like Hartley's *The Go-Between*, Golding's *Lord of the Flies* and Salinger's *Catcher in the Rye*. It is not just a question of drawing parallels, of cerebral instruction and comment. It is important that a boy should be emotionally involved in what he reads; dragged, from the character and situation in the book, through the hedge backward to self-awareness; moved, in discussion and when he writes, to new insights about himself and those around him.

To begin with, it didn't work for me. We were prescribed *Lord of the Flies* in the third form. I gave up halfway through. It was a distraction from *Match of the Day* and *Top of the Pops*. We were prescribed *The Catcher in the Rye* in the fourth form. It sparked a small romance with the idea of America, but again I gave up, finding Holden Caulfield a bit of a phony. I also failed to finish Alan Paton's *Cry, the Beloved Country*, which was especially shameful because one of the school's most charismatic teachers was the poet and novelist C. J. 'Jonty' Driver, exiled from his native South Africa after ninety days jailed in solitary confinement for his anti-apartheid activism.

In the fifth form, there was no choice but to read all the way through to the end of *The Go-Between*: it was O-Level year and this was one of the set texts.

The past is a foreign country: they do things differently there.

That, I liked. The past which was opened up seemed both familiar and strange. Many elements of the book transcended time: a boy who is bullied, but who outwits his rivals through clever use of language; shyness and embarrassment; long, slow summer days; the outsider peering into a world of beauty and elegance that may not be as happy or desirable a place as he imagines; the trauma at the climax (a suicide, a child's nervous breakdown, a mother dispatched to a mental institution); the onset of teenage years bringing a reckoning with the body, with sex and sexuality. The confusion of young Leo Colston as he falls in love with both the lovers he goes between, ethereal, blonde, upper-class Marian – the *Virgo* who proves not to be – and farmer Ted, ripped and tanned, was presumably a projection of L. P. Hartley's experience of being stifled in the closet. Other elements, meanwhile – the manners, dialogue, dress and customs of the characters – transported me to a lost time, the Edwardian summer of my grandparents.

And at the pivot of the plot, there was a cricket match (evoked in such detail that for the American edition Hartley had to rewrite it with an explanation of the basic principles of the game). When Leo made his miraculous catch, I could remember mine. I was twelve again, at my middle school. We would walk up to the playing field borrowed from West Heath, a boarding school for wealthy but not very academic young women (Lady Diana Spencer among them). One of my challenges as team captain was to resolve eager competition for the fielding position of deep square leg, adjacent to the hedge that divided the cricket pitch from the girls' swimming pool. That day, we were playing our local rivals, Sevenoaks Prep, who invariably won with ease. When they came out to bat, I decided to wrong-foot them by opening the attack with my own slow, looping leg spin instead of the conventional fast bowler. Their captain, Paul Downton, clearly destined to play for England, drove the first ball back at head height four feet to my right. I leaped with outstretched hand and held the catch. After that, it didn't matter that they still defeated us. The mighty Downton had, as Leo would have said, been *vanquished*.

The Go-Between was an ideal novel for classroom discussion because it was so rich in themes and symbols: class antagonism as well as sexual awakening; the eternal idea of childhood as a lost paradise, as well as the historical specificity of the coming Great War as the end of an era; the weather as emotional thermometer; the signs of the Zodiac as image of Leo's belief that he is among gods; the sense, as Leo describes it, of a magical *Midsummer Night's Dream* turned from comedy to tragedy. There was just enough erotic frisson to generate a sense of excitement for boys without causing offence to parents. The novel is a watered-down version of *Lady Chatterley's Lover*: whereas Lawrence's Sir Clifford has been literally emasculated by a war wound, Hartley's Viscount Trimingham merely has a Boer-inflicted scar on his face; where Lawrence wrote graphic sex scenes with four-letter words, Hartley was content with the shadow of the thrusting farmer's buttocks on the outhouse wall and the phallic image of a bicycle saddle which, *pulled out to its fullest extent for Marian to ride, disclosed a shining tube of steel six inches long.*

I loved the book so much that until recently I dared not return to it, for fear of disappointment. Now that I have done so, I recognize that the symbolism is sometimes heavy-handed and I can understand why its place on the examination syllabus has been taken by Ian McEwan's *Atonement* (I would wager that *The Go-Between* was one of his set texts in school). But my admiration for the perfect pacing of the plot and the evocation of place, time and feeling remains undiminished. And I am thankful that by being forced to study it at the age of fifteen I was relaunched into a life of reading. Re-reading it after all these years, I reached the final page, *when the south-west prospect of the Hall, long hidden from my memory, sprang into view*, and not only the lost Edwardian world but also my own past hovered in midsummer air, revisiting the light.

Next, we moved on to the other novel set for examination: *Wuthering Heights*. Again, I was transported to another country. My paternal grandmother had been born in Leeds, and even after moving south to Frinton-on-Sea and then Broadstairs, she still had the trace of a Yorkshire accent. Out of loyalty to her, I supported Leeds United, making myself very unpopular with my school friends, who were all fans of Tottenham, Chelsea, West Ham or Crystal Palace, the clubs you could actually get to. On one occasion I was nearly assaulted at Crystal Palace: they were playing my team, who were in their brutal, magisterial prime, and Jonny Giles turned on a sixpence and fired a perfect shot into the corner of the net. I yelled with delight before being rapidly stifled by my friend Robin – we were standing among the Palace supporters, not penned in the cage with the fearsome-looking followers of Leeds.

My family took a timely holiday walking on the Yorkshire moors, where we visited the Brontë parsonage in Haworth and hiked to the ruins of Top Withens, the farmhouse supposed to have inspired the location of the novel. I had no experience of the magnetic emotions that drew Cathy and Heathcliff together, but the wind on the moor taught me how the imagination could be fired by a place, an atmosphere. The book made me into a romantic, longing for the day when I could feel as Cathy felt when she says, *Nelly, I **am** Heathcliff – he's always, always in my mind – not as a pleasure, any more than I am always a pleasure to myself – but, as my own being.*

The language of *Wuthering Heights* was more alien than that of *The Go-Between*, the narrative structure far more complicated. Looking around the classroom, I could see that I was in a minority in my enthusiasm for it. It was so confusing that Catherine Earnshaw loves Heathcliff but marries Edgar Linton, with whom she has a daughter called Cathy, while Heathcliff takes revenge by marrying and abusing Linton's sister, and they have a son called Linton Heathcliff, who marries his cousin Cathy Linton, but soon dies, after which Cathy marries her other cousin, Hareton Earnshaw, the son of the first Cathy's cruel brother Hindley, who was hated by Heathcliff, who has no surname. Why did old Mr Earnshaw pick up this wild, 'dark' boy on the streets of Liverpool? Was he a 'gipsy' or Irish or a 'lascar' from the East Indies or a child of the plantations in the New World? Was he indeed Mr Earnshaw's illegitimate son, in which case he was Cathy's half-brother and there was even more intense incest than that of all the cousin-marrying? Did his dark character and the alcoholism of Hindley Earnshaw have something to do with Emily Brontë's bond with her charismatic but dissolute brother Branwell, who died the year after the novel was published, having claimed that he was its author? The narrative was braided together by eating disorders and episodes of insanity; the language peppered with *frenzy*, *disordered nerves*, *brain fever*, *alienation of intellect*, *mental illness*, indeed *the concentrated essence of all the madness in the world*. At times, the extremity of behaviour reminded the class of nothing so much as the excesses of the Piranha Brothers in everyone's favourite television show. *Monty Python*: 'Nail his head to the floor.' Emily Brontë: *I knocked over Hareton, who was hanging a litter of puppies from a chairback in the doorway.*

My brother, a mathematician and engineer, had been forced to study the novel for his English Literature O-Level. It had frustrated his powers of logic. The equation whereby Wuthering Heights equalled primitive passion and Thrushcross Grange equalled genteel elegance made sense to him, but his scientific mind could not bend to the paradox whereby Heathcliff is both hero and anti-hero, perpetrator of appalling domestic abuse and cruelty to animals, yet a man of absolute charisma and a monomaniacal capacity to love Cathy ceaselessly from their childhood play on the moors until the moment when he wills his own death in order to join her in the grave.

I didn't want to know Heathcliff's precise origin – he was the archetypal outsider who survives through the force of his own will. As a boy, he peers in through the window of Thrushcross Grange, rather as in *The Go-Between* Leo is given a glimpse of life at Brandham Hall; as a man, he becomes master of not only Wuthering Heights and Thrushcross Grange, but also the destiny of the next generation. His scheme of revenge for Edgar having become the legitimate lover of Cathy brings no joy. For the illegitimate Heathcliff, as for illegitimate Edmund in the equally foul-weathered *King Lear* (to which Mr Lockwood alludes early in the novel), the only satisfaction is death. I didn't believe in ghosts, but I understood the idea of Heathcliff being haunted by Catherine. Where *The Go-Between* felt real, as an evocation of a boyhood, a class and an historical moment, *Wuthering Heights* exposed the limits of realism by reaching towards a more mysterious, profounder truth beyond that of the everyday. I struggled to articulate the force of my reaction to the novel. I think that in the exam I fell back on the old staple of writing about the importance of the weather. Later, when I was a university student, Virginia Woolf gave me the words about Emily Brontë that I could not find myself:

We are given every opportunity of comparing Wuthering Heights with a real farm and Heathcliff with a real man. How, we are allowed to ask, can there be truth or insight or the finer shades of emotion in men and women who so little resemble what we have seen ourselves? But even as we ask it we see in Heathcliff the brother that a sister of genius might have seen; he is impossible, we say, but nevertheless no boy in literature has a more vivid existence than his . . . It is as if she could tear up all that we know human beings by, and fill these unrecognizable transparencies with such a gust of life that they transcend reality. Hers, then, is the rarest of all powers. She could free life from its dependence on facts; with a few touches indicate the spirit of a face so that it needs no body; by speaking of the moor make the wind blow and the thunder roar.

It was this rarest of all powers that readied me for Shakespeare.

The plaque on the wall on the way to school

3.

Falling in Love with Shakespeare

I fell in love with Shakespeare when I was not quite sixteen. Despite the fact that our first encounter, the previous year, had gone badly. Love affairs can be like that.

Who does get on with Shakespeare the first time they are made to read him? Our teacher had the right idea: a brisk warm-up in the archaic language before we slogged line by line through our O-Level set text. But I for one was too immature. Besides, it was the wrong play. *Othello*. What did a class of fourteen-year-old boys in white, middle-class Sevenoaks know or care about interracial marriage or the green-eyed monster of envy or the torment of the image of your beloved being made love to by another man? *Lie with her, lie on her . . .*

To make matters worse, we were forced to sit through a rickety reel-to-reel screening of the Laurence Olivier film, based on his National Theatre production. With the unthinking testosterone of our age, we lusted after the young Maggie Smith as Desdemona. But the blackface, the foaming at the mouth when

Othello has his fit, and the orotund faux-Caribbean delivery of such set pieces as *Like to the Pontic sea* and *It is the cause, it is the cause, my soul* reduced us all to fits of giggles. I cringe at the memory of our lunch-break imitations of his 'da' for 'the'. In those days, we were all as unwittingly racist as Olivier must have been when he thought it would be a good idea to have his face smeared with boot polish.

And then we were taken to see a production of *Julius Caesar* in suburban Croydon. Now that I am old and fascinated by politics, and know that anyone who gets to the top in any walk of life will sooner or later know what it feels like to be betrayed, I have enormous respect for the play. But it is the worst possible introduction to Shakespeare for teenagers. It has fewer jokes than any of the other plays and no sex whatsoever. I had never been so bored.

The following year, it was time for the set text. And it was the right play for teenage boys: *Macbeth*. This time, we came out abuzz from the screening in the school's Little Theatre. The Polanski version. Funded by Playboy Productions. Blood everywhere. The positively gothic shadow of the slaying of Polanski's heavily pregnant girlfriend Sharon Tate by the Charles Manson 'family'. And, to cap it all, a nude Lady Macbeth in the sleep-walking scene!

Now we had a different teacher, Mr Campbell. Softly spoken and straight out of training, he got *us* reading aloud, but stopping all the time to discuss the language, to relish the imagery:

> Light thickens,
> And the crow makes wing to the rooky wood.

It's usually a liquid that thickens, Mr Campbell observed. Shakespeare was the first to apply the verb to light, brilliantly capturing the smoky atmosphere of dusk. Taking a word that commonly belongs to one sphere and moving it to another – the process called metaphor – was one of Shakespeare's key techniques, as it was for all great writers. Shakespeare also loved to take a word more often used as one part of speech and turn it into another. *Light thickens* is much more powerful than 'the light is getting thicker' because the verb 'thicken' has an energy lacking in the adjective 'thick'. Then there is a reverse effect in the next line. Shakespeare could have just written 'flies' or 'wings its way', but *makes wing* is more evocative because it is a sort of double verb that includes the noun 'wing', making us see the slow flap of the crow's wing as it crosses the darkening sky. As I was marvelling at how Mr Campbell could find so much in a single sentence, he singled me out.

'You're a birdwatcher, Bate – what's the difference between a crow and a rook?'

'Well, sir, a crow has a black bill and a rook has a white one.' I thought for a moment. 'Crows are sinister, so maybe it's symbolic of the blackness in Macbeth's mind, the darkness in his heart.'

'What else?'

'I'm not sure, sir.'

'How do rooks nest?'

'Together, in a rookery. There's loads of them in the park.'

'Exactly: rooks are gregarious, but crows are solitary birds.'

I got it: Macbeth is the crow, isolated from the crowd of his fellow-thanes because he's about to commission the murder of Banquo and Fleance. Another boy suggested that we were being too deep, too clever; surely Shakespeare didn't intend all this.

Mr Campbell replied that *intention* didn't matter. What mattered was effect, the force of the poetry when Shakespeare's imagination took flight.

'Towards the rooky wood,' I added.

★

But the thing that really made me fall in love with Shakespeare's language was speaking it. Bob Taylor, the school's wild-haired, irrepressible, chain-smoking drama teacher, announced that we were going to *do* 'the Scottish play' as the inaugural production in the school's brand-new black-box theatre studio. The dark space would be perfect for Shakespeare's night vision. As light thickened and the crow made wing to the rooky wood of Knole Park, the ancient estate wrapped around the school, the audience would enter a world of witchcraft, betrayal and assassination. They would meet a ghost and a madwoman. Boys would play the Weird Sisters, but Lady Macbeth would be imported from Walthamstow Hall. And we wouldn't be playing the original text. Instead, Bob explained, we were going to do a 'cut-up' or 'collage' version – what would now be called a 'remix' or 'mash-up'. For a moment we thought he said that it was the Charles Manson version, which might have troubled the Parents' Association. Once we got our copies, we saw that it was Charles Marowitz's *A Macbeth*.

Bob explained that Marowitz was into something called 'group theatre'. He had teamed up with Peter Brook in directing the Royal Shakespeare Company's 1964 'Theatre of Cruelty' season, a series of experimental and often violent 'fringe' plays performed at a London theatre club. The style was inspired by the theories of Antonin Artaud, the French avant-garde poet and playwright who had died alone, clutching his shoe, in a psychiatric facility, probably from a lethal overdose of chloral hydrate. Artaud's *Le Théâtre et son double* had sought to transform playgoing from light, middle-class entertainment into a confrontation with the dark places of the human heart, rendered through an immersive audience experience created by the actors' focus on their physicality as much as their speech. One of the plays in the Theatre of Cruelty season – which was a prelude to Brook's startling production on the RSC main stage of Peter Weiss's *The Persecution and Assassination of Jean-Paul Marat as Performed by the Inmates of the Asylum of Charenton under the Direction of the Marquis de Sade* – was a condensed *Hamlet*, chopped up and rearranged by Marowitz.

He had gone on to give *Macbeth* the same treatment, having teamed up with an actor-producer called Thelma Holt. He had first encountered her when she was appearing in a play called *He Who Gets Slapped*, in which, as Marowitz remembered it, her costume consisted of a brocade corset, black fishnet stockings, high heels and a bowler hat. He added that 'She held a whip in one hand and her countenance was one of the most wicked I have ever seen in a woman,' which clearly meant that she was ripe for the part of Lady Macbeth. She played the sleepwalking scene in a see-through nightie, to symbolize the hollowing-out of her personality into madness, and Marowitz always insisted that Polanski ripped off this idea for his movie. Marowitz and Holt – who, as I write, is nearly ninety, but still has plans for new productions, that same wicked countenance, and a husky greeting of 'Darling' every time she sees you – found a disused basement on the Tottenham Court Road, painted the walls deep blue, stuck eight hundred egg boxes on the roof to improve the acoustic, and christened it the Open Space Theatre. The professional theatregoers were not best pleased with the liberties taken by *A Macbeth*. *The Times*'s critic thundered: *In Shakespeare, Macbeth is the man who advances towards horror with his eyes wide open. Marowitz's first action is to have his eyes put out with a branding iron.*

This was going to be our script. The blinding would be performed upon a Macbeth doll.

The books arrived. Calder and Boyars' Playscript 45, the price on the back in both old money and new (15 shillings, 75 pence). A suitably black cover, with an almost indecipherable image of the witches standing behind Macbeth, black-gloved hands over his eyes. The text in typewriter face, as if freshly composed. Before the play itself, a series of exercises which we duly performed during our rehearsals:

The Clothesline: A well-known line in Shakespeare is chosen . . . The Company is placed in a circle. Each actor is given one word of the line . . .

Death Circle: The actors form a circle and begin intoning any prayer of their own choice . . .

Macbeth Stew: Different scenes from the play are divided between five couples . . .

And my favourite,

Help Play: The room is littered with numerous obsta-cles; overturned chairs, banana-peels, balls, heavy equipment, trays of water, etc. One set of actors (the Movers) are blindfolded; alongside them a second set of actors (the Helpers) . . .

The adaptation was a clever choice for a young amateur cast: only eleven parts and the text stripped down to little more than an hour. We were agog to know who was going to play the lead when Bob explained that Marowitz had split the part into three. It was as if there was Macbeth himself, along with his good angel and his bad. The lines were carved up between them in order to represent different aspects of the character's personality: the Ambitious, the Nefarious and the Timorous, as Marowitz had it. I was to play Macbeth 3, the good guy, the conscience, a.k.a. the Timorous. My key lines would be:

We still have judgement here – that we but teach
    Bloody instructions, which, being taught, return
    To plague the inventor. This even-handed justice
    Commends the ingredient of our poisoned chalice
    To our own lips.

Win us with honest trifles, to betray's
    In deepest consequence.

And Pity, like a naked new-born babe,
    Striding the blast, or heaven's cherubim, horsed
    Upon the sightless couriers of the air,
    Shall blow the horrid deed in every eye,
    That tears shall drown the wind.

Nearly half a century later, I still know these speeches by heart, along with many more from the production.

The idea was that Macbeths 2 and 3 would keep popping up beside Macbeth 1 – the Ambitious, the main part, played by Bob himself – in order to urge him on or seek to hold him back. We would also double as the murderers and perform various important tasks, such as picking up Lady Macbeth and carrying her offstage when she pretends to faint as a distraction at the moment when Macbeth lets slip a piece of information that has the potential to reveal that they have been King Duncan's murderers. Bearing off Rachel Feldberg in her nightie was a moment to which I looked forward every night. She gave an astonishingly mature performance as a Lady Macbeth who has been possessed by the witches. In my mind's eye, I still see her on her knees with arms outstretched and the three witches standing behind her in grey monastic robes, their hands on her shoulders:

> Come, you spirits
> That tend on mortal thoughts, unsex me here
> And fill me from the crown to the toe top-full
> Of direst cruelty . . .
> Come to my woman's breasts
> And take my milk for gall, you murdering
> ministers.

The production was a triumph. There was even real blood on the last night, when Jeremy Keen, our Macduff, became over-enthusiastic with his heavy broadsword in the last battle and trenched a cut in Bob's finger. Someone must have broken the theatrical taboo and voiced the title backstage instead of calling it 'the Scottish play'.

The scene I could not get out of my mind was Lady Macbeth's sleepwalking. Her madness. She had been the strong one, but then something had happened. All her strength had evaporated. As the original text has it:

Falling in Love with Shakespeare

Canst thou not minister to a mind diseased,
Pluck from the memory a rooted sorrow,
Raze out the written troubles of the brain,
And with some sweet oblivious antidote
Cleanse the stuffed bosom of that perilous stuff
Which weighs upon the heart?

Doctor:

Therein the patient
Must minister to himself.

Easier said than done: the very thing about madness in all its
forms is that you're not in control of the mind diseased. You
can't wilfully pluck the sorrows from your memory precisely
because they are so rooted there. Macbeth has the right questions, but the doctors of Shakespeare's time did not have the
answers.

★

A few months later, in the autumn of 1974, the love affair
became serious. Doing Shakespeare as a schoolboy started the
engine; seeing him done at full throttle by professionals roared
me into top gear.

It didn't look like a theatre at all. The coach had pulled up
outside a red-brick building just off the Euston Road in north
London. Its appearance was exactly like that of the old army
drill hall in our town. Inscribed over the door were the words
'20th Middlesex Artists R. V.', which sounded like an odd
combination of military and artistic parlance. R. V.? Rendezvous,

maybe? What kind of meeting place was this? Its name was indeed now 'The Place'. It was a dance studio that had been temporarily converted into a studio theatre, with the audience raked on makeshift seating on three sides around a bare stage.

We had come to see another Shakespearean tragedy. None of us had read it, or knew much about the plot, though we had heard that it had a reputation for being demanding. We were, however, to be assisted by the fact that this was a stripped-down version designed especially for school groups. The cast was reduced to ten parts, the duration to a little over two hours. The programme was a single sheet of orange cardboard. In large black letters it said **Lear**, followed in small print by the explanation: 'A shortened version of Shakespeare's *King Lear*'. Then it listed the cast. Lear, King of Britain: Tony Church. Earl of Gloucester: Jeffrey Dench (his sister was an actor, too). Edgar, Gloucester's son: Mike Gwilym. Edmund, Gloucester's bastard son (bastard – a frisson there): Charles Keating. The Fool: David Suchet. Goneril: Sheila Allen. Regan: Lynette Davies. Cordelia: Louise Jameson (who, a couple of years later, would stir a thousand schoolboy hearts – or loins – in the leather-mini-skirted role of Dr Who's prehistoric warrior companion Leela). At the bottom of the page were some recommendations gathered from the production's first run, earlier that year, in a tin hut in Stratford-upon-Avon that the Royal Shakespeare Company had christened The Other Place. A teacher from Olton Court Convent, Solihull, was quoted as saying, 'I do hope we can have more Shakespeare like this again, particularly for the O-Level people who generally loathe him,' while a group of A-Level students offered the collective opinion: 'Seems for many of us to have created the sensation of sharing Lear's tragedy.'

And that is exactly how I felt. No, it is an understatement:

the effect was visceral. Our close proximity to the unencum-
bered stage, the small cast, the quietness of Tony Church's Lear
(the antithesis of the Olivier Othello that had almost turned
me into one of those O-Level people who loathe Shakespeare),
the pent-up anger of the two older daughters (their husbands
were omitted altogether, making the women all the more
powerful): every detail drew me in not only to Lear's tragedy,
but to the tragedy of those around him. I felt the prick of tears
when the father carried in the body of his beloved Cordelia
and vainly believed he could sense a feather-stir of breath. The
most powerful moment of all came at the end of the first half:
Regan plucked out the Earl of Gloucester's eyes and the whole
theatre was plunged into pitch-darkness. At that moment, we
were Gloucester.

It was not until I was at university some years later that I
learned the story behind this production. Mary Ann Goodbody,
known as Buzz because of the energy she exuded as a toddler,
was brought up in the posh London districts of St John's Wood
and Hampstead, and sent to the very posh private girls' school,
Roedean. Her father was an international lawyer who was
usually absent on business in Africa or the Far East. She rebelled,
joining the Communist Party at the age of fifteen. Consciously
rejecting Oxford and Cambridge, she went instead to Sussex,
the embodiment of the new left-wing 'plate-glass' universities
of the 1960s. Frustrated by the fact that most of the great parts
in the theatrical repertoire were written for men, she turned
from student acting to writing and directing. For her final
honours thesis, she was allowed to stage her own adaptation of
Dostoevsky's *Notes from Underground*. Following a victory at the
National Student Drama Festival, this was played at the Garrick
Theatre in London. John Barton, co-founder of the Royal

Shakespeare Company, saw it and recruited her as his personal assistant.

This was a typically canny move by Barton, who hid a razor-sharp mind behind a shambling manner. He and his co-founder Peter Hall were Cambridge men, intellectuals committed to nuanced readings of the Shakespearean text. He realized that in a world where edgy, small-scale experimental theatre companies were springing up everywhere, committed to more physical acting, there was a danger that the RSC, burdened with the 'Royal' imprimatur and the baggage of the Bard, would descend into the role of an Establishment behemoth. A radical Sussex woman would be just the ticket to prevent this. He gave Buzz Goodbody free rein. She soon staged one of the few Elizabethan plays in which the best part *was* written for a woman, the anonymous tragedy of adultery, marital discord and revenge murder, *Arden of Faversham*, which some scholars now think was partially written by Shakespeare. Then she came up with the idea of a small experimental theatre, with very cheap tickets and a mission to reach young audiences. The Other Place was born. At the age of twenty-seven, she became its artistic director.

I learned all this from her Lear, Tony Church. Negotiating the cliquey world of Cambridge student theatre, I had felt intimidated by Footlights and the ADC (Amateur Dramatic Club), inhabited as those companies were by charismatic contemporaries such as Emma Thompson, Hugh Laurie, Stephen Fry and Simon McBurney. I found my niche instead in the experimental company known as Mummers. This gave me the opportunity to direct small-scale productions of neglected modernist plays such as W. B. Yeats's *The Words Upon the Window-Pane*, T. S. Eliot's *Sweeney Agonistes* and – taking the palm of pretentiousness for sheer obscurity – the avant-garde Belgian Michel de Ghelderode's *Three Actors and Their Drama* (a half-size retake of Pirandello's *Six Characters in Search of an Author*).

At the annual Mummers dinner, the guest of honour was always a former member who had gone on to success in the professional theatre. So it was that I found myself sitting next to Tony Church. There was an initial misunderstanding, in which he asked what the current Mummers production was, and I replied *Magnificence*. 'That's very enterprising,' he said, 'to revive Skelton's medieval morality play.' 'Er, no,' I said, 'Howard Brenton's *Magnificence*.' Brenton was the communist darling of the 1970s theatre scene; this *Magnificence* was a typical production from the stable of the Royal Court, that ironically named hotbed of left-wing drama. It involved five revolutionaries squatting in an empty London house and a Conservative MP being blown up by plastic explosive. I sensed that it wasn't really Tony Church's cup of tea.

But he was full of praise for Buzz Goodbody. 'And it ended so tragically,' he said, 'just after her Ben Kingsley *Hamlet* opened to such rave reviews.' He registered my puzzled look. 'I'm sorry – did you not know that she took her own life, not long after we returned from doing that *Lear* in New York?' Then he added: 'No one really knew why. But I'll tell you something. One night Sheila Allen was off ill, so Buzz took the part of Goneril herself. And when I looked into her face as I delivered those lines *Into her womb convey sterility! Dry up in her the organs of increase!* I saw a look of such hatred that I was afraid. I don't think she had a very good relationship with her father.' Which may also explain why everybody who saw it considered her *Hamlet* as powerful as her *Lear*. I wish I had seen it: I was struggling with the language and the character of Hamlet – it was to be one of my A-Level set texts – and it would be many years before I saw a production that made me *get it*, let alone *love it*, as Goodbody's had instantly made me get and love *King Lear*, and feel that I could hold my own in an argument with one of my teachers who pronounced that no one could begin to understand the play until they turned the age of forty.

The Place, where I saw Buzz Goodbody's *Lear*

4.

Let Me Not Be Mad

For a long time, *King Lear* seemed either too vast or too horrific for the theatre. Charles Lamb, writing in the early nineteenth century, was typical in proposing that Shakespeare's anatomy of the human condition was so profound and tempestuous that the play could not be staged:

> To see Lear acted—to see an old man tottering about the stage with a walking-stick, turned out of doors by his daughters in a rainy night, has nothing in it but what is painful and disgusting. We want to take him into shelter and relieve him. That is all the feeling which the acting of Lear ever produced in me. The Lear of Shakespeare cannot be acted.

Lamb was speaking more truly than he knew. In 1811, when he wrote this, the Lear of Shakespeare could indeed not be acted. The madness of George III meant that the London theatre managers kept this play about an old, mad and despised king off the stage, for fear of offending the court.

A generation before, Dr Samuel Johnson confessed that even reading the play was almost too much to bear: *I was many years ago so shocked by Cordelia's death, that I know not whether I ever endured to read again the last scenes of the play till I undertook to revise them as an editor.* The shock for Johnson was both emotional and moral. The death of Cordelia – Shakespeare's boldest alteration of the older versions of the Lear story, in all of which the beloved youngest daughter survives – was an extraordinary breach of the principle that Johnson called 'poetical justice', whereby the good end happily and the bad unhappily. During the 1680s Nahum Tate, author of the hymn 'While shepherds watched their flocks by night', had indeed imposed poetic justice on the play by introducing a happy ending in which Cordelia is married off to Edgar. Dr Johnson had some sympathy with this alteration, which held the stage for a century and a half, whereas for Lamb it was yet one more indication that the theatre was not to be trusted with Shakespeare's sublime vision of universal despair.

I think that the way to make *King Lear* work in the theatre is, paradoxically, not to play it loud and large. I have only relived the intensity of Buzz Goodbody's production in 'black-box' chamber theatres: witnessing Ian Holm shivering nakedly in the little Cottesloe auditorium in Richard Eyre's farewell production as artistic director of the National Theatre; mesmerized by Lee Beagley, a worn-out Samurai warrior with a Cordelia in Doc Marten boots and a springy female Fool in a highly physical production directed for a company called Kaboodle by the Black British actor Josette Bushell-Mingo in Liverpool's tiny Unity Theatre; tuned to the pitch of Ian McKellen's voice in the Minerva studio, Chichester, in what he said would be his final Shakespearean role (though it wasn't, because he returned with an age-blind *Hamlet*). What they had in common was the ability to do not only the curse and the howl but, much more importantly, the whisper and the tear. McKellen had toured some of the biggest theatres in the world in an earlier *Lear*, but he wasn't satisfied. He knew that to truly own the part, he would have to do it again in a place where he could be up close and personal with both the other players and the audience.

The night that my son Tom and I saw it, we stayed with him in the unassuming little rented house which was his billet for the run. We talked about the play until three in the morning. 'What I've come to realize doing it this time,' he said, 'is that you don't play the part, you just let the words speak through you.' Many of the most important words are about the mind losing control of itself; if the actor tries too hard to control them, the effect will seem contrived or will be lost altogether.

The language does the work, not least through the changes that Shakespeare rings on the word *mad*. Studying ancient Greek at school, I had learned about the *optative* mood whereby a verb is formed in order to express a wish. Lear uses a negative optative, expressive of the wish for something *not* to happen:

O, let me not be mad, not mad, sweet heaven!
Keep me in temper: I would not be mad!

I prithee, daughter, do not make me mad.

O, that way madness lies: let me shun that:
No more of that.

But the onset of madness comes to seem inevitable. Afflicted with what the loyal Earl of Kent calls his master's *bemadding sorrow*, Lear shifts to the future tense: *O fool, I shall go mad!* And then the process is complete. He is, as another character says, *madded* by the cruelty of his daughters:

> Why, he was met even now
> As mad as the vexed sea, singing aloud,
> Crowned with rank fumiter and furrow weeds,
> With burdocks, hemlock, nettles, cuckoo-flowers,
> Darnel, and all the idle weeds that grow
> In our sustaining corn.

At school, we studied the play in the scholarly Arden Edition, edited by Kenneth Muir, the grandly titled King Alfred Professor of English Literature at the University of Liverpool. Taking his cue from these lines, Muir adopted the stage direction of an eighteenth-century editor: *Enter Lear, fantastically dressed with wild flowers* (Shakespeare's original texts are sparse in their stage directions, usually confining them to unadorned entrances and exits). For all the beauty of Shakespeare's floral bouquet, this romantic dressing-up seemed to me wrong: the topsy-turvy of the play would have been better reflected by a stage direction that read something like *Enter Lear, mad, wearing a crown not of gold but of smelly weeds*.

But what manner of madness was this?

Our teacher explained that the Elizabethans believed that excessive rage or grief could drive you over the edge into insanity. In the case of Lear, however, particular emphasis is given to his age:

I am a very foolish fond old man,
Fourscore and upward, not an hour more nor
   less,
And to deal plainly,
I fear I am not in my perfect mind.

I have been lucky enough to discuss the nature of Lear's imperfect mind with several actors who have played the role. One night over dinner, Simon Russell Beale told me about his approach. He is the son of Lieutenant-General Sir Peter Beale, an army medic who became Surgeon-General of Her Majesty's Armed Forces. Several of his family members pursued medical careers. He explained that while he was preparing to embark on playing Lear for Sam Mendes at the National Theatre, he spoke to his nephew, who was training in geriatrics at St Bartholomew's Hospital. He learned about various forms of dementia and was put in touch with a specialist in the disease of the brain known as dementia with Lewy bodies.

He discovered that a checklist of its symptoms mapped uncannily on to the development of King Lear's behaviour in the play. Changes in thinking and reasoning, often manifested by eruptions of rage: Lear's sudden, irrational decision to disinherit Cordelia because she will not play the game of flattery. Confusion and alertness that varies from one time of day to another, or from one day to the next: Lear is sometimes lucid but at other times does not know where he is or what time of day it is. Visual hallucinations: Lear has many of these, from monsters to mice. Trouble interpreting visual information: as the play progresses, he has increasing difficulty in recognizing familiar faces. Memory loss: Lear has moments of forgetting –

I will have such revenges on you both,
That all the world shall – I will do such things –
What they are yet I know not –

– but he does not undergo the fade into oblivion that is Alzheimer's disease. Furnished with this diagnosis, all that Russell Beale had to do was add some of the physical symptoms of dementia with Lewy bodies – a hunched posture, balance problems, rigid muscles, a tremor of the hand. In describing his approach, he stressed that dementia with Lewy bodies was not a 'blueprint' for the character, but that it had given him a way into the part of the aged king who says *I fear I am not in my perfect mind.*

McKellen, by contrast, found no signs of dementia in the part. For him, Lear's madness almost becomes a victory: 'I don't look on Lear's madness as being a frailty. Rather, it's a sign of his strength. It's almost a way of fighting back. I don't, therefore, connect it with what I know of dementia. Lear enters mad, as the stage direction has it. We may not quite be able to totally get into that world. But he's in a world of his own making. I never really think he's a victim of some mental disability . . . he discovers his weaknesses and then embraces them, and recognizes that love is more important than power. He becomes gentle. Yes. For me, my absolute favourite scene in the play is when he awakens after that sleep. And there – I don't like using the word madness, but there is this other-worldliness, isn't there? He almost thinks, am I still dreaming? Have I died and gone to heaven? Are you an angel?' He quoted the immensely moving lines,

I am bound
Upon a wheel of fire, that mine own tears
Do scald like molten lead.

'Don't tell me that's dementia.'

The essence of Lear for McKellen was the character's attempt to understand his physical, mental and emotional state, to come to terms with what it is to be a father, and indeed, what it is to be a human being. His periodic short-term memory loss (*I know not / Where I did lodge last night*) is just a part of the ageing process. 'So,' McKellen concluded, as he poured another glass of wine, 'I don't really relate it to my notions of what dementia is, where you're losing it. You're losing it. You're losing it the whole time. I feel, on the contrary, Lear is gaining it, gaining it, gaining it. But he does behave in some quite peculiar ways. I mean, it's a little strange for an old man, a former king used to being robed, to start taking his clothes off in a storm in the middle of the night.' That last point does suggest the behaviour associated with advancing dementia, but McKellen did not need to make the link in order to play Lear's physical and mental nakedness with profound courage and conviction.

What did I learn from the contrasting approaches of Russell Beale and McKellen? That Shakespeare's plays still live four hundred years after his death because he shares with the good physician the art of minute observation of human feelings and human bodies. But also because, again like the good physician, he never reduces a human being to a mere set of symptoms, labelled with a diagnosis. He respects the wild complexity of the whole person, with sympathy and without harsh judgement. He rejoices in human endurance, even as he pities the disintegration and sorrow that come with age.

★

Though Buzz Goodbody was irreplaceable, the spirit of her distinctive approach to Shakespeare lived on: not only in these later studio productions of *Lear*, but also in The Other Place itself. Without her example, Trevor Nunn could not, I think, have created that tin shed's most renowned production, the Ian McKellen-Judi Dench *Macbeth*. When it transferred to London, The Place was no longer available, so it went to another black box, the Young Vic, where I saw it on a May evening.

It begins with organ music. The stage is a black circle, with an acting area barely bigger than a suburban living room. The actors sit around the circumference on low wooden blocks. The three Weird Sisters gather in the middle of the room and begin to moan. King Duncan kneels and prays in Latin. Throughout the opening scenes, whenever he is not on stage, he is there on the edge, praying.

Banquo is at first more striking than Macbeth. The bloody captain speaks like an automaton. He has shell shock. One Weird Sister is a charming old lady, another limps and channels a disconcerting mix of punk and Down's Syndrome. When the messenger says, *The king comes here tonight*, Judi Dench screams because she thinks he means that the prophecy has been instantly fulfilled and her husband is already king. Then she kneels and invokes the night, reeling backwards on the word *cruel*. As at Goodbody's *Lear*, the audience is ranged on three sides and from the get-go we know that we are witnessing something special. There is heavy silence, and then the birdsong lull of the temple-haunting martlet. Macbeth plays with Banquo's son Fleance – fondles his neck. McKellen speaks his lines staccato, uneasy. And then the blood.

But wherefore could I not pronounce 'Amen'?

Macbeth is choking at this moment; Lady Macbeth goading, capable, but there are little glimpses that prepare us for her unravelling in the sleepwalking scene. And the knocking at the gate is so, so loud. A small pool of light descends and the Porter appears in it, then suddenly all the lights come on – the same coup as Goodbody's lights out upon the blinding of Gloucester, but in reverse – and we are dazzled as embarrassed members of the audience are picked out, identified as farmer, equivocator and tailor with French hose. When Macduff enters, the direction is counter-intuitive: it is in the most matter-of-fact voice that he says,

O horror, horror, horror!
Tongue nor heart cannot conceive nor name thee!

The old man with Ross, describing unnatural sights, is blind.

Macbeth is crowned in bright light, with solemn music and ill-fitting borrowed robes. The banquet begins and he passes round the loving cup. At each pass, he turns to his servant (one of the three murderers) to wipe it, and as he does so he asks about the murder of Banquo and Fleance. The ghost of Banquo does not appear. Only Macbeth sees it. He has a fit, spitting gouts of saliva. This Macbeth is a man of the senses. In private he fondles his wife's breasts and probes her mouth with his tongue.

The Weird Sisters blindfold him and leave the stage, so the apparition of Banquo's descendants, the line of kings stretching out to the crack of doom, exists only in his mind.

A murderer rocks Macduff's son on his knee. The boy says he has been murdered. We don't understand until he falls with bloody knife wound in his back. When Macduff is told, he keeps saying *all*, the unbelieving numbness of emotion too powerful for further words or tears.

In the sleepwalking scene, she whimpers. The sound continues for what seems like eternity. At the time, you only see Lady Macbeth; in retrospect, you begin to wonder by what art of breathing Judi Dench has accomplished this. She dies to an offstage wail. Macbeth's reaction is spoken with great deliberation. The first pause comes a beat later than the moment when you expect it (I love, by the way, that Macbeth's last loyal follower sounds as if he has the name of the devil):

SEYTON The queen, my lord, is dead.
MACBETH She should have died hereafter:
　　There would have been a time for such a word
　　tomorrow [*pause*]
　　　and tomorrow [*pause*]
　　　and tomorrow [*pause*]
　　Creeps in this petty pace from day to day
　　To the last syllable of recorded time:
　　And all our yesterdays have lighted fools
　　The way to dusty death. Out, out, brief candle.

Then Macbeth arms. Five planked fruit boxes are gathered centre-stage. McKellen stands on them. The other actors, around the circumference, get to their feet. They become Malcolm's army. McKellen says, *I 'gin to be a weary of the sun.* He is lit by a single suspended spot, which he grabs and sets swinging around the auditorium. It revolves for the rest of the battle – darkness otherwise – lighting sections of the audience. We see fear in each other's faces.

Macduff enters with blood on his hands, a look of horror, a

sense of the cycle of blood starting again. Malcolm leads off, Ross last, picking up the crown. Lights and three curtain calls. It has been accomplished in just over two hours, with no interval.

We have seen into the heart of darkness.

McKellen and Dench

5.

The Lunatic, the Lover and the Poet

A rite of passage for any lover of Shakespeare is the first pilgrimage to Stratford-upon-Avon. I had just left school, but I cadged a place on a minibus filled with thirteen boys, driven erratically from Sevenoaks to Oxford by Bob Taylor, and then more smoothly into Warwickshire by one of the English masters, Hugh Pullan. Once in Stratford, we checked into the youth hostel and walked into town, where at a grim little café I ate a 'Choppy Grill' followed by a 'Peach Delight', each mouthful the embodiment of the full awfulness of 1970s English food. Then we wandered down to the Royal Shakespeare Theatre by the Avon and sat high in the gallery, looking down on Trevor Nunn's production of *The Comedy of Errors*.

Since this is Shakespeare's shortest play, it is often padded out with extra stage business. Never, the critics agreed, had it been so well stuffed as here. Farcical pressing of door buzzers, a chase timed in synchrony with an old Western movie projected on a screen, an assortment of dances and acrobatic acts, a rousing musical finale. The stage set was a café in a square, with brightly coloured laundry suspended from washing lines across the street. Roger Rees, as Antipholus of Syracuse, wore a white suit and a very 1970s red and white checked shirt with an enormous collar. A camera was strapped around his neck to indicate that he was a tourist in a strange town.

The Comedy of Errors is an early play, Shakespeare's first comedy of mistaken identity. Twins, both called Antipholus, have been separated since infancy. They each have a servant called Dromio. The two Dromios are also twins. The reason for the doubling of names is that, after the shipwreck in which the two pairs were separated and the father assumes that his wife and one child plus servant have been drowned, the surviving child and servant are given the names of their lost siblings. This detail is explained in a long and clunky expository speech early in the play, but we aren't supposed to trouble ourselves with its implausibility, since realism is not the mode of farce.

The best scene in the production – which must have been filmed for television, because you can find it on YouTube – has Judi Dench striding on in the role of Adriana, wife of Antipholus of Ephesus, and accusing him of having an affair. It is one of the most powerful and poignant speeches to come from the mouth of a Shakespearean wife. Especially when delivered with the force and nuance of Judi Dench in her prime. She is actually addressing Antipholus of Syracuse, who has just arrived in town and has no idea who she is, let alone what she is talking about. *Plead you to me, fair dame?* he replies at the end of her tirade, getting as big a laugh as any Shakespearean line ever gets.

I didn't notice the twist in Antipholus' next words – *I know you not* – even though we had been told in school that in

Elizabethan usage 'know' could mean 'have sex with', which added irony to his innocence, since Adriana's accusation is precisely that her husband is 'knowing' a mistress instead of her. Nor did I think about her pain – or the double standard to which she unerringly points. The language of her speech was too closely packed for my ear to follow:

> How comes it now, my husband, O, how comes it,
> That thou art then estrangèd from thyself?
> Thy self I call it, being strange to me,
> That, undividable, incorporate,
> Am better than thy dear self's better part.
> Ah, do not tear away thyself from me!
> For know, my love, as easy mayst thou fall
> A drop of water in the breaking gulf,
> And take unmingled thence that drop again
> Without addition or diminishing,
> As take from me thyself, and not me too.

I only saw below the surface of the marital spat when I was back at home, reading the play in the double-columned Oxford Edition that my parents, who never fought, had given me. Adriana seemed to be suggesting that a partner in love is a second self. We spend our lives in search of our lost other half. If we are lucky enough to find them, the two halves will be joined and we will be whole, *undividable, incorporate.* Two selves become one body in sexual and emotional union. *Wherefore they are no more twain, but one flesh,* as St Matthew's Gospel has it in the verse immediately before the words we hear in the liturgy of the wedding service: *What therefore God hath joined together, let not man put asunder.* The division carved by adultery is accordingly, for Adriana, a taking of her own self from herself. The irony that shadows her anguish is the fact that the Antipholus to whom she is speaking is not her 'other half' in the sense of her sexual partner, but her other half's biological other half, the twin from whom he has been separated.

No playgoer can instantly take in all these layers of thought. Shakespeare's friends the actors must have known this. When they collected his plays after his death and published them in the great book that we call the First Folio, they wrote in their Preface: *Read him, therefore, and again, and again, and if then you do not like him, surely you are in some manifest danger not to understand him*. The demand sounds a bit coercive, but it chimed with what I was learning from my stellar group of English teachers: persevere with Shakespeare, read him repeatedly and closely, and you will be rewarded. To get an education out of him you need a little education into him. You have to put in some work, by way of a close reading of his words – a line-by-line thoughtfulness of the kind you don't have time for in the transience of the theatrical moment.

*

Some special arrangement must have been made. After *The Comedy of Errors*, we were allowed to go backstage. The house manager showed us the prop store, rehearsal space and dressing rooms. We caught a glimpse of Judi Dench deep in conversation with Trevor Nunn. And then we walked on to the stage, looked out into the darkened auditorium and I fantasized about becoming an actor or maybe a director myself.

The next morning I became a tourist, but Anne Hathaway's cottage seemed only quaint, not relevant to what I wanted from

Shakespeare. In the afternoon, we sat through a marathon (nearly four-hour) matinee of *King Lear*. This was a full works production, with Donald Sinden in Donald Wolfit mode. It left me cold. I barely remember a single detail, apart from the well-staged rain. Was there a risk of overexposure? Was I going cold on Shakespeare?

The school party headed home and I stayed on alone for the evening show: *The Winter's Tale*. My faith was reawakened. This was a play that took you through a dark tunnel into the light beyond. The language of the opening scenes was crabby and harsh, though rendered with great lucidity by Ian McKellen as Leontes under the direction of John Barton. This Leontes was a ramrod-backed soldier, ruling Sicilia as a one-party state – McKellen anticipating the buttoned-up Iago he created a decade later and the Richard III as anglicized Hitler that he brought to both stage and screen in the 1990s. After the interval, the play was transformed into a joyful country romp, with young love, a lost one found, and finally a magical return to life. For the Bohemian shepherding scenes, Barton handed over the direction to Trevor Nunn and Barry Kyle. McKellen did not like the disjunction. 'Three directors are two too many,' he remarked wryly when asked to look back on the production many years later. But at the time, I loved the contrast: the tragic first half and comic second made *The Winter's Tale* feel like a two-for-the-price-of-one special offer.

Returning home on the train the next morning, I reflected on the astonishing variety of the three plays I had seen. By good fortune, the sequence had followed their order of composition. *The Comedy of Errors* was early Shakespeare, finding his way, experimenting and having fun. *King Lear* was middle Shakespeare, written in the full maturity of his tragic voice. *The*

Winter's Tale was late Shakespeare, moving into a vein that critics call 'romance'. So what was the unifying thread? Most obviously, family.

In *The Comedy of Errors*, husband, wife and twin children all lose and find each other. In *King Lear*, bad children turn against their parents, leading intemperate fathers to exile their good children, actions for which they pay a terrible price (Gloucester blinded, Lear driven mad) and then, piling on the tragedy, they pay a second time when, after the briefest of reunions, they are separated again through death. In *The Winter's Tale*, Leontes pays an equally great price for his false accusation that the child in his wife Hermione's womb is not his own, but that of his best friend Polixenes: his only boy Mamillius is struck dead and for sixteen years he has to live with the belief that he has also caused the deaths of his wife and baby daughter. The early play ends in comic reunion, the middle one in tragic desolation, the late one in the 'romance' twist of a seemingly magical return from death. The progression mirrors that of many lives: you lark around when young, encounter adversity in middle age and, if you allow yourself to *awake your faith*, as Paulina puts it in *The Winter's Tale*, you may achieve a certain serenity and hope in old age, a recognition that things have a way of falling into a pattern.

I had packed a slim volume of poetry to read on the train, the *Four Quartets* of T. S. Eliot. My eyes fell on a passage towards the end of 'Little Gidding':

> See, now they vanish,
> The faces and places, with the self which, as it could, loved
>   them,
> To become renewed, transfigured, in another pattern.

Sin is Behovely, but
All shall be well, and
All manner of thing shall be well.

But all wasn't well at home. The problem in my family was not infidelity of the kind imagined by Leontes or ingratitude as embodied by Goneril and Regan. I thought about the character of Hermione: what must it have been like for her to be kept locked up by Paulina in a secluded house for sixteen years? The image of a woman who had once been so loving, so active, so charming, as a wife, a hostess, a mother, now just sitting there all day, alone with her thoughts of her lost children, never venturing out. The circumstances were very different, but I was led to think of my own mother, who, almost as soon as my brother left home, had retreated into the house. And could not make herself get up from her chair.

Then I realized that the three plays had something else in common, and I remembered again the words of the Doctor in *Macbeth* about ministering to a mind diseased. Mental illness. Lady Macbeth had gone mad. A running gag in *The Comedy of Errors* is the way that the mistakes of identity caused by the presence of two sets of twins lead people again and again to accuse each other of being mad. When the Duke comes on in the final scene, to try and sort everything out, he encapsulates the play in a single line:

I think you are all mated or stark mad.

In Shakespeare's time – as in the Bible – madness was often thought of as a symptom of being possessed by devils. Adriana, believing that her husband is so afflicted, calls on a mad doctor named Pinch to conjure the devils out of him. His spell does not work, so he resorts to an equally age-old practice:

Mistress, both man and master is possessed,
I know it by their pale and deadly looks.
They must be bound and laid in some dark room.

The same remedy is tried for Malvolio in *Twelfth Night*, Shakespeare's other twin play: when the authorities are conned into thinking that he is mad, he is locked up in a dark room. In Shakespeare's London, people branded with madness might be incarcerated in Bethlem Hospital, known as Bedlam. Edgar in *King Lear*, disguising himself as a Bedlam escapee, pretends to be possessed by devils:

My face I'll grime with filth,
Blanket my loins, elf all my hairs in knots,
And with presented nakedness outface
The winds and persecutions of the sky.
The country gives me proof and precedent
Of Bedlam beggars, who with roaring voices
Strike in their numbed and mortifièd arms
Pins, wooden pricks, nails, sprigs of rosemary,
And with this horrible object, from low farms,
Poor pelting villages, sheepcotes, and mills,
Sometimes with lunatic bans, sometime with prayers,
Enforce their charity. Poor Turlygod, poor Tom!
That's something yet: Edgar I nothing am.

Bedlam was located in the parish of Bishopsgate, where Shakespeare lodged for much of his career. The 'hospital' was very close to the Shoreditch theatres for which he wrote in the years before his company built the Globe on the south bank of the Thames. The father of Ned Alleyn, the man who dominated the London stage in the years when Shakespeare was beginning his career as an actor and playwright, had actually been keeper of Bedlam. He retained the keeper's house even after leaving the post, and Alleyn seems to have been brought up there. If Shakespeare's best friend, Richard Burbage, lead actor in his company, was in any way like a modern method actor, he could easily have prepared to play his madmen's parts by going along to Bedlam, which was – shamefully, we now say – a place of public spectacle.

Shakespeare did not, however, exploit the twenty or so inmates confined at Bedlam in the way that some of his fellow-dramatists did. Edgar merely plays the role of Poor Tom, whereas in *The Changeling* by Thomas Middleton and William Rowley, an entire strand of the plot is set in a lunatic asylum based on Bedlam, with much slapstick comedy at the expense of the mentally ill. For Shakespeare, in the plays I saw on that first trip to Stratford, mental disturbance was a wide spectrum, a phenomenon to which any one of us could be subject. Dr Pinch in *The Comedy of Errors* was a joke: he gets his diagnosis wrong. Antipholus is not really mad. When Donald Sinden quietened down in the closing scenes of *Lear* we witnessed a man coming out of madness, recovering self-knowledge. And McKellen's Leontes was infected with a different kind of madness, the paranoia that comes from sexual jealousy, his mind racing to false conclusions, the intensity of his love for Hermione creating suspicion and then seeming certainty on the basis of pure delusion. Madly, he believes his own dream of cuckoldry:

Affection? – thy intention stabs the centre.
Thou dost make possible things not so held,
Communicat'st with dreams – how can this be? –
With what's unreal thou coactive art,
And fellow'st nothing. Then 'tis very credent
Thou mayst co-join with something, and thou
    dost,
And that beyond commission, and I find it,
And that to the infection of my brains
And hard'ning of my brows.

'Affection' could mean 'delusion' as well as 'passion': a single word holds the brainworm of Hermione making love to Polixenes together with the madness of Leontes' belief that his fears must be true merely because he has dreamed them.

The intriguing thing about *The Winter's Tale* was its turn from the infection of Leontes' brain in the first half to the joyful affection of the young lovers, Florizel and Perdita, in the second. After Time bid us imagine the passing of sixteen years, and the action moved from the chilly Sicilian court to the country warmth of Bohemia, the poetry began to tiptoe with grace and ease. Watching the play from the gods in the Shakespeare Memorial Theatre, I imagined myself in Florizel's shoes. I wanted to be infatuated with a girl again, to hold her in a slow dance at the end of a disco, and to say,

    when you do dance, I wish you
A wave o' the sea, that you might ever do
Nothing but that. Move still, still so,
And own no other function.

I think I loved the play because it was reversing my own story: the previous year, I had been Florizel, in love for the first time. But now I was Leontes, convinced that she had left me for someone else. *The Winter's Tale* meant so much to me because it offered the hope that you could lose someone, but then get her back.

Shakespeare thought that being in love is another kind of madness:

The lunatic, the lover and the poet
Are of imagination all compact.
One sees more devils than vast hell can hold:
That is, the madman. The lover, all as frantic,
Sees Helen's beauty in a brow of Egypt.
The poet's eye, in a fine frenzy rolling,
Doth glance from heaven to earth, from earth to
    heaven,
And as imagination bodies forth
The forms of things unknown, the poet's pen
Turns them to shapes and gives to airy nothing
A local habitation and a name.

Did this mean that the gift of poetry was compensation for the frantic heartache of love? Now that seemed to me an interesting idea.

★

Among our set texts for A-Level English Literature was the Penguin selection of *The Metaphysical Poets*. I still have the copy – an orange paperback with a leaf design – that I somehow forgot to return to the English department's book cupboard when I left school. The poems were printed in their original spelling, which made them seem more challenging than Shakespeare, whose olde wordes had been smoothed out by his editors. Our teacher warned us that we would be in for some mental gymnastics. 'John Donne makes Tom Stoppard seem like tennis for rabbits,' he pronounced.

Cunningly, he got us started with a local reference. The key technique, he explained, was a kind of metaphor known as a *conceit* ('Yes, it was a way of showing off'), in which, as Dr Johnson put it when coining the term 'metaphysical poets', *the most heterogeneous ideas are yoked by violence together*. One of Johnson's examples was the poet Abraham Cowley, a disciple of Donne, comparing a lover's heart to a hand grenade. A modern poem was handed around the class in order to illustrate the idea of a conceit. 'In 1617, Donne preached a sermon in St Nick's just across the road,' we were told. This inspired the poem, 'A Letter to John Donne' by C. H. Sisson:

> I understand you well enough, John Donne
> First, that you were a man of ability
> Eaten by lust and by the love of God
> Then, that you crossed the Sevenoaks High
>   Street
> As Rector of St Nicholas:
> I am of that parish.
>
> To be a man of ability is not much
> You may see them on the Sevenoaks platform
>   any day
> Eager men with dispatch cases . . .

Bring out your genitals and your theology.
What makes you familiar is this dual obsession.

It was easy to see that a double conceit was at work here: John Donne giving a sermon and stockbrokers commuting from Sevenoaks was one pair of heterogeneous ideas yoked together, genitals and theology another.

Naturally, the genitals pricked our interest more than the theology. When we turned to Donne himself, although we wondered what the hell was meant by such lines as *The general balme th'hydroptique earth hath drunk* in the eerily titled 'A Nocturnall upon S. Lucies day, Being the shortest day', the rewards were ample: poem after poem was about sex. In one, he was undressing his girlfriend to a state of *full nakedness*; in another, he was telling the busy old sun not to rise so that he could have another shag before going to work. There was a poem for every stage of a relationship, from fancying –

> Twice or thrice had I lov'd thee,
> Before I knew thy face or name

to seducing –

> My face in thine eye, thine in mine appeares,
> And true plaine hearts doe in the faces rest

to the transition from talking about it to doing it –

> For Godsake hold your tongue, and let me love

to parting with the assurance that you will be back –

> Sweetest love, I do not goe,
> For weariness of thee

to getting angry after being dumped –

> When by the scorne, O murdresse, I am dead.

Our anthology of the Metaphysical Poets also included Andrew Marvell's 'To his Coy Mistress':

> Had we but World enough, and Time,
> This coyness Lady were no crime . . .
>   But at my back I alwaies hear
> Times winged Charriot hurrying near:
> And yonder all before us lye
> Desarts of vast Eternity.
> Thy Beauty shall no more be found;
> Nor, in thy marble Vault, shall sound
> My ecchoing Song: then Worms shall try
> That long preserv'd Virginity:
> And your quaint Honour turn to dust;
> And into ashes all my Lust.
> The Grave's a fine and private place,
> But none I think do there embrace.

Now let us sport us while we may . . . Great sport in the classroom, too, as we found double entendres in such images as *private place* and the echo of a forbidden word in *quaint*. Chaucer's ribald *Miller's Tale* was another of our set texts, so we were familiar with an attention-grabbing line that centuries later would be unknowingly paraphrased by Donald J. Trump: *And prively he caught hir by the queynte.*

For the romantic in me, best of all was John Donne's 'The Extasie', which turned on the same idea as that of Adriana in *The Comedy of Errors*:

> Love, these mixt soules, doth mixe againe,
> And makes both one, each this and that.

Like so many of Donne's poems, it is a seduction workout, the argument being that if love makes two souls into one, then the two bodies must be joined forthwith in sexual intercourse. The poet and his lover are in the outdoors, on a grassy bank purpled with spring flowers, their hands interlocked, their mutual gaze magnetic, their souls reaching towards union,

> And whil'st our soules negotiate there,
>   Wee like sepulchrall statues lay;
> All day, the same our postures were,
>   And wee said nothing, all the day.

Imagine that, I thought: to lie under the sun with your lover, *all the day*, souls and bodies united and with no need for words. Shakespeare and Donne: they were writing four hundred years ago and yet they understood my desires, my dreams.

I wondered whether Shakespeare invented the idea of the teenager in love. He wasn't the first to tell the story of Romeo and Juliet, but he was the first to make Juliet so young (not quite fourteen) and to get inside her head, to find words for that dizzy yearning of first love:

Come night, come Romeo, come thou day in night,
For thou wilt lie upon the wings of night
Whiter than new snow on a raven's back.
Come, gentle night, come, loving, black-browed night,
Give me my Romeo, and, when I shall die,
Take him and cut him out in little stars,
And he will make the face of heaven so fine
That all the world will be in love with night
And pay no worship to the garish sun.

In a culture where young women were thought of as passive objects, to be handed from father to husband, Shakespeare makes Juliet into a hot-blooded subject. Where her father wants to sell her as a wife, she speaks here of buying the mansion of love and she can't wait to possess it. To enjoy sex. We had learned that a central conceit in Donne was the double entendre whereby an orgasm was perceived as a little death. Here, Juliet is suggesting that when she comes ('dies'), she literally sees stars. In a poetic tradition where the beautiful attributes of the female body were customarily surveyed and enumerated by the rapacious male eye, here the imaginative gaze falls on the lovely white body of the boy. In Donne, it was always the man's voice, hungry for the woman's body. In Shakespeare, even though the lines were written to be spoken by a boy actor, the girl has a voice. She shares both the love and the lust.

The summer school for Greek children was my first experience of teaching. To finance Interrail excursions into the Italian Renaissance, I worked there each July during my university years. There was chatter at the time about whether teenagers are put off Shakespeare by having to study him from the age of fourteen. I thought that it was a question of how you introduce him. Choose the right play – *Romeo and Juliet* or *A Midsummer Night's Dream* – and begin with a performance, then set the class to work on a few key passages, not worrying about the meaning of every word. I tested my approach. VHS cassettes had just become available, so I was able to show the Franco Zeffirelli film of *Romeo and Juliet* (now I'd begin with Baz Luhrmann). Then we spent an hour discussing Juliet's speech and Romeo's response to the light at her window. 'What do you think is conveyed by the line, *It is the east, and Juliet is the sun?*'

'Juliet is bright as the sun, an angel.'

'The directing light of Romeo's life.'

'The life-giving force of Romeo.'

This was a class of thirteen- and fourteen-year-olds, English their second language. One of them even cried out 'ἴαμβος': she had recognized the iambic pentameter.

★

It was typically bold of our teachers to choose the story of the middle-aged *Antony and Cleopatra* as opposed to the teenage Juliet and her Romeo for our A-Level tragedy of love. It is a much longer, more demanding and ultimately more grown-up play. But they were an inspiring team and they brought it alive for us.

Classes alternated between Alan Hurd, a Cambridge man who had become a county cricketer, and John Adams, who could have been an Oxford don but was committed to school-teaching. Hurdy and JA, we called them. Hurdy coached the cricket team, which included two future England players; he took special delight in hearing a master from Tonbridge complaining on the boundary that it was 'A fine state of affairs when we can't beat the grammar school down the road'. Hurdy was a great admirer of E. M. Forster, who had been miserable as a pupil at Tonbridge. His own tone of teaching was Forsterian, probing but never coercive. *'School,'* says the headmaster in *The Longest Journey*, a novel based on Forster's experience at Tonbridge and then Cambridge, *'School is the world in miniature.' Then he paused, as a man well may who has made such a remark.* Hurdy loved the quiet subversion of the public-school ethos in that.

JA, meanwhile, was master of the bon mot, as in the one about John Donne making Tom Stoppard seem like tennis for rabbits. And such pronouncements as 'To say that Fielding's character of Tom Jones is an insufficiently deep psychological entity is like saying that Mozart makes inadequate use of the electric guitar.' He had the whole of Western culture at his fingertips. He launched us into the first ten lines of *Antony and Cleopatra*, spoken by a Roman soldier who doesn't contribute anything else to the play:

Nay, but this dotage of our general's
O'erflows the measure: those his goodly eyes,
That o'er the files and musters of the war
Have glowed like plated Mars, now bend, now
    turn,
The office and devotion of their view
Upon a tawny front. His captain's heart,
Which in the scuffles of great fights hath burst
The buckles on his breast, reneges all temper
And is become the bellows and the fan
To cool a gipsy's lust.

Nay, but: see how Shakespeare pulls you into the moment by beginning the play in the middle of a conversation. *Dotage*: what does that mean? Yes, old age. They're worried that Antony is over the hill, past his prime. But what else does it mean? Doting, yes, falling in love. Unwisely. Excessively. Overflowingly. And see how the line itself overflows the measure of the iambic pentameter, runs on into the next line. Enjambment, a good word to use in the exam, but use it purposefully, showing its dramatic effect, don't just tick it off to show the examiner you know the technical terms. *Plated Mars*: Mars, the god of war, but there's a story in Ovid – Shakespeare's favourite poet – about Mars being snared in a net as he makes love to Venus, the goddess of love. We'll see Cleopatra as Venus when we come to Enobarbus' great speech about Antony's first sight of her on the barge at Cydnus. This is a play about big hearts and broken hearts. And about excess. *Reneges all temper*: this is what Empson would call a seventh-type ambiguity, in which two opposite things are said at once. Antony and Cleopatra are both wildly hot-tempered – each has a scene where they berate a messenger – but *temper* here also means temperance, moderation, restraint. The oxymoronic pattern continues in *the bellows and the fan*: bellows are used to heat a fire – the fire of lust, as it were – whereas fans are for cooling yourself in the Egyptian heat – gypsies were thought to come from Egypt, where the people were dark-skinned, hence *tawny front*. Though as a matter of historical fact, Cleopatra was an Alexandrian Greek, not a native Egyptian.

One part of my brain was befuddled by the time he got to seventh-type ambiguity, but the exposition of Shakespeare's way of opening up the whole world of a play within its very first speech was mesmerizing. It made me want to become a teacher if I failed in my theatrical ambitions.

The Lunatic, the Lover and the Poet

As the exam season approached, we reached the final act. The Clown has brought Cleopatra the asp, wishing her *joy o' th' worm*. She dresses herself for death:

Give me my robe, put on my crown: I have
Immortal longings in me. Now no more
The juice of Egypt's grape shall moist this lip.
Yare, yare, good Iras! Quick! Methinks I hear
Antony call: I see him rouse himself
To praise my noble act. I hear him mock
The luck of Caesar, which the gods give men
To excuse their after wrath. Husband, I come!
Now to that name my courage prove my title!
I am fire and air: my other elements
I give to baser life. So, have you done?
Come then, and take the last warmth of my lips.
Farewell, kind Charmian. Iras, long farewell.
Have I the aspic in my lips? Dost fall?
If thou and nature can so gently part,
The stroke of death is as a lover's pinch,
Which hurts and is desired.

We spent an entire class taking these lines to pieces and putting them together again. The patterns of repetition and variation. Those run-on lines. The internal rhymes (*grape/lip, mock/luck*). The double meanings (the *stroke of death* suggesting the blow of a sword as well as the caress of a lover). The interplay between the abstraction of *Immortal longings* and the sensuous immediacy of the almost entirely monosyllabic line *The juice of Egypt's grape shall moist this lip*. The shifts between Cleopatra talking to herself, talking to her handmaids Charmian and Iras, talking to the dead Antony as she imagines him becoming the husband in death that he could not be in life. Our discussion veered from the Renaissance theory that everything is made from a mix of the four elements of *fire and air* (the light ones, reaching towards the heavens) and earth and water (the *baser*, heavier ones) to ribald questioning as to whether there was a double meaning in *Husband, I come*. 'The only comparable moment in Western culture that comes immediately to mind,' said JA, 'is Isolde's Liebestod at the end of *Tristan*, so I suspect that we may answer in the affirmative.'

For a long time, I thought that *Antony and Cleopatra* was one of the few plays with respect to which I agreed with Charles Lamb: Shakespeare was just too big for the stage. How could any production sweep across the entire Mediterranean world as the play does, how stage the adamantine pillars of Rome and the eunuch's playground of Egypt with equal conviction? How could any actor do justice to the transcendent language of Cleopatra's closing arias?

I have been confounded twice. First in 1987. Critics were sceptical when Peter Hall, who had by then moved from the Royal Shakespeare Company to the National Theatre, cast Judi Dench as Cleopatra, alongside Anthony Hopkins, who shared a toughness as well as a name with Antony. Would she really have it in her to melt his military demeanour? Dench had doubts herself: 'I hope you know what you are doing,' she allegedly said to Hall, 'you are setting out to direct Cleopatra with a menopausal dwarf.' He knew exactly what he was doing. Cleopatra's allure comes not from her looks but from her mercurial behaviour, her playfulness and above all her language. Peter Hall knew that no actor could command the twists and turns of the Shakespearean pentameter better than Judi Dench. He could trust Shakespeare and trust her to make it work, and it did. Every line came freshly minted from her tongue as she ran the gamut from flirtation to joking to fury to the fire and air of those final speeches. As I looked around the sweeping amphitheatre of the Olivier auditorium, I saw that every male face was enchanted by her every move and word. Here was a Shakespearean education for us men: the lasting beauty is that which comes from within. The lover with whom you will stay in love is not the one with the pretty face, but the one who makes you laugh and makes you cry and is always one step ahead of you and never ceases to surprise.

Further education came two decades later. The Manchester Royal Exchange cast Josette Bushell-Mingo as Cleopatra. She had been the director of the highly physical chamber version of *King Lear* in Liverpool that I numbered among the most memorable productions of that play. The Manchester auditorium was in-the-round, the action played on a stone floor that mixed Roman numerals and Egyptian hieroglyphics. Stunted pillars for the Romans were played off against a stagey platform for Cleopatra, adorned with scarabs. There was no doubt who held the power here. The magnetic Bushell-Mingo dominated every scene in which she appeared, camp and playful one moment, threatening the next. As one reviewer wrote, she was truly a drama queen.

The production was praised for casting a Black actor, but for Bushell-Mingo that was not the point. 'Cleopatra's colour is completely irrelevant,' she said in an interview. The key to her view of the character was not race, but command: 'Cleopatra was the first woman in history to be completely in control of her own image – she's like Madonna, no – Ginger Rogers, in that *New Yorker* cartoon where Fred Astaire dies and goes to heaven and she says, "What kept you?"'

'The most helpful thing I read about *Antony and Cleopatra* was Harley Granville Barker's Preface,' she added, 'which was all about the importance of pace. Tempo. Thinking ahead of the line.' Yes, Shakespeare on the stage needs pace above all else.

★

Virginia Woolf once wrote that *The merest schoolgirl, when she falls in love, has Shakespeare, Donne, Keats to speak her mind for her.* Reading Shakespeare's sonnets, another of our set texts, I found a darker variation on this idea:

> O know, sweet love, I always write of you,
> And you and love are still my argument:
> So all my best is dressing old words new,
> Spending again what is already spent.
>> For as the sun is daily new and old,
>> So is my love still telling what is told.

Dressing old words new: were the words 'I love you' and 'you are so beautiful' no more than an echo of what had been spoken by millions of people before? *Spending again what is already spent*: the verb 'spend', we learned in class, could refer not only to financial transactions but also to the expending of a person's life-force in orgasm – that little death again. Did this mean that the act of love, as well as the words, was at best an age-old routine, at worst a quasi-commercial transaction, never a manifestation of unique passion? If this sense of verbal inadequacy and sexual cynicism was felt even by the genius who created a simile such as *new snow on a raven's back* and the injunction to take a lover *and cut him out in little stars*, what hope would there be for a word-poor teenager such as me, as opposed to a creature of his imagination such as Juliet?

Allowing Shakespeare (and the Metaphysical Poets) to speak my mind for me, as Woolf suggested, seemed like the best solution. As with Donne, it took a while to work my brain around the knotty language of the sonnets. Some of them could be grasped immediately: *Shall I compare thee to a summer's day? / Thou art more lovely*. That could be quoted at the right moment. Others, though, were baffling: *They that have power to hurt, and will do none . . . They rightly do inherit heaven's graces*. What was going on there? Was he praising his gilded but adamantine beloved or condemning him? It didn't help when Hurdy sent me off to read an essay by William Empson – he of the seven types of ambiguity – which began with the claim that this particular sonnet, number 94, was open to 4,096 different interpretations. Too clever by half.

Slowly, by reading a few sonnets aloud each night before bed, I began to grasp that it didn't matter who the Dark Lady was or whether Will Shakespeare the man really was in love with a Lovely Boy. What we were witnessing was this capacious imagination at play, spinning every conceivable variation on the theme of love. Spiritual and physical, gay and straight, finding yourself and losing yourself, the joy of presence and the ache of absence, the paranoia and the jealousy, the ecstasy and the agony. And the stupidity of it. Our classroom favourite was the parody of conventional love poetry: *My mistress' eyes are nothing like the sun . . . If snow be white, why then her breasts are dun*. Though, as always with Shakespeare, there was a twist in the tail: *And yet, by heaven, I think my love as rare / As any she belied with false compare.*

Another of the Dark Lady sonnets caught an element that was familiar to me, but that laddish Jack Donne didn't seem to worry about. The sexual liberation of the 1960s hadn't fully reached middle-class, churchgoing Sevenoaks, so in homes such as mine teenage fumbling was always accompanied by secrecy and shame. Shakespeare proved himself as good at expressing the shame as he was at voicing Juliet's sexual liberation:

Th' expense of spirit in a waste of shame
Is lust in action, and till action, lust
Is perjured, murd'rous, bloody, full of blame,
Savage, extreme, rude, cruel, not to trust,
Enjoyed no sooner but despisèd straight,
Past reason hunted and, no sooner had,
Past reason hated as a swallowed bait
On purpose laid to make the taker mad,
Mad in pursuit and in possession so,
Had, having, and in quest to have, extreme,
A bliss in proof and proved a very woe,
Before, a joy proposed – behind, a dream.
    All this the world well knows, yet none knows well
    To shun the heaven that leads men to this hell.

Extreme. Bliss, then woe. Joy in anticipation, vanishing afterwards into a dream. Despised as soon as enjoyed: before, during and after, the business of desire could drive you mad. *Mad in pursuit and in possession so.*

Equally unsettling was the discovery that in Elizabethan usage *hell* was a euphemism for the vagina. Was Shakespeare projecting his own dark feelings about *lust in action* on to his mistress, implicitly blaming her for his self-disgust? When this question came up, Hurdy responded by talking about a writer he especially admired, Ezra Pound. 'He was a fascist and an anti-Semite, but that didn't make him a lesser poet. As Auden said of Yeats, time will pardon him for writing well.' (A prediction belied, at least for now, by the 'cancel culture' of the 2020s.) 'Our business as critics,' he continued, 'is not to make moral judgements about the author, but to pay close attention to the quality of the writing. Pound's prerequisite for a good poem was *To use absolutely no word that did not contribute to the presentation.*'

To test the proposition, Hurdy showed us the text of sonnet 129 in its original printed form. The accumulation of epithets in a single sentence; the breathless pace of it, imitating the mad pursuit of which it spoke; the wordplay (*waste* suggesting 'waist', below which the action takes place); the repetition and variation (*Past reason hunted . . . Past reason hated . . . well knowes . . . knowes well*); the possibilities opened up by the absence of conjunctions (was it *blouddy* and *full of blame* or *blouddy full* of it?) and indeed by the habits of the printing-house – *v* was printed as *u*, so the word printed as 'proved' in our modern edition originally looked like 'proud', which, we were delighted to learn, was a term used for an erect penis, which was pretty much the situation at this moment in the pursuit.

All this, Hurdy suggested, answered to Pound's demand for every word to do its work. Then he added: 'Pound also said that literature is news that STAYS news. And that's what makes Shakespeare so extraordinary: he has stayed news for four hundred years.'

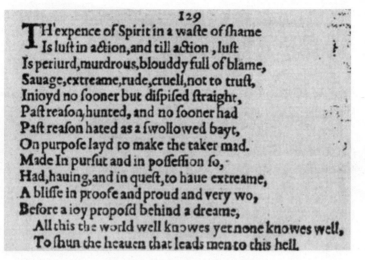

TH'expence of Spirit in a waſte of ſhame
Is luſt in action, and till action , luſt
Is periurd, murdrous, blouddy full of blame,
Sauage, extreame, rude, crueli, not to truſt,
Inioyd no ſooner but diſpiſed ſtraight,
Paſt reaſon, hunted, and no ſooner had
Paſt reaſon hated as a ſwollowed bayt,
On purpoſe layd to make the taker mad.
Made In purſut and in poſſeſſion ſo,
Had, hauing, and in queſt, to haue extreame,
A bliſſe in proofe and proud and very wo,
Before a ioy propoſd behind a dreame,
    All this the world well knowes yet none knowes well,
    To ſhun the heauen that leads men to this hell.

Sonnet 129 in its original spelling

Josette Bushell-Mingo as Cleopatra
and Tom Mannion as the dying Antony

6.

The Understanding Spirit

Shakespeare didn't work on me alone. He had many able assistants on hand. One of my favourite Falstaff lines was *I am not only witty in myself, but the cause that wit is in other men.* I was beginning to see that this was true of Falstaff's creator: he was not only educating me in himself, but he was the cause that other writers were educating me too. His influence seemed to be everywhere. The school's bespoke A-Level Literature syllabus demanded that we should not be narrowly English, so we were introduced to the plays of Ibsen and Chekhov. When John Gabriel Borkman went out half deranged into the snowstorm, he seemed to be another King Lear; and when in *Three Sisters* the scheming Natasha crossed the stage *carrying a candle* to exit left *without saying anything*, she was another Lady Macbeth. Chekhov's kindly fools, meanwhile, were reincarnations of Shakespeare's sad clowns.

Then there were Shakespeare-loving poets discovered outside of class. Shortly before I met my first love, a girl called Sarah

Jane, my friend Karim introduced me to the voice of Edward Thomas. This was his gentle way of suggesting that the best poetry – or at least the right poetry for the present – was a lot quieter, more conversational and matter-of-fact, than the pseudo-Romantic effusions of my own that I had shown him. Thomas made me see that what a writer really needs is an eye for things that most of us fail to notice, and maybe an acceptance that there is more grace to be found in the little things of the earth than in the showy gestures of rose bouquets and love songs:

> Tall nettles cover up, as they have done
> These many springs, the rusty harrow, the plough
> Long worn out, and the roller made of stone:
> Only the elm butt tops the nettles now.
>
> This corner of the farmyard I like most:
> As well as any bloom upon a flower
> I like the dust on the nettles, never lost
> Except to prove the sweetness of a shower.

But then Karim lent me the memoir written by Edward Thomas's wife. This was fatal: my relationship with Sarah Jane would founder because I put on too much pressure. Because I tried to replicate a romance that had played out in the long, hot summers before the end of the world that came with what would be named the Great War.

Helen Noble was shy, bookish, rather gawky, but with a deep reserve of passion waiting to be unlocked. The daughter of a literary man, she is living in a little villa in suburban London in the closing years of the Victorian age. An equally shy boy, an Oxford undergraduate with literary aspirations of his own, comes visiting. He has a *most striking face, recalling a portrait of Shelley in its sensitive, melancholy beauty.* He writes essays about nature, clouds, sky, trees, landscapes. They walk on the common and he brings her birds' nests and wild flowers. His jacket has deep pockets, from which he pulls volumes of Keats and Shelley, Shakespeare and Donne. She says goodbye and moves to Broadstairs to take a job as a nanny. Broadstairs, where we spent every summer holiday under the cry of seagulls, our lungs filled with the same salt air that Helen felt on her face when she slipped out of the house and ran along the beach *reciting aloud Shelley's 'Ode to the West Wind' or 'Adonais'.*

They become lovers, they marry while he is still a student. He struggles to earn a living as a freelance writer. An endless grind of reviews and hackwork, of rented homes and sleepless nights with crying babies. For a time, they find happiness at a farmhouse in the village of Weald, just outside Sevenoaks:

A large square farmhouse standing away from the road in the midst of its own fields. Oast houses, cow sheds, stables, hayricks and a huge barn were grouped about it on two sides. On the other side was a large garden and orchard, and in the front was a little garden opening into a field in which stood great oak trees, and in whose coppice-like hedges sang innumerable nightingales.

On a still summer afternoon like the ones captured in 'Tall Nettles' and Thomas's best-known poem, 'Adlestrop', Karim and I went to find it. It was exactly as she described it, save that a barking dog and a surly farmhand chased us off. I vowed to return at night in the hope of hearing a nightingale, but never did.

Edward Thomas suffered from severe depression. He grew more and more difficult to live with. Harsher and harsher with Helen. Just before the outbreak of the Great War, he forged a close friendship with the American poet Robert Frost, who encouraged him to turn away from prose and become a poet himself. Now he found a voice for his dark thoughts. Poetry allowed him to write about depression more honestly than any previous poet – save Emily Dickinson and Gerard Manley Hopkins, though they habitually wrote at a slant, not with Thomas's quiet directness:

> so that if I feared the solitude
> Far more I feared all company: too sharp, too rude,
> Had been the wisest or the dearest human voice.
> What I desired I knew not, but whate'er my choice
> Vain it must be, I knew.

Yet he also found that grace in simple, natural things: those lightly dusted nettles, a willow, blackberries in the hedgerows, a fallow doe moving silently across the snow, Shakespeare's image of icicles hanging by a wall.

It was love of the English land and landscape that made him join up. *When asked what he was fighting for*, reported Eleanor Farjeon, a young woman with whom he had a (probably platonic) affair, *he answered, 'Literally, for this,' crumbling a pinch of earth between his fingers*. He enlisted in a regiment called the Artists Rifles. Only now, as I piece together my memories of falling in love with Shakespeare and with Edward Thomas, does the synchronicity reveal itself: the place where he went to enlist and to train was The Place, Duke's Road, Camden, the old drill hall where I saw Buzz Goodbody's *Lear*, the words 'Middlesex

Artists R. V.' still carved above the door. Artists R. V. meant not artists' rendezvous but Artists Rifles Volunteers.

★

Immediately after passing my driving test, I borrowed the family Mini and headed over to the home of my friend Chris, filled with a mixture of exhilarated freedom and the apprehension of being alone at the wheel for the first time. We talked about books, as we had often done at school. But this was also the first time I saw his room. It was lined with books from floor to ceiling. Always impressionable, I decided on the spot that I must build a library of my own. Chris told me that the best place to start hunting for good-value second-hand copies of the classics was Hall's Bookshop in the Pantiles at Tunbridge Wells.

The shop soon became a favourite haunt, where I picked up foxed Everyman editions and faded Penguins for next to nothing. I made a particular search for books by Edward Thomas. I wanted to know if all that prose he churned out in order to make a living in the Edwardian years really was mere hackwork, as he claimed. The first volume of his that I found had the unpromising title *Feminine Influence on the Poets*. Interested in feminine influence on anything, I bought it, even though, being a first edition, it cost a little more than I could properly afford. Though the style was of its time, I didn't think it was hackwork at all. The first chapter was called 'The Inspiration of Poetry'. It began with a quotation from Shakespeare bringing together the very things that interested me about Edward Thomas: love, poetry and depression: *'By Heaven,' says Biron in 'Love's Labour's Lost', 'I do love; and it hath taught me to rhyme and to be melancholy.'*

Before long, though, Thomas was writing not about feminine influence on poets but women as poets. Anne Killigrew, Katharine Phillips, Aphra Behn: it was curious that Edward Thomas, a man, had unearthed these intriguing seventeenth-century poets, whereas Helen Gardner, the female Oxford don who edited the Penguin anthology of *The Metaphysical Poets*, fielded an all-male line-up.

The book really took flight in a chapter called 'Women, Nature and Poetry'. Here Thomas turned to Shakespeare's sonnets and argued that, paradoxically, *love-poetry seems so often to have little to do with love*. There are, he says, matters in the presence of which even Shakespeare himself is silent:

The love-poem is not for the beloved, for it is not worthy, as it is the least thing that is given to her, and none knows this better than she unless it be the lover. It is written in solitude, is spent in silence and the night like a sigh with an unknown object. It may open with desire of woman, but it ends with unexpected consolation or with another desire not of woman. Love-poetry, like all other lyric poetry, is in a sense unintentionally overheard, and only by accident and in part understood, since it is written not for any one, far less for the public, but for the understanding spirit that is in the air round about or in the sky or somewhere.

I only half understood the thought, but it seemed to me profound and true. The true purpose of poetry was not to get a girl into bed, but to connect with the mysterious *understanding spirit* towards which all creative artists are forever reaching. Call it imagination, or the motion and the spirit that impels all things, or the soul of the world. Even call it God. Whatever it is, it is always lost, just beyond reach. We imagine we touched it in childhood and that we will recover it in the moment of creation or the act of love, but somehow it always vanishes. Maybe this accounts for the old saying, *post coitum omne animal triste est.*

Thomas went on to suggest that the most unanswerable testimony to his theory was the later poetry of the nineteenth-century agricultural labourer John Clare. I learned of how Clare spent the last twenty years of his life in a lunatic asylum where he wrote poetry, at once ethereal and earthly, about his lost childhood sweetheart Mary Joyce, making her at one with the past, with his own childhood, and with the meadows and woods that had been his domain:

> Come with thy maiden eye, lay silks and satins
>   by;
> Come in thy russet or grey cotton gown;
> Come to the meads, dear, where flags, sedge, and reeds
>   appear,
> Rustling to soft winds and bowing low down.

Was it, I wondered, because Edward Thomas had endured depression, and John Clare madness, that they had come to the understanding that loss is the mother of beauty?

Helen Thomas seems to have thought so:

> I could not be borne high upon the crest of ecstasy and joy unless I also knew the dreadful depths of the trough of the great waves of life. I could not be irradiated by such love without being swept by the shadow of despair . . . as I grew up I learned that life is richer and fuller and finer the more

you can understand, not only in your brain and intellect but in your very being, that you must accept it all; without bitterness the agony, without complacency the joy.

★

She learned it the hardest way. Edward Thomas returned for leave just after Christmas 1916, before being posted to the Western Front. By this time, they were living in the village of High Beech in the Epping Forest, a stone's throw from the site of the private lunatic asylum where John Clare had first been confined. Helen's account of their last night is the most moving passage of her memoir *World Without End*:

I sit and stare stupidly at his luggage by the walls, and his roll of bedding, kit-bag, and suitcase. He takes out his prismatic compass and explains it to me, but I cannot see, and when a tear drops on it he just shuts it up and puts it away. Then he says, as he takes a book out of his pocket, 'You see, your Shakespeare's Sonnets is already where it will always be. Shall I read you some?' He reads one or two to me. His face is grey and his mouth trembles, but his voice is quiet and steady. And soon I slip to the floor and sit between his knees, and while he reads his hand falls over my shoulder and I hold it with mine.

'Shall I undress you by this lovely fire and carry you upstairs in my khaki overcoat?' So he undoes my things, and I slip out of them; then he takes the pins out of my hair, and we laugh at ourselves for behaving as we often do, like young lovers.

They draw closer to the fire and he picks up another book, a volume from his miniature set of Shakespeare's plays. He tilts it to catch the light of the fire and he puts his other hand over her naked breast and she puts her hand over his. He reads from the closing scenes of *Antony and Cleopatra*, until she can bear it no longer because for them the words are so full of poignancy.

My body is torn with terrible sobs. I am engulfed in this despair like a drowning man by the sea. My mind is incapable of thought. Only now and then, as they say drowning people do, I have visions of things that have been – the room where my son was born; a day, years after, when we were walking together before breakfast with hands full of bluebells; and in the kitchen of our honeymoon cottage . . . So we lay, all night, sometimes talking of our love and all that had been, and of the children, and what had been amiss and what right. We knew the best was that there had never been untruth between us. We knew all of each other, and it was right. So talking and crying and loving in each other's arms we fell asleep as the cold reflected light of the snow crept through the frost-covered windows.

Morning comes, and in the last minutes all that she can say is *Beloved, I love you*, and he says, *remember that, whatever happens, all is well between us for ever and ever.* Then he says goodbye to their three children and he walks away. A thick mist hangs over the valley as he disappears into the grey with a shout of 'Coo-ee!' She marks the day of his departure, 11 January 1917, in the copy of Shakespeare's sonnets that she has given him, inscribing it 'To Edward from Helen'. It is strange that she does not add the words 'with love'.

All roads now lead to France, he had written in one of his poems. He kept the sonnets in his breast pocket, close to his heart. He also had with him his full set of Shakespeare's plays in a nine-volume miniature edition of 1825, each book no larger than the palm of a hand. At night in the dugout, he read, keeping notes in his pocket diary. He was now in the artillery, as my father would be in the next war.

> February 13. Evening censoring letters and reading Sonnets; others writing – when I began to talk to Rubin, the Captain said 'You get on with your Sonnets' and then all was silent. Awful fug.

> April 3. Snow just frozen . . . A fine day, filling sandbags. MACBETH.

> April 5. A dull morning turns misty with rain. Some 4.2s coming over at 10 . . . Sun and wind drying the mud. Firing all day, practising barrage etc. Beautiful pale hazy moonlight and the sag and flap of air. Letters to Mother and Helen. HAMLET.

On Easter Day, he was lucky. A 5.9 shell fell a few feet from him as he stood at a Forward Observation Post. A piece of dust scratched his neck, but the shell did not explode. It was a rare dud. His pocket diary and a photograph of Helen that he was carrying seem to have been creased by the force of air when the shell landed.

Early the next morning, a small 77-millimetre shell known as a pip-squeak pierced him clean through the heart. His effects were returned to Helen, among them his volumes of Shakespeare.

They are now in the library of Cardiff University. The page is turned down at a battle scene in *Henry VI Part 3*. It still bears the mud of Flanders, staining the text just below the very line that had come to mind when I read the letter written by the mother of Lance-Bombardier Fisher in the next war: *Say how he died, for I will hear it all.*

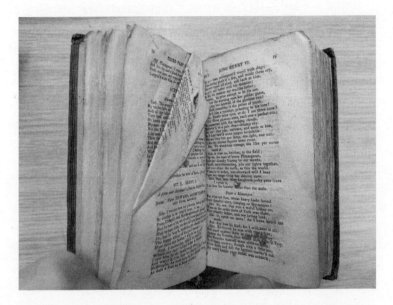

Edward Thomas's pocket Shakespeare,
returned to Helen after he was killed in Flanders fields

7.

Dr Johnson's Prescription

Hurdy and JA explained that, as well as our selection of Shakespeare's plays and sonnets, we would be studying Dr Samuel Johnson's Preface to his edition of the Complete Works.

At first this seemed a curious choice, a work of secondary as opposed to primary literature, but, to me at least, it proved inspired. Johnson crafted supremely balanced sentences; he would teach us how to write while at the same time introduce us to some of the central questions of literary criticism. He would show by example how to punctuate a complex sentence; he would teach us not to be afraid to have our own opinions about the books we read, so long as we supported them with a forceful and well-supported argument.

What makes a work of art into a classic? Johnson said that it required endurance for more than a hundred years. 'A good test,' said JA. 'It means that no one will be obliged to read the collected poems of Trumbull Stickney.' We assumed that he was making up the name; decades later, after the arrival of the Internet, I stumbled across the fact that there really was such a poet, a young American who had failed the test.

Why is Shakespeare so great? Because, Johnson told us, he holds a mirror up to nature. 'Remember, though,' said JA, 'that when you see your pimpled faces in a mirror you do not see them in the way that I see them as I am looking at you now.' For a moment, I was puzzled. He could not have meant that when we look in a mirror we fail to see our own ugliness and that the corollary was that Shakespeare represents the world without the ugly bits. Then a classmate who was brighter than me teased out his meaning: 'A mirror shows us our image in reverse – you know, like mirror writing – and it only has two dimensions, but gives the illusion of three, so was Johnson saying that Shakespeare's plays are true to life without being *realistic*?' 'Exactly,' – Adams was pleased – 'nobody in real life speaks in blank verse, but that does not prevent Shakespeare from reflecting life, just as an opera can mirror life, even though no one, so far as I am aware, goes through life singing arias.'

He went on to explain about the history of dramatic *rules*, the fact that in Dr Johnson's time English criticism was dominated by French theory, notably that of Voltaire, who in turn was influenced by Aristotle's *Poetics*, which argued that you shouldn't mix tragedy and comedy, high style and low, and that the action of a play should obey the three unities of time, place and action. Voltaire called Shakespeare a *barbarian* for including jokes and a comic Gravedigger in *Hamlet* and for veering between verse and prose, lyricism and banter. This was what Johnson was arguing against. 'Let's take a close look at the following splendid sentence,' said JA:

Shakespeare's plays are not in the rigorous and critical sense either tragedies or comedies, but compositions of a distinct kind; exhibiting the real state of sublunary nature, which partakes of good and evil, joy and sorrow, mingled with endless variety of proportion and innumerable modes of combination; and expressing the course of the world, in which the loss of one is the gain of another; in which, at the same time, the reveller is hasting to his wine, and the mourner burying his friend; in which the malignity of one is sometimes defeated by the frolick of another; and many mischiefs and many benefits are done and hindered without design.

Granted, this was not a simple sentence; you had it to read it slowly, pausing one beat for the commas and two for the semi-colons; Johnson made me into an admirer of the semi-colon, that now almost lost punctuation mark which, when used correctly, is grammatically no different from a full stop, but rhetorically so subtle and useful because it is only a half-stop, not a full period, in your train of thought.

JA explained that 'sublunary', literally beneath the moon, simply meant the real everyday world. He then asked us to think about Johnson's phrase *at the same time, the reveller is hasting to his wine, and the mourner burying his friend*. 'All Shakespeare's plays are in fact tragi-comedies. Discuss.' That would be the kind of examination question for which we should be prepared, he warned us, as he distributed copies of W. H. Auden's poem 'Musée des Beaux Arts', together with a reproduction of Pieter Bruegel the Elder's painting *Landscape with the Fall of Icarus*. In the foreground it showed a ploughman ploughing and a shepherd shepherding; on the sea, ships sailing. It took us a while to locate a pair of legs sticking out of the water towards the bottom right-hand corner. Nobody had noticed the fallen Icarus, who had flown too close to the sun and burned his wings made of feathers secured by beeswax. Auden:

> About suffering they were never wrong,
> The Old Masters: how well they understood
> Its human position; how it takes place
> While someone else is eating or opening a window or just
>   walking dully along.

Life goes on. A tragic hero may be the centre of his own world, but he is not the centre of the world. The tragi-comedy or comi-tragedy of everyday life will always be with us. The Porter will get drunk as the King is being murdered in *Macbeth*; the Gravedigger will make bad jokes as Hamlet meditates upon the skull of the dead jester Yorick; King Lear needs a Fool to prick his ego. Comedy in tragedy. In *The Winter's Tale*, Mamillius dies and does not, like Hermione, come magically back to life; at the end of *Twelfth Night*, Antonio is left alone, betrayed by his beloved Sebastian. Tragedy in comedy. Holding up a mirror to life. *At the same time, the reveller is hasting to his wine, and the mourner burying his friend.* On the eve of the day when we buried my father, it was the 'wrap' party for Magic Circus. I went along for a few minutes, but could not revel. Instead, I drove to an empty church and practised my funereal reading of Horace's ode for his dead friend Quintilius:

> praecipe lugubris
> cantus, Melpomene, cui liquidam pater
> vocem cum cithara dedit.

Teach me the saddest song,
O Tragic Muse, blessed by your father with the gift
Of voice so sweet in lyric song.

I was the mourner at the very moment when my friends were revellers.

★

JA looked rather like Dr Johnson himself, especially when he twisted his ankle and came into class with a hefty walking stick that he periodically banged on the floor, trying to stimulate a class of seventeen-year-old boys into an argument about literary form. Above all, he wanted us to learn from Johnson the art of clear thinking and forceful expression. He suggested that Dr Johnson was the most lucid writer of critical prose in the English language, with the possible exception of William Hazlitt ('his true successor – Johnsonian in intelligence but a Radical as opposed to a Tory – well worth making his acquaintance'). 'When you write your essays, you could do worse than follow Johnson's example – this is Boswell's account of his literary craft':

> Sir Joshua Reynolds once asked him by what means he had attained his extraordinary accuracy and flow of language. He told him, that he had early laid it down as a fixed rule to do his best on every occasion, and in every company: to impart whatever he knew in the most forcible language he could put it in; and that by constant practice, and never suffering any careless expressions to escape him, or attempting to deliver his thoughts without arranging them in the clearest manner, it became habitual to him.

JA assumed we would know that James Boswell was Johnson's biographer; if we didn't, we were expected to find out for ourselves. Like all great teachers, he directed us well beyond the set syllabus. With no Internet, no personal phones and only three television channels, there was all the time in the world to devote to reading. We were taught to weed out our own *careless expressions* and to find examples of *forcible language* in extracts from Johnson's other writings, such as an essay in *The Rambler* where he proposed that

> The cure for the greatest part of human miseries is not radical, but palliative . . . the armies of pain send their arrows against us on every side, the choice is only between those which are more or less sharp, or tinged with poison of greater or less malignity . . . The great remedy which heaven has put in our hands is patience, by which, though we cannot lessen the torments of the body, we can in a great measure preserve the peace of the mind.

Reading and writing as palliative care, as education in the patience that eases the troubled mind: this was an idea, JA suggested, that Johnson found in the classical philosophy of Stoicism, especially the letters of Seneca. In Shakespeare, he would have encountered many characters who have to learn patience. King Lear pleads for it, while in *Twelfth Night* Viola associates it with a love that dare not speak its name:

> She never told her love,
> But let concealment, like a worm i'th'bud,
> Feed on her damask cheek: she pined in thought,
> And with a green and yellow melancholy

She sat like patience on a monument,
Smiling at grief. Was not this love indeed?

But is it really a good idea to bottle up your emotions in this
way? Wasn't Malcolm right to tell Macduff to let his feelings
out when hearing the news that his wife and all his children
have been slaughtered by Macbeth's henchmen?

Give sorrow words. The grief that does not speak
Whispers the o'er-fraught heart and bids it break.

We were beginning to learn that every time a character in
Shakespeare gives you an idea, another character elsewhere in
Shakespeare will give you the opposite idea. Sometimes, you
even get contradictory ideas in adjacent lines. Like Mark Antony
himself, I was bewitched by Cleopatra's contrariness:

That time? O times!
I laughed him out of patience, and that night
I laughed him into patience, and next morn,
Ere the ninth hour, I drunk him to his bed,
Then put my tires and mantles on him, whilst
I wore his sword Philippan.

Into patience and out of patience. Putting on each other's
clothes. Cleopatra laughs and hastes Antony to his wine in the
first half of the play, then buries her beloved in the second,
climaxing (in several senses, we persuaded ourselves) when she
makes her agony into an ecstasy.

JA had passed the baton of teaching *Antony and Cleopatra* to
Hurdy. The classroom joker thought he was ripe for testing. 'Is

the sword Philippan a phallic symbol, sir?' 'To judge from the later line, *The soldier's pole is fallen*, you're probably right,' replied Hurdy, 'but we should remember that Freud said that a cigar is sometimes just a cigar – when I was at Cambridge, I was a great fan of E. M. Forster, who was living next door in King's College, and I wrote to him asking whether the tree in *Howards End* was a symbol of England and he replied very politely with the suggestion that I might consider the possibility that the tree was meant to be a tree.'

Dr Johnson loved his female friends, especially Hester Thrale, who comforted him in his darkest hours, but he was a man of his time, so it is not surprising that he had a low opinion of what he called Cleopatra's *feminine arts*. Just as he had a low opinion of Shakespeare's relentless wordplay. *A quibble*, he wrote in the Preface,

> is to Shakespeare, what luminous vapours are to the traveller; he follows it at all adventures, it is sure to lead him out of his way, and sure to engulf him in the mire. It has some malignant power over his mind, and its fascinations are irresistible . . . A quibble, poor and barren as it is, gave him such delight, that he was content to purchase it, by the sacrifice of reason, propriety and truth. A quibble was to him the fatal Cleopatra for which he lost the world, and was content to lose it.

Passages such as what JA called 'the expostulation upon the quibble' taught us that it was acceptable to criticize Shakespeare. And equally acceptable to disagree even with a critic as lofty as Johnson. His opinions were always his own. He made no pretence at objectivity. He was as fulsome in praise as he could be excoriating in criticism:

The arguments by which Lady Macbeth persuades her husband to commit the murder, afford a proof of Shakespeare's knowledge of human nature. She urges the excellence and dignity of courage, a glittering idea which has dazzled mankind from age to age, and animated sometimes the housebreaker, and sometimes the conqueror; but this sophism Macbeth has for ever destroyed, by distinguishing true from false fortitude, in a line and a half; of which it may almost be said, that they ought to bestow immortality on the author, though all his other productions had been lost:

I dare do all that may become a man,
Who dares do more, is none.

The indecorous juxtaposition of the housebreaker and the conqueror as exemplars of courage was quintessential Johnson. He wanted none of Voltaire's classical rules of art. The only authority he accepted was that of his own experience.

*

Since Johnson endured lifelong illness and dejection himself, he took the view that literature should not shy away from dark matter. He told Boswell that

If nothing but the bright side of characters should be shown, we should sit down in despondency, and think it utterly impossible to imitate them in *anything*. The sacred writers (he observed) related the vicious as well as the virtuous actions of men; which had this moral effect, that it kept mankind from despair.

Though he was a dedicated Christian, who wrote many heart-felt prayers and religious meditations, by *sacred writers* he did not mean the authors of the Bible or the early theologians. He meant the great secular writers, among whom he never doubted that Shakespeare was the greatest. Conversely, he loved nothing more than to launch thunderous denunciations of bad writing and ill-thought argument. In this, said JA, he in certain respects anticipated the only other literary critic who was regularly cited with an academic title, Dr F. R. Leavis. 'Who's Dr Leavis?' asked a boy who rejoiced in the name John Milton. 'Some people think he's God,' replied JA. An Oxford man, he was always a little suspicious of the earnest Cambridge-educated Leavisites of his generation who devoted themselves to the messianic creed of literature as the discipline that uniquely cultivated the *felt life* of both the individual and society. He granted that such passion for literature was admirable, but, with his voracious reading and catholic taste, he had no time for Leavis's policing of 'the canon', his absurd suggestion that *Hard Times* was the only decent novel of Charles Dickens and that 'the Great Tradition' of the English novel consisted exclusively of Jane Austen, George Eliot, Henry James and Joseph Conrad. 'And now,' he said, 'the poor old boy sees himself as the victim of some strange Marxist conspiracy with Raymond Williams as chief commissar.'

'Dr Johnson was a contentious old noddy,' Adams opined in class one day, before launching into an account of a book review in which the 'good doctor', as he called him, had eviscerated a second-rate moralist called Soame Jenyns. He quoted a remark from the review that has stayed with me to this day.

In 1755, the Lisbon earthquake destroyed an entire city in five minutes. It took the lives of about thirty thousand people.

This was hard to reconcile with the idea, preached from every pulpit in the Western world, of a beneficent God. We knew about this from Voltaire's *Candide*, which was one of our A-Level French texts. The catastrophe makes a fool of the character of Dr Pangloss, who claims that all is for the best in the best of all possible worlds. Across the Channel in England, the earthquake prompted the gentleman author Jenyns to pen *A Free Enquiry into the Nature and Origin of Evil*. The argument was essentially the same as that of Dr Pangloss. Building on Alexander Pope's *Essay on Man* ('Whatever is, is right'), Jenyns proposed that inequality is inevitable, that poverty is a blessing because it makes us appreciate small things, and that sickness is a good thing because it makes us value health. Thus, says Jenyns,

> The universe resembles a large and well-regulated family, in which all the officers and servants, and even the domestic animals, are subservient to each other, in a proper subordination: each enjoys the privileges and perquisites peculiar to his place, and, at the same time, contributes, by that just subordination, to the magnificence and happiness of the whole.

Since the universe is a well-ordered machine of this kind, it must follow that God ordained the Lisbon earthquake for some beneficent purpose.

Dr Johnson, JA told us, thought that this was, if we would pardon the expression, bollocks. The consummate professional, always struggling to earn a living by his pen in Grub Street, he hated the slack argumentation of amateurs such as Jenyns. He nailed the contradiction at the heart of the *Free Enquiry*. Jenyns had written that

Happiness is the only thing of real value in existence, neither riches, nor power, nor wisdom, nor learning, nor strength, nor beauty, nor virtue, nor religion, nor even life itself, being of any importance, but as they contribute to its production. All these are, in themselves, neither good nor evil: happiness alone is their great end, and they are desirable only as they tend to promote it.

Johnson agreed that we are all in search of happiness, though – in one of the glorious put-downs that led his opponent to describe him as a brute – he remarked that Jenyns's pompous phrasing of the idea *may serve to show how the most common notion may be swelled in sound, and diffused in bulk, till it shall perhaps astonish the author himself.* Besides, the question that needed to be asked was whether Jenyns's book itself promoted human happiness.

What is the purpose of writing? To assist readers (and writers, who are always their own first readers) in the pursuit of happiness:

The only end of writing is to enable the readers better to enjoy life, or better to endure it: and how will either of those be put more in our power by him who tells us, that we are puppets, of which some creature not much wiser than ourselves manages the wires.

Jenyns's argument that suffering – whether individual pain or the Lisbon earthquake – is part of some divine plan puts into the reader's head the idea *That a set of beings unseen and unheard, are hovering about us, trying experiments upon our sensibility.* That, in the words of Gloucester in *King Lear,*

As flies to wanton boys are we to th' gods:
They kill us for their sport.

Physical pain: *putting us in agonies, to see our limbs quiver.* Mental illness: *torturing us to madness, that they may laugh at our vagaries.* Digestive disorders: *sometimes obstructing the bile, that they may see how a man looks when he is yellow.* Road traffic accidents: *sometimes breaking a traveller's bones to try how he will get home.* Starvation: *wasting a man to a skeleton.* Obesity: *and sometimes killing him fat for the greater elegance of his hide.* How can a reader possibly be made happy by the thought that the gods are pulling our strings in these ways? The argument is a recipe for depression, not happiness. Dr Johnson therefore concluded that Jenyns's *Free Enquiry* is not good for our health.

JA singled out that phrase *The only end of writing is to enable the readers better to enjoy life, or better to endure it.* He suggested that we should use it as a yardstick in judging every book we read. I've stuck by it all my life (with the proviso that sometimes, as in a diary, the *only* intended reader is the writer). It is a standard that licenses one to cast aside unfinished any book that is not offering either enjoyment or mental fibre.

The enjoyment can be taken for granted. All sorts of people read all sorts of books for pleasure. But can writing really enable us to endure the pains of life? That was Johnson's great hope.

He had much to endure. Among his ailments were: aphasia, asthma, bronchitis, dropsy, emphysema, gout, insomnia, madness (bouts of), melancholy, near-blindness, nervous tics, nightmares, sarcocele, scrofula, scurvy, smallpox, stroke, sweats and almost certainly Tourette Syndrome. *Disease produces much selfishness,* he wrote late in life, *A man in pain is looking after ease.* Among his prescriptions for finding ease were: bloodletting, Cantharides (tincture of), cold bathing, country air, the elastication of bodily fibres, electricity, opium, the royal touch, rue, tea, the waters of Bath. And above all, reading and writing.

For Dr Johnson, literature was a form of therapy, a means of survival, a prescription against despair.

Mr Adams looked rather like Dr Johnson . . .

8.

The Black Dog

O ne day in class, John Adams, in his characteristic manner, veered far from the text of the *Preface to Shakespeare* and told us about Dr Johnson's particular compulsion. Back in the 1970s, we didn't have the technical term OCD. The story is told in the famous biography. Johnson told Boswell that he was inordinately fond of orange peelings:

BOSWELL And pray, Sir, what do you do with them? You scrape them, it seems, very neatly, and what next?
JOHNSON Let them dry, Sir.
BOSWELL And what next?
JOHNSON Nay, Sir, you shall know their fate no further.

The original observation of this peculiar habit had been at the Club, where the Doctor met with his cohort of friends. Bozzy had consulted all who survived, and they had confirmed his own memory of how the Doctor had frequently been observed squeezing the juice of fresh Seville oranges into a drink that he had made himself, then putting the remnants in his pocket. It had been on the morning after an especially raucous carousing at the Club that Bozzy had plucked up the courage to ask the question. He had seen on the table the spoils of the previous night, some fresh peels nicely scraped and cut into pieces. He pressed Johnson further, but the big man refused to reveal what he did with them. The inquisitive Boswell did discover that twenty years earlier Johnson had recommended to a certain Miss Boothby that dried orange peel, finely powdered, taken in a glass, was a serviceable remedy for indigestion. Which was one of his many ailments. But no one ever saw him drink such a concoction himself.

JA invited speculation around the class. Assorted preposterous usages for dried orange peel, some of them unprintable, were duly weighed and rejected. We were left with a mystery. And then we saw what JA was getting at: this was how we should read literature, Shakespeare especially. There isn't a solution. A great literary work is made of striking images and ideas, painted in evocative prose or verse. As critics, we carve them into little pieces, as Johnson did with his orange peelings. But we don't then give a simple *answer*. The carving-up serves to sharpen our attention, but we shouldn't look for a *particular* use of what Adams called 'the *disjecta membra*, as Sherlock Holmes or Samuel Beckett might have put it'. However, by thinking deeply about the language of the texts we were studying ('and perhaps learning some quotations to use in the exams'), we would carry their insights with us, as Johnson carried his orange peelings in his pocket as a mundane talisman, giving us a perpetual resource for enjoyment and endurance.

I liked this idea of words as a resource that you could carry around in your pocket. I wondered if anyone had ever written a book that gathered all the wisdom to be learned from a lifetime of reading. What would a full complement of literary orange peelings look like? Dr Johnson gave me an answer.

He struggled to get out of bed in the morning. This was a symptom of what he called his 'black dog'. He described the condition memorably in a letter to Hester Thrale in 1783:

> When I rise my breakfast is solitary, the black dog waits to share it. From breakfast to dinner he continues barking . . . After dinner, what remains but to count the clock, and hope for that sleep which I can scarce expect? Night comes at last, and some hours of restlessness and confusion bring me again to a day of solitude. What shall exclude the black dog from an habitation like this?

Modern psychiatry has a term for the advent of the black dog: Major Depressive Episode. According to the bible of the profession, the *Diagnostic and Statistical Manual of Mental Disorders*, such episodes involve the presence of five or more of nine symptoms during the same two-week period and representing a change from previous functioning. For there to be a formal diagnosis, symptoms one and/or two – *Depressed Mood* and *Diminished Interest or Pleasure in Life* – must be present, along with some of the following: *Significant Weight Change*; *Insomnia or Hypersomnia*; *Psychomotor Agitation or Retardation* (which is to say anxious restlessness and involuntary movements); *Fatigue or Loss of Energy*; *Feelings of Worthlessness or Inappropriate Guilt*; *Diminished Concentration or Indecisiveness*; *Recurrent Thoughts of Death*.

When the black dog came calling on Dr Johnson, it drove out all his pleasure in conversation, company, tea, entertainment and everything else; his weight ballooned; he couldn't sleep; he was afflicted with a perpetual nervous tic; he lost the prodigious appetite for work which awed all who knew him; he tormented himself in prayers and meditations wracked with feelings of worthlessness *and* inappropriate guilt; he lost concentration, became indecisive and thought obsessively about death. In every symptom, a textbook presentation.

According to Boswell, there was a single book that gave Johnson the will to get out of bed at a reasonable hour. It was one that described the very condition with which he wrestled all his life: Robert Burton's *The Anatomy of Melancholy*. I imagine Johnson fiddling with the orange peelings in his ample pocket as he imparted to Boswell, who suffered from severe bouts of depression himself, a valuable piece of advice about how to keep away the black dog that he had found in this book: *The great direction which Burton has left to men disordered like you, is this, 'Be not solitary; be not idle.'* He added that the advice should be modified to the effect that those of an idle disposition should not be solitary and those who are solitary should not be idle.

The 'direction' quoted by Johnson comes from the last page of Burton's compendium of psychiatric lore, first published in 1621 under the pseudonym Democritus Junior, and revised and expanded on many occasions before the author's death in 1640. Its full title was *The Anatomy of Melancholy, What it is: With all the Kinds, Causes, Symptomes, Prognostickes, and Several Cures of it. In Three Partitions, with their several Sections, Members and Subsections, Philosophically, Medicinally, Historically, Opened and Cut Up.* As Andreas Vesalius had revolutionized the understanding of the body's physical anatomy by opening cadavers and cutting them up, so, two generations later, Burton, an Oxford don who spent almost his entire life in his study and his university's great libraries, set out to anatomize the human mind.

★

I found out about Johnson's love of Burton around the time that Sarah Jane called off the love affair in which I'd pushed too hard because of my reading of Helen Thomas's memoir. Right, I thought, literature got me into this mess, so can it get me out of it? Hall's second-hand bookshop gave me what I needed: *The Anatomy of Melancholy* reprinted in three musty-smelling Everyman Library volumes, with torn yellow dust jackets, tiny print and great swathes of Latin. Much skimming would be required.

I very much liked the account of Burton's method given in the Everyman Introduction:

> The *Anatomy* looks like a crude assembly of quotations and is indeed a vast mobilization of the notions and expressions of others, yet it is not they but the rifler who is revealed on every page, it is he, not they, who peeps from behind every quotation . . . He is an artist in literary mosaic, using the shreds and patches he has torn from the work of others to make a picture emphatically his own. Books are his raw material. Other artists fashion images out of clay, contrive fabrics and forms of stone, symphonies of words, sounds, or pigments. Burton makes a cosmos out of quotations. He raids the writings of the past, which he often finds neglected or in ruins, and reassembles them in a structure of his own, much as the ruins of Rome were pillaged by the builders of the Renaissance and worked into the temples and palaces of a new civilization.

That's the kind of book I would like to write one day, I said to myself. A collage of quotations.

The Editorial Introduction was followed by Burton's own Preface. Which went on for 120 pages. The gist of it seemed to be that we are all mad, all foolish, all *so carried away with passion, discontent, lust, pleasures* that we hate the virtues we should love and love the vices we should hate. But then Burton explains that he wants to distinguish between these everyday follies – that is to say, the behaviour of those of us who are *metaphorically mad, lightly mad, or in disposition stupid, angry, drunken, silly, sottish, sullen, proud, vain-glorious, ridiculous, beastly, peevish, obstinate, impudent, extravagant, dry, doting, dull, desperate, harebrain, etc.* (which is to say, all humankind) – and the symptoms of those who are suffering from the disease of melancholy.

I was tempted to give up after this looping and digressive preliminary address to the reader, but fortunately the main text was preceded by a wonderfully detailed flow diagram, with dozens of arrows, offering a summary guide that allowed one to pick out the bits that sounded most interesting. Symptoms of melancholy? Hollow eyes, *much trouble with wind and a griping in their bellies*, belching, *dejected looks*, tinnitus, vertigo, light-headedness, *little or no sleep, terrible and fearful dreams, continual fears, griefs and vexations*, headaches, and an inability to *go about any business*. Strange behaviours of the melancholiac? Fear of walking alone, fear of small, enclosed rooms. *Not daring to go over a bridge, come near a pool, rock, steep hill, lie in a chamber where cross-beams are.* This was a veritable seventeenth-century *Diagnostic and Statistical Manual*.

Flicking through the second volume, devoted to cures for melancholy, I found a few tips for my own dejection over the end of the affair with Sarah Jane. The starting point, Burton suggested, should be improved diet. He recommended *such meats as are easy of digestion, bread of pure wheat well-baked, water clear from the fountain, wine and drink not too strong*, together with plentiful fish, herbs, fruit and root vegetables. No snacking, he adds, and not overmuch of any one dish. I tried vainly to persuade my mother to make some changes in the weekly cycle of shepherd's pie, baked beans on white toast and toad in the hole. Burton continued with a long digression on the subject of air, in which he discoursed, in the learned free-form manner of JA in the classroom, on everything from the merits of building houses on higher ground with a good view, to the importance of opening and closing windows, to the recreational benefits of a landscape that is *rather hilly than plain, full of downs, a Cotswold country, as being most commodious for hawking, hunting, wood, waters, and all manner of pleasures.*

Then there was a chapter called 'Exercise Rectified of Body and Mind'. Though warning against the dangers to the body caused by exercising to excess, Burton (surprisingly for a sedentary Oxford don) regarded physical activity as crucial to mental health: exercise is *much conducing to this cure and to the general preservation of our health*. Sport is good for the body – country pursuits are ideal, he says, but every city has its *several gymnics and exercises*, while dancing and singing are also commended. And it is equally important to exercise the mind: Burton helpfully suggested playing chess, going to the theatre, museums and art galleries, and above all reading everything you can lay your hands on, especially the classics.

The next necessity for the rectification of the mind, he said, was friendship. I was lucky in that regard, having Karim and Chris and the future spymaster Jonathan Evans as confidants. And the best cure of all, Burton claimed, is humour. If you can find a friend who makes you laugh, mirth will purge melancholy. My memory of sixth form is indeed of constant laughter, in class and out of it. The school was divided into houses, named after famous figures from Kentish history. (Mine was Wordsworth: the poet's brother Christopher was rector of a parish just outside Sevenoaks and sent his son to the school, where, according to the *Dictionary of National Biography*, 'he began to show his taste for Latin verse and cricket'.) My housemaster was Ian Huish, the funniest man I'd ever met, who started every day by reading out the notices in a voice that was a pitch-perfect parody of the school's registrar, a former Royal Air Force squadron leader for whom two o'clock in the afternoon was always fourteen hundred hours and the CCF was the backbone of the school.

It was in the third volume that I found what I was looking for: the cure for 'Love-Melancholy'. Burton discovered its symptoms in numerous ancient and modern literary works: *as the poet describes lovers: love causeth leanness, makes hollow eyes, dryness . . . lovers pine away, and look ill with waking, cares, sighs*. In *Hamlet*, Polonius is convinced that Hamlet has been driven mad with love, because of the behaviour that Ophelia describes to him: Hamlet has appeared in her closet, dishevelled, pale and sighing, his socks around his ankles. Burton offered an entire literary casebook of lovers in distress, demonstrating how being unrequitedly in love can quickly lead to loss of appetite and of sleep. In so doing, he could as well have been describing me after Sarah Jane sent her 'Dear Jon' letter.

As cures for 'Love-Melancholy', Burton offered me a typically practical set of suggestions: throw yourself into your work, improve your diet, take exercise, share banter with your friends, do everything you can to avoid seeing your lost love, travel, keep thinking about the freedom enjoyed by people who are single, and, for the particular benefit of men, spend time with other beautiful women so the one who has rejected you will not seem so special. Several of these remedies proved effective. I would put Simon and Garfunkel on my portable record player and repeat a line from their song 'I Am a Rock' as if it were a mantra: *I have my books / And my poetry to protect me.* Then I would read, read, read. Hiding in my room, I touched no one and no one could touch me. I determined to work so hard that I would follow my father and my brother to Cambridge. I became such a swot that Hurdy compared me to Harry Hotspur in *Henry IV Part 1*: *he that kills me some six or seven dozen of Scots at a breakfast, washes his hands, and says to his wife 'Fie upon this quiet life! I want work.'*

The suggestion of spending time with other beautiful women was less effective, mainly because all the prettiest girls were out of my league. With one girl, by coincidence also called Jane, I tried to relive the romance I had shared with Sarah Jane: walking in Knole Park as deer rustled in the dusk while we plunged into the bracken for ardent kisses followed by laughter at the penalty of mosquito bites, then strolling home as slowly as possible under the stars with our hands interlocked. But neither the romance nor the laughter returned. Jane phoned the next day to say that she was in agony with the bites and didn't think it would be a good idea to see me again.

It was with despair – the extreme of melancholy that can end in suicide – that Burton concluded his vast book. This struck home. There were so many lives of quiet desperation even in prosperous, middle-class Sevenoaks. One day around this time, I came home from school to the smell of woodsmoke, a police car parked in front of a house four doors up the road, and my mother ashen-faced. A neighbour, who to me had always seemed perfectly cheerful, had left a note on the kitchen table for her husband saying, 'Don't go into the garden, just call the police.' She had then immolated herself on an autumn bonfire.

★

When the black dog weighs upon you, you struggle to do anything. Voracious reader and furious writer that he was, Dr Johnson was so often overcome by the forced idleness of melancholy that he tried to turn it into a virtue. JA explained that one of the pen names under which he published his essays was 'The Idler'.

'Why so?' Because, Johnson wrote, *Every man is, or hopes to be, an Idler . . . as peace is the end of war, so to be idle is the ultimate purpose of the busy.* 'This is probably true for a class of idlers such as your good selves,' said JA. 'When someone is asked at the immigration desk whether the purpose of their visit is business or leisure, and they reply "business", they are not then asked, "What is the ultimate purpose of your busy-ness?" If they were, I doubt that many would say with Jeremy Bentham, "To increase the sum of human happiness." For most of us, the honest response would be "I pursue my business, make myself busy, to earn enough money to look after my family and to find a little time for idling" – whether that be pottering around the garden or perusing the Sunday newspaper.'

So perhaps the point of reading is that it is a very good form of idling. To enjoy a book is to add to the Idler's enjoyment of life. That would certainly be the main point of the paperback novels most of us read while lounging by the swimming pool in the sunshine on our well-earned summer holiday. The airport bookstore provides fast food to the Idler. But what kind of books offer the most nutritious diet?

Johnson gave his answer to the question in number 84 of *The Idler*, published on Saturday, 24 November 1759: *Biography is, of the various kinds of narrative writing, that which is most eagerly read, and most easily applied to the purposes of life.* Or, as he said to Boswell when they were on their tour to the Hebrides, *I esteem biography as giving what comes near to ourselves, what we can put to use.* And the best kind of biography, he claimed, is auto-biography: *Those relations are commonly of most value in which the writer tells his own story.* The reason for this, he explained, is that biography can give us examples of what makes people happy and what makes them unhappy, and there is no better person to give an account of that than the person who has been through the experience.

Had Dr Johnson written his own Life, James Boswell wrote on the first page of the book that laid the foundations of modern biography, *had he employed in the preservation of his own history, that clearness of narration and elegance of language in which he has embalmed so many eminent persons, the world would probably have had the most perfect example of biography that was ever exhibited.* But he didn't. Instead, we have the imperfect telling of his life by Boswell – which still happens to be one of the most rewarding examples of biography that has ever been written. *The Life of Samuel Johnson, LL.D.* lives through the immediacy of the narrative voice, the presence of the biographer himself. There is no attempt at objectivity, no desire for balance or comprehensiveness. Because the book is more like a dialogue with Johnson – much of it is a record of his conversations – the reader has the feeling of being in the room, joining the club, sharing the stories, reasoning and feeling, joshing and idling, alongside the subject himself. Boswell brings back to life the laughter and the friendships that kept Dr Johnson from despair.

Yet our teachers at school were none too keen on biography. We were taught to focus on the text, not the author. We learned about 'the intentional fallacy'. Sometimes, the rule was broken. You can't really understand the leap from John Donne's youthful erotic verse to the *Holy Sonnets* of his later years without knowing that he himself made a distinction between Jack Donne, lad about town, and Dr Donne, Dean of St Paul's Cathedral. But in the case of Shakespeare, his impersonality, his elusiveness, was the thing. Every action, every opinion in the plays belongs to the character, not the dramatist. He never gets into his pulpit, as the later Donne did. If a character starts preaching at you, their sermon is almost bound to be undone by experience. *All friends shall taste / The wages of their virtue*, intones the well-meaning but ineffective cuckold Albany in the final scene of *King Lear, And all foes / The cup of their deservings*. At which point Lear enters bearing the dead body of his daughter, most undeservedly murdered.

Sermons are intended to give answers to the meaning of life. Plays are there to pose questions. Like the one that Lear addresses to his dead daughter:

Why should a dog, a horse, a rat have life,
And thou no breath at all?

There is no answer to that, which is why the end of *King Lear* was too much for Johnson to stomach.

But a moment later, the loyal Earl of Kent steps forward. Hapless Albany has proposed that, following all the carnage, Britain should be jointly ruled by Kent and Edgar. Given that the treachery and civil war began with a division of the kingdom, this proposal to crown two new kings simultaneously does not seem a very good idea. So Kent gracefully takes his leave:

> I have a journey, sir, shortly to go:
> My master calls me, I must not say no.

Is he, like Gloucester and Lear before him, undergoing a heart attack? Or is he intending to commit suicide? Either way, he is answering the call of death out of loyalty and love towards Lear. There is no answer to the question about the dog, the horse, the rat and the dead daughter, but in its witness to the force of loyalty and love, even this play that seems to foreshadow the *promised end* of everything can enable its readers – and its spectators – better to endure life.

With the assistance of Burton and Boswell, Dr Johnson had given me another prescription. Like all Oxford dons in the seventeenth century, Burton was ordained in the Church of England. He accordingly urged his readers towards orthodox Christian faith and hope as the antidote to despair. But, with supreme honesty, he acknowledged the difficulty of maintaining hope and staving off despair, especially when one is lonely. That is what led him to end *The Anatomy of Melancholy* with the memorable advice that meant so much to Dr Johnson:

> As thou tenderest thine own welfare in this and all other melancholy, thy good health of body and mind, observe this short precept: give not way to solitariness and idleness. 'Be not solitary, be not idle.'

The avoidance of solitude needs love; of idleness, work. Burton's prescription for a good life was in this respect an anticipation of Leo Tolstoy's in a letter to his fiancée: *One can live magnificently in this world if one knows how to work and how to love.*

For Burton himself, as for Dr Johnson, the work was literature: he said that the purpose of writing *The Anatomy* was *by being busy to avoid melancholy.* The book was the cure for the disease that it diagnosed.

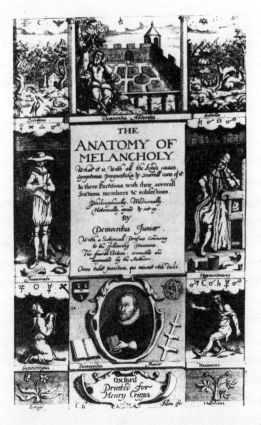

Of the several kinds of melancholy depicted on Burton's
title page, mine was that of the Inamorato with
hat pulled down upon his brows (middle left)

9.

Like Mad Hamlet

When it came to the A-Level Shakespeare exam that would play a big part in determining our university futures, we only had to write about two of the four Shakespeare plays we had studied. This was a good thing, because I loved *Henry IV Part 1* and *Antony and Cleopatra*, but was indifferent to the third play and could not get on at all with the fourth.

Dr Johnson opined that Shakespeare's natural instinct was for comedy, not tragedy. When we discussed this in class, most of us thought the idea was perverse. Wasn't it generally agreed that the tragedies of *Hamlet, Macbeth, Othello* and *King Lear* were Shakespeare's very greatest plays – the 'four big ones', as the influential critic A. C. Bradley had dubbed them? Did Johnson really think that *As You Like It*, our set comedy, was in that league? His own summary judgement didn't sound especially enthusiastic:

Of this play the fable is wild and pleasing. I know not how the ladies will approve the facility with which both Rosalind and Celia give away their hearts . . . The character of Jaques is natural and well preserved. The comick dialogue is very sprightly, with less mixture of low buffoonery than in some other plays.

His own melancholy must have drawn him to the melancholy Jaques, whom I found a bit of a bore. And, for all JA's patient explication of the analogy between a wit combat and a duel, we were all bored by the stand-up routines of the clown Touchstone. Then the four weddings at the end seemed just too good to be true. Shakespeare played the same trick in *Love's Labour's Lost*, a comedy I discovered later, but there he had the good sense to throw in a funeral.

Professor Christopher Ricks tossed off an aside in one of his dazzling lectures when I was at university: 'Tragedies make us happy because we think *life cannot be that bad*, whereas comedies make us sad because we think *life cannot be that good*.' My jaundiced view of *As You Like It* might have been due to the fact that my life didn't seem that good at the time. We were supposed to laugh at the gloomy and verbose self-indulgence of Jaques. Fair enough, since he was in many ways *playing the part* of the melancholy man. But was depression really a laughing matter? Besides, real depression was characterized by silence, withdrawal into the shell of the self that feels itself empty, not sermons about the sorrows of the deer and the resemblance of human life to a seven-act play.

As for the love-plot, the class divided into two: the cynics who made jokes out of such lines as Rosalind's *My affection hath an unknown bottom* and the frustrated romantics who, like Orlando, mooned around writing bad poetry but, unlike Orlando, never got the girl. Or, as in my case, got the girl and then made a mess of it and lost her. The only scene I really liked was the one where Rosalind, disguised as the boy Ganymede, pretends to be Rosalind training Orlando for his encounter with the real Rosalind. She has commissioned herself with the task of offering him a cure for love, since

> Love is merely a madness; and, I tell you, deserves as well a dark house and a whip as madmen do: and the reason why they are not so punished and cured is that the lunacy is so ordinary that the whippers are in love too.

If we didn't all find ourselves in thrall to the madness of love, we'd lock up those who succumb to it in a *dark house* – the place where Malvolio is confined in *Twelfth Night* when he is tricked into the presumptuous belief that the lady he serves is in love with him.

The good thing about a literary work, which is usually not the case with a love affair, is that you can give it a second chance at a much later date. *As You Like It* seems to me one of those Shakespeare plays that has to be seen to be loved. When it is staged well, you leave the theatre thinking that there could be no more life-affirming way of spending an evening. My relationship with the play was redeemed in 1994, courtesy of the touring company Cheek by Jowl.

Their production showed me how it was possible to be simultaneously true to Shakespeare in his own time and to make him our contemporary. The staging was in many respects authentically Elizabethan. No proscenium arch or realistic scenery; just an empty platform stage like that of Shakespeare's Globe. The exiled Rosalind, Celia and Touchstone walked round and round the bare boards: that was enough to take them to the Forest of Arden. Dress was modern, but more colourful and larger than life than that of everyday – as it would have been in the 1590s, when costumes included the cast-off robes of courtiers, second-hand wear, but still of a lavishness beyond the purse of most playgoers. Touchstone wore different-coloured socks, in allusion to the fool's motley. The eclecticism reminded me of the earliest surviving Shakespeare illustration, a drawing of *Titus Andronicus*, in which Titus wears a Roman toga and Tamora the Goth a medieval-looking robe, while the men-at-arms are 'modern-dress' Elizabethan halberdiers.

The irreverent style of performance, with frequent direct addresses to the audience and occasional improvised interjections on the part of Touchstone, an Elizabethan pun one moment, a bunch of flowers used as an interview microphone the next, answered to what Peter Brook in *The Empty Space*, my theatrical bible, called 'rough theatre':

It is always the popular theatre that saves the day. Through the ages it has taken many forms, and there is only one factor that they all have in common – a roughness . . . The arsenal is limitless: the aside, the placard, the topical reference, the local jokes, the exploiting of accidents, the songs, the dances, the tempo, the noise, the relying on contrasts, the shorthand of exaggeration, the false noses, the stock types, the stuffed bellies. The popular theatre, freed of unity of style, actually speaks a very sophisticated and stylish language: a popular audience usually has no difficulty in accepting inconsistencies of accent and dress, or in darting between mime and dialogue, realism and suggestion.

Le Beau touched up Orlando on the line *I shall desire more love and knowledge of you*. This was an all-male production, unashamedly gay at a time still scarred by the Aids epidemic. Best of all was Adrian Lester as Rosalind. With his beautiful voice and grace of movement, when he played the female Rosalind playing at being the male Ganymede, he seemed more like a woman playing a man than a man playing a woman. And when he played at Rosalind playing Ganymede playing Rosalind, one simply gave up trying to work out whether one thought he was a woman playing a man playing a woman or a man playing a woman playing a man playing a woman. When the text drew attention to the idea of the male actor, as in the Epilogue, one thought about it, but for most of the time the audience was held so spellbound by the strength and the wit and the pain of Rosalind that the actor's gender, let alone the colour of his skin, was forgotten.

Some feminists condemned the production, arguing that it perpetuated the exclusion of women from the Shakespearean stage and that by flaunting its drag it reduced the play to a homosexual romp; a campy Celia and an obviously cross-dressed Phebe provided hostages to such an attack, but the androgynous delicacy and subtlety of Lester's Rosalind seemed to me to nullify it. It probably helped, though, that the person I was sitting next to in the auditorium had the wit, intelligence, kindness and fortitude of Rosalind and that we were newly and madly in love. It was April when I wooed and, contrary to Rosalind's warning, did not become December when we wed. How we feel about a Shakespeare play when we encounter it will usually be affected by – and have an effect upon – the way we are feeling about life.

★

The fourth play, the one I really didn't like at all, was *Hamlet*. Oh God, how weary, stale, flat and unprofitable it seemed to me. The Prince of Denmark just droned on and on, in maudlin self-examination just like . . . me? That was the problem: it was all too close to the bone.

Hurdy guided us through the many possible interpretations of Hamlet's character, working from a sheet of key quotations cyclostyled on pink paper. One was T. S. Eliot saying that the play was a failure because it lacked an 'objective correlative', whatever that was. Another was a brief extract from a poem called *Daiphantus, or the Passions of Love*, published very soon after the play was first performed, which parodied the affected behaviour of a lovesick university student who

Puts off his clothes; his shirt he only wears,
Much like mad Hamlet.

This was a clear allusion to Ophelia's account of Hamlet coming to her chamber with his doublet all unbraced and no hat upon his head, in the style of the man affected with love-melancholy. It presumably also reflected the original staging of the play. But, as Hurdy pointed out, the undress may be a performance on Hamlet's part, an attempt – which certainly convinces Polonius – to put everyone off the scent. It comes after he says that he will *put an antic disposition on*, pretend to be mad. That was the question: to what extent was Hamlet really mad?

It was easy to see that Hamlet ticked all the boxes for melancholy in the Renaissance equivalent of the *Diagnostic and Statistical Manual of Mental Disorders*: disillusionment with the world, propensity for satiric and misogynistic outbursts, dislike of sunshine, obsession with death as manifested by a tendency

to lurk about graveyards and pick up skulls, simultaneous delight
and scorn in the scholar's life:

POLONIUS What do you read, my lord?
HAMLET Words, words, words.

Above all, inability to act. If JA resembled Dr Johnson, Hurdy's
avatar was Samuel Taylor Coleridge. His brilliant mind was
tainted by the inability ever to finish the books he was planning,
not least because of the irresistible lure of alcohol (at least he
never turned to opium). Coleridge said that he had a smack of
Hamlet himself, and so did Hurdy. He leaned very much to
the interpretation offered in the passage from one of Coleridge's
lectures in our compendium of critical quotations:

Hamlet was the play, or rather Hamlet himself was the character, in the intuition and exposition of which I first made
my turn for philosophical criticism, and especially for insight
into the genius of Shakespeare . . . Man was distinguished
from the animal, in proportion as thought prevails over sense:
but in healthy processes of the mind, a balance was maintained
between the impressions of outward objects and the inward
operations of the intellect: if there be an overbalance in the
contemplative faculty, man becomes the creature of meditation, and loses the power of action. Shakespeare seems to
have conceived a mind in the highest degree of excitement,
with this overpowering activity of intellect: and to have placed
him in circumstances, where he was obliged to act on the
spur of the moment. Hamlet, though brave and careless of
death, had contracted a morbid sensibility from this overbalance in the mind, producing the lingering and vacillating

delays of procrastination; and wasting in the energy of resolving, the energy of acting. Thus the play of Hamlet offers a direct contrast to that of Macbeth: the one proceeds with the utmost slowness, the other with breathless and crowded rapidity.

That was indeed the problem: my love of Shakespeare had been sparked by the breathless and crowded rapidity of *Macbeth*, doubled by the compression of the Marowitz remix, so I simply did not have the patience for the slow unfolding of *Hamlet*. I wrote an essay making this complaint. In response, Hurdy quietly rebuked me for using the word 'prevaricate' when I meant 'procrastinate'.

In this case, the theatre did not help. The timing should have been propitious. Just as we were in the final run-up to exams, in the spring term of 1976, the long-delayed National Theatre building was supposed to open on the south bank of the Thames with a production of *Hamlet* directed by Peter Hall and starring Albert Finney. Snagging problems caused more Hamlet-like delay, so the company stayed in their old home, the Old Vic. Discounted seats were procured for our school group. Up went the curtain and on went the show. And on and on. It was nearly three hours before we even reached the interval. Hall, a textual purist if ever there was one, had elected to play the whole thing uncut. It lasted four and a quarter hours. Reviews were mixed. For some, Finney was the best Hamlet since Michael Redgrave in the 1950s, but I agreed with Harold Hobson in *The Sunday Times*:

In an age that puts only a low value on grace, style and subtlety, Mr Finney is an appropriate enough choice. His voice is monotonously rasping, his mind does not respond to the text, and his way of taking curtain calls suggests insufferable conceit.

I learned only one thing from the production: slow Shakespeare was the kiss of death to a young audience. Has anyone ever left one of his plays saying, 'That was a great production, but I wish it had been longer?'

There was another problem. There seemed to be no emotional connection between Finney's Hamlet and Angela Lansbury's Gertrude. She never seemed to do anything other than wring her hands. The interpretative quotation that generated some discomfort in our class was the one from Freud about Hamlet's alleged Oedipus complex: he wants to kill Claudius not because Claudius has killed his father, but because his uncle is in bed with Gertrude, which is where Hamlet would really like to be himself. I couldn't see the incestuous desire, but it was obvious that the student prince had a difficult relationship with his mother. He is broken-hearted, grieving, isolated, indeed suicidal, *before* he meets the ghost and finds out about the murder of his father. That is because while he has been away at university, his mother has married his uncle with indecent haste. To say the least, she has let his father down. Which is enough to make Hamlet mad.

And what I could not forgive him for was the way in which his half-real, half-feigned madness makes Ophelia truly mad. I could not bring myself to sympathize with a hero who was so cruel to his girlfriend: dumping her, publicly humiliating her with his coarse jokes about lying between her legs and engaging in 'country matters', killing her father (albeit in a case of mistaken identity), ultimately driving her to distraction, to hysterical songs of sexual frustration and to a watery death.

Mark Rylance's mad Hamlet for the RSC in 1989:
the first production that held my attention

10.

Essentially Made or Essentially Mad?

In the 1970s, the Royal Shakespeare Company opened their productions in Stratford-upon-Avon, then transferred them to the Aldwych Theatre, just off the Strand in London. By good fortune for our study of *Henry IV Part 1*, they staged the full trilogy of *Part 1*, *Part 2* and *Henry V* around the same time as that National Theatre production of *Hamlet*. One Saturday, our sixth-form group sat through the endurance test of watching Alan Howard begin as Prince Hal in *Henry IV Part 1* at ten o'clock in the morning, reject Sir John Falstaff (Brewster Mason) at five in the afternoon at the end of *Part 2*, and still have the stamina to lead his men into the Battle of Agincourt as Henry V in the evening.

Prince Hal flees the dysfunctional court of his father, King Henry IV, who has usurped the throne from the legitimate but weak King Richard II. The Prince finds a substitute father in the fat knight, Sir John Falstaff; they carouse in the Boar's Head Tavern in the East End of London and, together with his friend Poins, Hal plans a botched highway robbery that will reveal Falstaff to be a coward. When they taunt him for this back in the pub, in one of the most theatrically rich scenes that Shakespeare ever wrote, Falstaff has an answer at every turn: *I knew ye as well as he that made ye. Why hear me, my masters, was it for me to kill the heir-apparent? . . . I was a coward on instinct.*

Falstaff and Hal then go on to enact their imagining of the moment when the Prince will return to the court and be upbraided by his father for wasting his time with rogues and layabouts. First Falstaff plays the King and the Prince plays himself; then they swap roles, allowing Falstaff to plead his own cause:

No, my good lord, banish Peto, banish Bardolph, banish Poins, but for sweet Jack Falstaff, kind Jack Falstaff, true Jack Falstaff, valiant Jack Falstaff, and therefore more valiant, being, as he is old Jack Falstaff, banish not him thy Harry's company, banish not him thy Harry's company: banish plump Jack, and banish all the world.

In response, Hal turns to stone and forewarns him of what will happen at the end of *Henry IV Part 2*: *I do, I will.*

Witnessing the full arc of the narrative that day at the Aldwych made all the pieces fit together. Very early in the story, Hal confides to the audience that he is only playing the part of the rebel:

I know you all, and will awhile uphold
The unyoked humour of your idleness.
Yet herein will I imitate the sun.

By pretending to be bad, he will seem not just good but unexpectedly good when he redeems himself. Then he will defeat the real rebel, the other Harry, Hotspur. *I know you all*: but does he know himself? Is he only playing? Getting to learn the language of the common people so that they will be loyal to him when he turns them into *food for powder* on the battlefield? Or is he really one of the lads? What will make him a good king? Is the person synonymous with the office, or does becoming an effective governor depend on a rejection of the pleasures and gifts of private life?

When Falstaff, accused of running away during the robbery, pretends that *I knew ye as well as he that made ye*, we might recall that *he that made* Hal is not only God, but also his father, Henry IV, who was a rebel himself. What is Prince Hal ultimately made of?

One day in class, Hurdy took us through a maddening problem. The original printed editions of the play – the scrappy little text published soon after its first performance and the handsome 'First Folio' of Shakespeare's complete plays – have Falstaff saying, in response to the threat of banishment at the climax of the play-acting scene, *Never call a true piece of gold a counterfeit: thou art essentially made, without seeming so*. This was ambiguous enough in itself. Falstaff appears to be saying that Hal is essentially true to his friends even though he has counterfeited, pretended, seemed to say that he will reject them. But the meaning could also rebound on Falstaff: Hal is essentially a true prince, not a rebel, so it is inevitable that he will eventually reject his own wild youth. To complicate it further, Hurdy explained that the printers of the Third Folio, published a generation later, suspected a misprint and changed the line to *thou art essentially mad, without seeming so*. He reminded us of the turning-point in sonnet 129, which he had shown us in its original: *On purpose layd to make the taker mad. / Made In pursut and in possession so.* Though one could just about make sense of the reading that lust is 'made in pursuit', a misprint seems far more likely, so all modern editions of the sonnets print 'Mad in pursuit'.

Opinion is more divided on Falstaff's line, but many editors have gone for *essentially mad* on the grounds that *essentially made*, 'made of an essence', doesn't really make sense and that the closest parallel phrasing elsewhere in Shakespeare is Hamlet saying

That I essentially am not in madness,
But mad in craft.

In other words, Hamlet is only pretending to be mad, but crafty Hal is only pretending to be a good chap when really he is a madcap. *Essentially made* and *essentially mad* give us two diametrically opposed readings of the character of Hal. The two options open up multiple possibilities of interpretation for both actor and student.

At the Aldwych, Alan Howard, torn between his duty to the cold and distant biological father who is obsessed with power and his affection for the warm but shameless substitute father in Eastcheap, seemed able to hold open both possibilities until the very moment when he rejected Falstaff in his devastating speech at the end of *Part 2*:

I know thee not, old man . . .
I have long dreamed of such a kind of man,
So surfeit-swelled, so old and so profane,

But being awake, I do despise my dream . . .
  I have turned away my former self,
So will I those that kept me company.

I know thee not: the opening words of this chilling, crafted public proclamation echo back to Hal's initial *I know you all* in *Part 1*. Yes, he has been planning this all along. But at such a price! Falstaff is left speechless as the newly crowned king and his procession leave the stage. Then he turns to Justice Shallow and says, *I owe you a thousand pound*. And for those of us in the theatre who had remained attentive all through the day, there was another echo back to *Part 1*, when Falstaff tells a lie that reveals a deeper truth. Mistress Quickly, the tavern-keeper, tells Prince Harry that Falstaff has told her that the Prince owes him a thousand pounds, which will enable him to pay his gargantuan bill for food and drink:

PRINCE Sirrah, do I owe you a thousand pound?
FALSTAFF A thousand pound, Hal? A million. Thy love is
  worth a million: thou ow'st me thy love.

By reverting to the sum of *a thousand pound* at the moment of rejection, Shakespeare subtly reminds his audience on the one hand that Falstaff is a disreputable sponger and on the other that what Hal has rejected is love.

Thinking about all this the morning after seeing the three plays in a day, I turned to Dr Johnson:

But Falstaff unimitated, unimitable Falstaff, how shall I describe thee? Thou compound of sense and vice; of sense which may be admired but not esteemed, of vice which may be despised, but hardly detested. Falstaff is a character loaded with faults, and with those faults which naturally produce contempt. He is a thief, and a glutton, a coward, and a boaster, always ready to cheat the weak, and prey upon the poor; to terrify the timorous and insult the defenceless. At once obsequious and malignant, he satirises in their absence those whom he lives by flattering . . . Yet the man thus corrupt, thus despicable, makes himself necessary to the prince that despises him, by the most pleasing of all qualities, perpetual gaiety, by an unfailing power of exciting laughter.

Hilaire Belloc once wrote a poem saying that nothing matters more in life than laughter and the love of friends. In order to become a king, Prince Hal has to reject these two things. *What, is it a time to jest and dally now?* he says to Falstaff on the battlefield near the end of *Part 1*. Recognizing that Falstaff's jests would deflate the heroics of Agincourt, Shakespeare broke the promise he made to his audience at the end of *Part 2*, and did not send Sir John to France in *Henry V*. Instead he killed him off, his heart broken by his friend's rejection of him. Pistol, whose humour is cruder and crueller, takes his place, and by the end of *Henry V* the victorious King Harry fails in the power to excite laughter – mine, at least – when he woos Kate, the French princess, by means of threats veiled in bad jokes (*in loving me, you should love the friend of France, for I love France so well that I will not part with a village of it; I will have it all mine*). Dr Johnson was puzzled that King Henry V is now speaking and behaving in the same way as Harry Hotspur (who also has a Kate), whom he mocked back in *Part 1*. That, it seemed to me, was the point. He has become a soldier and a braggart, a second Hotspur, at the expense of Falstaff and of Poins, of friendship and of play.

Johnson knew in his head all the responsibilities of morality, law and government that were vested in the King. But in his heart, he shared the sentiment of Falstaff on the battlefield of Shrewsbury: *Give me life.*

★

No sooner had Dr Johnson finished single-handedly compiling a complete dictionary of the English language on historical principles, with a legion of quotations giving examples of the usage of every word, than he set to work on his new edition of the complete plays of Shakespeare, with commentary. Where the words of Jesus gave him his model of virtue, in those of Shakespeare he found the perfect account of human failings, especially his own. His perpetual restlessness, for example. Hurdy introduced us to the Duke's sermon on mortality in the third act of *Measure for Measure* and Johnson's footnote explaining its purport:

> Thou hast nor youth, nor age;
> But as it were an after-dinner's sleep,
> Dreaming on both.

This is exquisitely imagined. When we are young we busy ourselves in forming schemes for succeeding time, and miss the gratifications that are before us; when we are old we amuse the languor of age with the recollection of youthful pleasures or performances; so that our life, of which no part is filled with the business of the present time, resembles our dreams after dinner, when the events of the morning are mingled with the designs of the evening.

I could see how a quotation such as this, moving from Shakespeare to life (and death), together with the critical principles articulated in the Preface, was of value in making us better readers and writers, and indeed more thoughtful people. But I was bored, as was everyone in class, by the latter part of the Preface, in which Johnson started quarrelling with the prior Shakespearean editions of Mr Rowe, Mr Pope and Mr Warburton. There didn't seem to be much to learn from this, other than the art of damning:

> Pope was succeeded by Theobald, a man of narrow comprehension and small acquisitions, with no native and intrinsick splendor of genius, with little of the artificial light of learning, but zealous for minute accuracy, and not negligent in pursuing it.

In later years, I would encounter one or two minds of the Theobald kind. Not to mention some that resembled the authors of various other works of textual criticism mentioned by Johnson:

> One ridicules errors with airy petulance, suitable enough to the levity of the controversy; the other attacks them with gloomy malignity, as if he were dragging to justice an assassin or incendiary. The one stings like a fly, sucks a little blood, takes a gay flutter, and returns for more; the other bites like a viper, and would be glad to leave inflammations and gangrene behind him.

Along with its dedicated teachers and brilliant scholars, the academic world still has its vipers and men (they are always men) of gloomy malignity. Some will strike at this book with forked tongue, hoping to infect the author with emotional gangrene.

'Why does Shakespeare have to be *edited*?' a boy asked in class. JA showed us some facsimiles of the original texts, with their weird spellings and the long printed 's' that looks like an 'f'. 'Potentially a little problematic when Ariel in *The Tempest* sings *Where the bee sucks, there suck I*', he joked, in order to gain our attention. And it was mildly intriguing that *Hamlet* existed in three distinct early texts, the strangely named Bad Quarto, Good Quarto and First Folio. We learned with some incredulity that the first printed text contained the immortal line, *To be or not to be, ay, there's the point*. We learned, too, that there were cuts in the Folio texts, suggesting that, unlike Peter Hall with his full-length *Hamlet*, Shakespeare's acting company saw that some of the plays were too long. And we were told about the baffling line, at the time of the report of Sir John Falstaff's death in *Henry V*, about *a table of green fields*. Mr Pope had come up with the explanation that this was really a misplaced stage direction for a stage manager called Greenfield to bring on a table; Johnson had followed Theobald in dismissing this ludicrous proposition and emending the line, so that as Falstaff died he *babbled of green fields* in a vein of English pastoral. Interventions of this kind, along with such questions as whether Hal is essentially made or essentially mad, made me see that, yes, Shakespeare has to be edited.

★

Thirteen years after being introduced by Dr Johnson and JA to this necessity, I saw another of those studio productions of

Shakespearean tragedy that changed my life. It was in The Pit, a white box in the basement of the Barbican in London. A young director called Deborah Warner staged *Titus Andronicus*, not as the stylized high drama that it had once been in a famous production starring Laurence Olivier and Vivien Leigh, directed by the young Peter Brook in the 1950s, but as a raw, intimate study in human suffering. Lavinia, the daughter of Titus, is gang-raped. So that she cannot reveal the identity of her attackers, they chop off her hands and cut out her tongue. In Warner's production, thanks to Sonia Ritter's performance and some very convincing make-up and costuming, Lavinia's mutilated body looked real, whereas in Brook's the blood had been represented by red silk streamers coming from Leigh's wrists and mouth. And when Titus cut off his own hand, a metal bucket and a piece of cheese wire made the audience gasp with horror. The production veered between black humour and darkly beautiful poetry.

> If there were reason for these miseries,
> Then into limits could I bind my woes:
> When heaven doth weep, doth not the earth o'erflow?
> If the winds rage doth not the sea wax mad,
> Threat'ning the welkin with his big-swoll'n face?
> And wilt thou have a reason for this coil?
> I am the sea. Hark how her sighs do blow!
> She is the weeping welkin, I the earth:
> Then must my sea be movèd with her sighs,
> Then must my earth with her continual tears
> Become a deluge overflowed and drowned,
> For why my bowels cannot hide her woes,
> But like a drunkard must I vomit them.

Brian Cox, who played Titus, said that this was without doubt the best stage performance of his life. It turned me into a huge admirer of Shakespeare's first tragedy, which Dr Johnson had condemned as so *barbarous* in its *general massacres* that it could not possibly have been by Shakespeare. JA had taught me that we should always stand up for our own literary opinions – 'as long as they are well supported by evidence in the text' – so there would be times when one could heartily disagree with the 'good doctor'. For me, *Titus* was not a self-indulgent spectacle of barbarism but a profound meditation on how human beings cope, or fail to cope, with extreme suffering. The most powerful moment in the play was when Titus was confronted not only with his violated daughter and his own chopped-off hand, but with the severed heads of his two sons. His kindly brother Marcus tells him that it is time to weep, rage and rend his garments. But all Titus can do is laugh. He has no more tears to shed. Cox rode the emotional rollercoaster and rendered the part completely true to life. From moment to moment, he was mad then sane, hilarious then heart-rending. His vocal range was astonishing – as you can still see in a grainy YouTube video in which he replays for a group of drama students the speech in which Titus prepares to slit the throats of the boys who raped and mutilated his daughter before baking them in a pie and serving them up to their mother. *For worse than Philomel you used my daughter, / And worse than Progne I will be revenged*: the full heft of the character's grief and anger was borne in Cox's stretching of the 'you' sound in 'used'.

Sitting in the Swan Theatre in Stratford-upon-Avon, watching another Deborah Warner production (the *King John* in which Ralph Fiennes played the Dauphin), I shared my enthusiasm for her *Titus* with Jane Armstrong, managing editor of the authoritative Arden Edition of Shakespeare, which had been our text when we were studying for A-Level. 'We're about to redo the Ardens,' she said, 'and *Titus* is one of the plays most in need of a fresh edition. Would you be interested?'

That was how I became a scholarly editor. Most people would imagine that it is a tedious task to collate textual variants and delve into obscure Shakespearean vocabulary, but I relished the variety of the task: other than staging it, there is no better way of getting to know a play than having to examine every word, every stage direction, every nuance of interpretation, while also writing an Introduction setting it in its context and opening up avenues for students to explore. The old Arden *Titus* had followed in the tradition of trashing the play. I think that, along with Warner's production and, a few years later, Julie Taymor's film with Anthony Hopkins in the lead role, my edition helped to rehabilitate it by taking its emotional range, its wit and its stagecraft seriously.

Having so enjoyed the process, I could not refuse when the Royal Shakespeare Company asked me to edit a new edition of the Complete Works under their imprimatur. The challenge was to do something new. What would be the point of a Complete Works that merely echoed the dozens of other editions that had appeared down the ages? In devising my own editorial principles, I looked back on the history of Shakespeare's text and found myself returning to Dr Johnson's Preface.

Half the sum of Shakespeare's plays were published in his own time, in little pocket editions in 'quarto' size. Then, seven years after his death, all thirty-six of his 'authorized' works were gathered in the handsome double-column Folio Edition over-seen by John Hemmings and Henry Condell, the leading surviving actors of the company for which he wrote. There are, however, significant differences between the quarto and Folio texts. It was only in Dr Johnson's era, the eighteenth century, that anyone began to worry about this.

In a pioneering edition of 1709, Nicholas Rowe, a playwright himself, systematically modernized Shakespeare's spelling and punctuation, organized the plays into act and scene divisions, added stage locations and *dramatis personae* lists. He followed the Folio texts, with one important exception: he noticed that the quarto text of *Hamlet* included an extra soliloquy, in which Hamlet castigates himself for doing nothing about his father's murder, in contrast to Fortinbras, who sends an army off to fight for a little patch of land, a far inferior cause. Not wanting to lose this, Rowe dropped it into his Folio-based text. So began a long tradition of 'conflating' the early texts. The habit endured until the late twentieth century, at which point editors began to suggest that many of the differences between quartos and Folio might be attributable to authorial revision or theatrical alteration. After all, plays go through a constant process of modification in rehearsal, performance and revival.

In 1725, Alexander Pope became the first editor to make substantial use of the quartos, but he made his decisions on aesthetic more than bibliographic grounds: what he called *shining passages* of poetic excellence were highlighted by means of marginal quotation marks, while *excessively bad* lines, especially those with too much wordplay, were *degraded* to the foot of the page. Then came Lewis Theobald, who, despised as he was by Johnson, must be credited as the first editor to undertake a sustained collation of Folio and quartos, and to make conjectural emendations on bibliographic rather than aesthetic grounds, under the influence of editorial techniques learned from classical and biblical scholarship.

Essentially Made or Essentially Mad?

In 1768, a very learned man called Edward Capell became the first editor to argue that the choice of which of the 'old editions' – quartos or Folio – should be used as the 'ground-work' for the editorial task should be determined by asking which version was the earliest authoritative text (thus some quartos were deemed 'authoritative' and others 'corrupt' – later editors would use the terms 'pirated' or simply 'bad'). And in 1790, an even more learned man, Edmond Malone, an Irish friend of Johnson's, became the first editor to apply principles of 'authenticity' to all aspects of the preparation of an edition, seeking not only to get back to the Shakespearean originals behind the texts 'corrupted' by printers and copyists, but also to attend to the chronology of the creation of the plays, together with contextual and historical determinants of meaning. By the end of the eighteenth century, the principles of Shakespearean editing were all there; through the twentieth century, the Ardens would put them into practice with unprecedented rigour, based on quasi-scientific principles for establishing the 'correct' copy-text for each play by means of bibliographic minutiae.

By this account, Dr Johnson's edition was not notably inno-vative. He prepared it by marking up copies of two earlier editions – Theobald's and that of a bishop called William Warburton. But in the Preface he laid out a series of conser-vative principles that seemed to me eminently sensible. His adoption of Theobald's *babbled of green fields* was the exception, not Johnson's rule: generally, he eschewed such bold editorial interventions. He had particular respect for the actor-authorized text of the First Folio. He took pride in never introducing new emendations of his own into the text, but rather *confining his imagination to the margin*. His rule was not to correct the early printed text unless he was fully confident that error had been

introduced by a scribe or printer. If there was difficulty or
obscurity, he sought to explain possible meanings before
emending to something less obscure:

> To alter is more easy than to explain, and temerity is a more
> common quality than diligence. Those who saw that they
> must employ conjecture to a certain degree, were willing to
> indulge it a little further. Had the author published his own
> works, we should have sat quietly down to disentangle his
> intricacies, and clear his obscurities; but now we tear what
> we cannot loose, and eject what we happen not to understand.

He reminded readers that the text of the plays is often obscure,
not because of corruption in the printing-house but because
*the style of Shakespeare was in itself ungrammatical, perplexed and
obscure.* Explanatory annotation was accordingly more important
than emendation. *It has been my settled principle, that the reading
of the ancient books is probably true, and therefore is not to be disturbed
for the sake of elegance, perspicuity, or mere improvement of the sense*:
we may grant that the printers of the plays were far from perfect,
yet *they who had the copy before their eyes were more likely to read
it right, than we who read it only by imagination.* When a passage
was obscure, he began by trying to recall it to sense with the
least possible violence: *I have adopted the Roman sentiment, that
it is more honourable to save a citizen, than to kill an enemy, and
have been more careful to protect than to attack.* In short, on the
matter of emendation, when in doubt, don't. Or, if the reading
of the original text is defensible, then retain it.

Re-reading this, an idea came to me. Might it not be an
honourable thing to *save* the Folio, to *protect* rather than to *attack*
its readings? To respect the work of the actors who had been

in the plays and stayed loyal to Shakespeare all their working lives. In their Prefatory Address 'To the great Variety of Readers', Hemmings and Condell, to whom Shakespeare had bequeathed mourning rings in his will, wrote of their *care, and pain, to have collected and published* the works of their friend. They claimed that the earlier editions were *stolen and surreptitious copies, maimed and deformed by the frauds and stealths of injurious impostors*, whereas their volume presented the plays *absolute in their numbers, as he conceived them*. This was not strictly true – some of the quartos do seem to have been printed from Shakespeare's original working manuscripts, while the Folio was sometimes deformed by censorship – but it struck me that the appropriate way of creating an edition for the Royal Shakespeare Company might be to reproduce, with old spellings modernized and manifest printers' errors corrected, the text created by the original royal Shakespeare company: the King's Men (formerly known as Lord Chamberlain's Men) for whom he wrote. So that is what I did, ably assisted by my fellow-editor, Eric Rasmussen, an unflappable American with the sharpest eye for a misprint of anyone I have ever met; assisted by a team of dedicated graduate students, we produced the first modern-spelling Folio-based Shakespeare since that of Nicholas Rowe in 1709, and the first ever edition of the Folio to be provided with annotations explaining Shakespeare's obscure language, together with contextual and interpretive Introductions, as well as supplementary texts of works, notably his non-dramatic poems, that were excluded from the Folio.

It was the most arduous task of my working life. What kept me going, along with the Johnsonian principles that inspired it, was the Johnsonian example of hard work as a bulwark against despair. Because those were years when, nursing a sick child, I was very close to despair.

not him thy *Harryes* companie; banish plumpe *Iacke*, and banish all the World.

Prince. I doe, I will.

Enter Bardolph running.

Bard. O, my Lord, my Lord, the Sherife, with a most most monstrous Watch, is at the doore.

Falst. Out you Rogue, play out the Play: I haue much to say in the behalfe of that *Falstaffe.*

Enter the Hostesse.

Hostesse. O, my Lord, my Lord.

Falst. Heigh, heigh, the Deuill rides vpon a Fiddle-sticke: what's the matter?

Hostesse. The Sherife and all the Watch are at the doore: they are come to search the House, shall I let them in?

Falst. Do'st thou heare *Hal*, neuer call a true peece of Gold a Counterfeit: thou art essentially made, without seeming so.

Prince. And thou a naturall Coward, without in-

The Folio text: 'essentially made'

11.

The Man from Stratford

One autumn there was a curious announcement when we returned for the new school year. Mr Frank Dawson, who taught me for O-Level Latin and Greek, had changed his name by deed poll. He would now be LEMA instead of FD. Lewis Edward Mithras Alexis. In our first lesson of term, he explained the names. Lewis was the anglicized form of Ludwig, chosen because Beethoven was the greatest of all composers. Mithras because he was a believer in the Roman mystery cult of that bull-slaying god. Alexis because the greatest of ancient poets, Virgil, devoted his second Eclogue to a lovely boy of that name. I am not sure that a schoolmaster could advertise this predilection today. And what of Edward, which seemed a mundane choice in such company? It was in honour of Edward de Vere, 17th Earl of Oxford, the 'true' author of the plays attributed to William Shakespeare.

LEMA would shuffle into class wearing a long grey and not very clean raincoat. To picture his pale face and long black hair, you only have to visualize Alan Rickman as Snape in the Harry Potter films. 'After God,' he told us, quoting the French novelist Alexandre Dumas, 'Shakespeare has created most.' He had a quick wit. 'Or, as Hollywood mogul Samuel Goldwyn said on first leafing through the collected works, *Fantastic! And it was all written with a feather!*' But the mere grammar-school boy from rural Warwickshire: how could he have known enough about courts and kings to create *Hamlet* and *Lear*, about Italy to have written *The Merchant of Venice*, about war to have written *Henry V*? Where did he get his vast vocabulary and his knowledge of the law? Aren't the surviving documents about his life mysteriously silent about his plays?

LEMA was a bit of a conspiracy theorist. He believed that Nero was a Christian emperor and that Akhenaten, father of Tutankhamun, was actually Moses. But because I admired him as a teacher, I wanted to believe him. I started reading books such as Dorothy and Charlton Ogburn's *This Star of England*, which argued that the lovely boy of the sonnets was Henry Wriothesley, 3rd Earl of Southampton (which may well have been true), offspring of an illicit union between the Earl of Oxford and Queen Elizabeth (which was news to my history teachers). Then there was Broadway press agent Calvin Hoffman's *The Murder of the Man Who Was 'Shakespeare'*, which proposed that Christopher Marlowe wasn't really killed in a brawl over the bill for the booze in a house in Deptford, but that a dead sailor was substituted in his place and he was whisked away to Italy by the secret service, from where he wrote the plays and sent them back to be passed off as Shakespeare's. All these theories did seem a lot more exciting than the idea of a middle-class grammar-school boy going to London and making some money in the nascent entertainment industry, then returning home to quiet retirement in his native town.

The Man from Stratford

It is, of course, the first question I am always asked by taxi drivers when they ask me what I do. 'Shakespeare professor, are you, guv? So tell me, did he write all those plays himself?'

The doubting began two and a half centuries after Shakespeare's death, with an American woman called Delia Bacon. She proposed that the plays were really written by . . . the philosopher and lawyer Sir Francis Bacon, a proper scholar and courtier. But the unfortunate Delia couldn't find any evidence, so she attempted to dig up Shakespeare's grave in the hope of finding a secret message from Sir Francis. Not long after, her family reported with regret that she had been 'removed to an excellent private asylum at Henley-in-Arden – in the forest of Arden'. Eight miles from Stratford-upon-Avon, as it happens.

Then along came an Edwardian schoolmaster with a new theory: Shakespeare's plays were really written by the 17th Earl of Oxford. That the Earl was an enthusiastic and sometimes violent pederast is not necessarily an impediment to his candidacy. A little local difficulty comes with his death in 1604, before half the plays were written. He would also have struggled to collaborate with the actors during the long period when he was in exile abroad for having committed the unpardonable offence of breaking wind in front of Queen Elizabeth. The story is told by the biographer John Aubrey, who also happens to have had reliable information that the actor from Stratford was indeed the author of the plays attributed to him:

This Earl of Oxford, making of his low obeisance to Queen Elizabeth, happened to let a Fart, at which he was so abashed and ashamed that he went to Travel [for] 7 years. On his return the Queen welcomed him home, and said, 'My Lord, I had forgot the Fart'.

The schoolmaster who pioneered the 'Oxfordian' theory was called J. Thomas Looney, though he liked to pronounce it 'Loney'.

As I investigated the 'Authorship Controversy', I found that no shortage of candidates had been put forward at one time or another: 17th Earl of Oxford, 8th Lord Mountjoy, 7th Earl of Shrewsbury, 6th Earl of Derby, 5th Earl of Rutland, 2nd Earl of Essex, Sir Walter Raleigh, the Countess of Pembroke, Queen Elizabeth I and King James I. These names seemed to have something in common. Did it all boil down to snobbery, the conviction that such high genius could not have come from a lowly place? Americans, including Mark Twain of all people, have often taken this line, which is curious in a country where it's supposed to be possible to go from a log cabin to the White House.

Conspiracy theorists dismiss 'the Man from Stratford' as an imposter. They suppose that he was an illiterate actor mouthing some nobler man's words. It wasn't quite clear how the actor could have learned his parts if he couldn't read.

I stuck with the Oxford theory for as long as I could, even trying to convince my college tutor. By then, though, I was only doing it to be contrary. The benefit of my dalliance with heresy was that it had made me look very hard at the evidence. This proved invaluable when, many years later, I was accosted by Prince Charles during the interval of a performance of *Henry V*: 'I wonder if you can help me out? We always have a family row at Christmas because my father doesn't believe that Shakespeare wrote his plays. Can you send me a single page laying out the key facts, so that I can win the argument next time?'

This is what I told him.

In his will, Master William Shakespeare of Stratford-upon-Avon left legacies to his fellow-actors John Hemmings and Henry

Condell. They in turn edited the First Folio of his collected works, referring there to his writing techniques and their close friendship with him. The First Folio also includes poems by Ben Jonson attesting to the authentic likeness of the engraving of Shakespeare on the title page, to Shakespeare's authorship of the plays and to his coming from Stratford (*Sweet swan of Avon*). In both his notebook and his conversations with the Scottish poet Drummond of Hawthornden, Jonson spoke (sometimes critically) about Shakespeare, who acted in his plays, as a writer.

Many other contemporaries also referred to Shakespeare as a poet and playwright. They range from Sir George Buc, Master of the Revels at court, to other dramatists such as Francis Beaumont and Thomas Heywood, to Leonard Digges, a family friend of Shakespeare's who was also a writer himself. Shakespeare's monument in Holy Trinity Church represents him as an author and refers to his literary greatness. It was seen by a visiting poet soon after his death, negating the claim of some conspiracy theorists that it was altered at a later date.

How did a man who did not go to university write such 'learned' plays? They are actually much less learned than the plays of his contemporaries George Chapman and Ben Jonson, neither of whom went to university. The simple fact is that the education in Latin language and literature that Shakespeare received at the Stratford grammar school meant that by the age of twelve he would have had a command of the discipline as good as that of a university Classics student today.

How did he know about courts, how see into the minds of dukes and kings? Through his reading and through witnessing the court by acting there. Payments to him for writing plays for court performance survive in the Chamber accounts of the royal household. His knowledge of Italy? Better to ask how someone who had been to Italy could write two plays set in Venice and never mention a canal. The real questions should be: how could anyone but a glover's son have put in his plays so much accurate technical detail about leather manufacture and the process of glove-making? And how could anyone but a professional actor have filled his plays with inside information about the nitty-gritty of making theatre?

★

The truth of the Authorship Controversy is that it is an offshoot of the cult of Shakespeare that emerged with the Romantic movement of the late eighteenth and early nineteenth centuries. No one had any doubts about his identity before then. But once you turn someone into a god, sects and heretics are bound to emerge.

There is a rather glorious lunacy to the whole thing. No one has exposed this better than the word-magician Vladimir Nabokov. Reading his second English-language novel, *Bend Sinister*, when I was at university, I warmed to his account of how anti-Stratfordianism has the same allure as *men of bizarre genius, big-game hunters, chess players, prodigiously robust and versatile lovers* and *the radiant woman taking her necklace off after the ball*. The protagonist, a philosopher called Adam Krug, and his friend Ember consider the authorship question from a strictly epistemological point of view:

Theoretically there is no absolute proof that one's awakening in the morning (the finding oneself again in the saddle of one's personality) is not really a quite unprecedented event, a perfectly original birth. One day Ember and he had happened to discuss the possibility of their having invented in toto the works of William Shakespeare, spending millions and millions on the hoax, smothering with hush money countless publishers, librarians, the Stratford-on-Avon people, since in order to be responsible for all references to the poet during three centuries of civilization, these references had to be assumed to be spurious interpolations injected by the inventors into actual works which they had re-edited; there still was a snag here, a bothersome flaw, but perhaps it might be eliminated, too, just as a cooked chess problem can be cured by the addition of a passive pawn.

Ember then comes up with a fantastically perverse reading of *Hamlet* in which

The real plot of the play will be readily grasped if the following is realized: the Ghost on the battlements of Elsinore is not the ghost of King Hamlet. It is that of Fortinbras the Elder whom King Hamlet has slain. The ghost of the victim posing as the ghost of the murderer – what a wonderful bit of farseeing strategy, how deeply it excites our intense admiration!

There was nothing to stop Nabokov from inventing a character who seeks to reinvent *Hamlet* as a cypher in the manner of his own novels, which are full of doubles and shadows, poses and stratagems (Humbert Humbert and Clare Quilty in *Lolita*, the *Twelfth Night*-like twinning of the narrator V and his biographical subject in *The Real Life of Sebastian Knight*, and many more). And since there is no way of proving definitively that what you think of as the real world is not a dream, that this morning was not your first morning, that the past is not a fiction, and that the plot of *Hamlet* is not a hoax, you can't prove definitively that the identity of Shakespeare is not a hoax.

Before writing *Bend Sinister*, Nabokov read a classic conspiratorial treatise, *Bacon is Shake-speare* by Sir Edwin Durning-Lawrence, BART., B.A., LL.B., ETC. Following in his footsteps, I ventured into Durning-Lawrence's book:

> In Camden's 'Remains' of 1616 in the Chapter on Surnames, because the head ornament is printed upside down, we may be perfectly certain that we shall find some revelation concerning Bacon and Shakespeare.
>
> Accordingly on p. 121 we find the name of a village 'Bacon Creping.' There never was a village called 'Bacon Creping.' And on page 128 we read 'such names as Shakspeare, Shotbolt, Wagstaffe.' In referring to the great Cryptographic book, we shall realise the importance of this conjunction of names.

I love the assurance of *we may be perfectly certain*.

Durning-Lawrence then introduces his prize exhibit, a facsimile of the title page of *the great Cryptographic book*, a sixteenth-century treatise by Gustavus Selenus (a pseudonym, naturally) entitled *Cryptomenytices et Cryptographiae*. He invites the reader to look closely at its triptych of images.

Nabokov pillages and dilates upon Durning-Lawrence's analysis. Ember has the images on his wall, allegedly annotated in the hand of a contemporaneous scholiast:

> Number one represents a sixteenth-century gentleman in the act of handing a book to a humble fellow who holds a spear and a bay-crowned hat in his left hand. Note the sinistral

detail . . . Note also the legend: 'Ink, a Drug.' Somebody's idle pencil (Ember highly treasures this scholium) has numbered the letters so as to spell *Grudinka* which means 'bacon' in several Slavic languages.

Number two shows the rustic (now clad in the clothes of the gentleman) removing from the head of the gentleman (now writing at a desk) a kind of shapska. Scribbled underneath in the same hand: '*Ham-let*, or *Homelette au Lard*.'

Finally, number three has a road, a traveller on foot (wearing the stolen shapska) and a road sign 'To High Wycombe.'

Never mind that Nabokov has divided the top-left image into two and ignored the one on the top right, while also neglecting to point to the shaking spear in the sky, facing left, in the heraldic position known as *bend sinister*, just like the spear on Shakespeare's coat of arms, which was reproduced on the covers of the old Temple Edition, bound in maroon limp leather, some volumes of which Nabokov took from his father's library when fleeing St Petersburg at the time of the October Revolution. You must be convinced by now. Why have you not seen before that *Hamlet* sounds like *Homelette au Lard*, which is French for Bacon Omelette? After his tour de force of decipherment, Durning-Lawrence could proudly proclaim:

> The hour has come when it is desirable and necessary to state with the utmost distinctness that
> BACON IS SHAKESPEARE.

That should have been the rousing conclusion to the book, but he couldn't resist adding a chapter in which his theory was 'Proved mechanically in a short chapter on the long word Honorificabilitudinitatibus'. This involved converting the longest word in Shakespeare into numbers (A=1, B=2 etc.), reaching a total of 287, and since 'Honorificabilitudinitatibus' is the 151st word on page 136 of the First Folio and 151 + 136 = 287, this proves ('mechanically') that Bacon is Shakespeare. Oh yes, and that the ludicrously voluminous word conjured by the clown Costard in *Love's Labour's Lost* contains an anagram of Bacon's name (in Latin). On reading this, I could think only of Polonius:

I will be brief: your noble son is mad.
Mad call I it; for, to define true madness,
What is't but to be nothing else but mad?

Being the most playful of writers, Nabokov flirted with anti-Stratfordianism himself, yet in the very next paragraph of *Bend Sinister* he both explains why the Authorship Controversy became possible and why, word games aside, we should not have any doubt as to Shakespeare's true identity:

His name is protean. He begets doubles at every corner. His penmanship is unconsciously faked by lawyers who happen to write a similar hand. On the wet morning of November 27, 1582, he is Shaxpere and she is a Wately of Temple Grafton. A couple of days later he is Shagspere and she is a Hathway of Stratford-on-Avon. Who is he? William X, cunningly composed of two left arms and a mask. Who else? The person who said (not for the first time) that the glory of God is to hide a thing, and the glory of man is to find it. However, the fact that the Warwickshire fellow wrote the plays is most satisfactorily proved on the strength of an applejohn and a pale primrose.

Plays for the Elizabethan stage were not autobiographical confessions exposing court intrigue and secret love affairs, as the Oxfordians and other anti-Stratfordians believe. Shakespeare did not fill his works with portraits of his acquaintances (though he occasionally made joking references to members of his own acting company and to friends such as his schoolmate Richard Field, who became the publisher of his first printed work). What we can unearth in the plays is better described as the experiential DNA of the author. This is Nabokov's point.

Shakespeare was always a countryman, as is revealed by the precision of his country language: *the fact that the Warwickshire fellow wrote the plays is most satisfactorily proved on the strength of an applejohn and a pale primrose.*

Disappointing as it is to acknowledge, the mighty dramatist was provincial and middle-class, and his life was distinctly uneventful. His rival Christopher Marlowe moved in a world of espionage, thuggery, buggery and skulduggery. His collaborator George Wilkins had a second career as a brothel-keeper, with a history of beating up the girls who worked for him. As for Ben Jonson, both friend and rival, he fought in the Dutch wars, killed a fellow-actor in a street brawl and was thrown into prison for writing subversive plays.

Will Shakespeare was neither a fabulous aristocrat nor a flamboyant gay double agent. He was a grammar-school boy from an obscure town in middle England, whose main concern was to keep out of trouble and to better himself and his family. He came from a perfectly unremarkable background, which is the most remarkable thing of all.

Maybe it was because Shakespeare was a nobody that he could become everybody. He speaks to every nation in every age because he understood what it is to be human. He didn't lead the life of the pampered aristocracy. He was a working craftsman who had to make his daily living and face the problems that we all face every day. His life was ordinary; it was his mind that was extraordinary. His imagination leaped to distant lands and ages past, through fantasy and dream, yet it was always rooted in the real.

He shows us what it is to be human. But what was it like *being Shakespeare?*

★

Spring 2009. The message – fountain pen, black ink, flamboyant hand – arrived out of the blue on a thick white postcard embossed with the name Simon Callow. He was familiar with my work. I might have been familiar with his one-man play *The Mystery of Charles Dickens*, in which he told the story of the author's life, interweaving it with dramatized readings from the novels. He had long wanted to do something similar with Shakespeare. Might I be interested in writing the script?

We met in a little private members' club tucked into a Dickensian alleyway near Charing Cross station. He explained how, as a drama student in Belfast, he had become dresser to Micheál Mac Liammóir. Born Alfred Willmore in London, Liammóir had reinvented himself as an Irishman and, together with his partner Hilton Edwards, founded the famous Gate Theatre in Dublin, where Orson Welles made his stage debut. Liammóir played Iago in Welles's film of *Othello* and Poor Tom in the extraordinary 1953 live telecast of a stripped-down *King Lear*, directed by the young Peter Brook, with Welles as Lear (not yet forty years old, but with *Citizen Kane* behind him, he was guarded throughout by the Inland Revenue Service, who took his wage as a contribution to his mountain of unpaid tax). In this version, Edmund and Edgar were omitted and Tom was a real madman, a role which Liammóir executed with panache. Then for the last twenty years of his life he toured his pioneering one-man show *The Importance of Being Oscar*, which dresser Callow, with some temerity but ultimately huge satisfaction, revived in London twenty years after the actor's death. It was, Simon explained, a kind of living biography. The actor does not pretend to *be* Wilde; rather, he evokes him through anecdotes from his life, revelations of his character and his creative language. The aim was to move seamlessly between narrative and quotation in a way that finally began to bring the subject into the room.

'That's all very well for Wilde and Dickens,' I said, 'where we have wonderful stories about their lives, but the surviving documents that give us Shakespeare's biography aren't exactly dramatic, are they? All those petty legal disputes and property deals in Stratford, the odd payment for performance at court. How are we going to make theatre out of that? Shakespeare didn't write about his own childhood in the way that Dickens did in *Copperfield*.'

'We're going to mine the plays for little details that reveal his inner life. Childhood – where are the child characters in Shakespeare?'

'I get it,' I replied. 'Mamillius in *The Winter's Tale*, that lovely scene with Hermione and her ladies.'

'I'd *love* to play Mamillius,' boomed Simon, banging on the lunch table.

I warmed to the idea: 'And we could link the death of Mamillius, Leontes' only son, to that of Hamnet, Shakespeare's only son. Then maybe bring in Queen Constance, grieving over the loss of her child in *King John*.'

'I don't know that one,' said Simon, 'but I certainly want to play some female parts. What I need you to do is find me a structure.'

Simon playing many parts. It came to me. Shakespeare's own structure for a life. 'One man in his time plays many parts.'

'The Seven Ages?' Simon looked doubtful. 'Isn't that a bit obvious? Gielgud did it. *The Ages of Man*, based on that anthology by Dadie Rylands.'

'Obvious, but effective. Wouldn't you like to outdo Gielgud? He just used Jaques's speech as a peg on which to hang his beautifully spoken monologues. We use it to tell a story. Map it on to Shakespeare's life. The schoolboy: his grammar-school education, that scene with the Latin lesson and the Welsh schoolmaster in *Merry Wives of Windsor*. The lover: the sonnets. The soldier: the history plays. Second childhood: Justice Shallow, Lear.'

'Definitely Lear. You have it, my boy.' Then he turned his head, winked, and directed my gaze across the room to a table where fellow-actor Sir Derek Jacobi was holding forth. 'You see, what I want to do is show those who have gone over to the dark side, like my good friend, that the plays could *only* have been written by the Man from Stratford.'

'The Man from Stratford?' I said: 'Good title.' It pained me that Jacobi – the most glorious Benedick in *Much Ado About Nothing* – had become an Oxfordian. And that Bacon was the favoured candidate of Mark Rylance, whose pyjama-clad Hamlet with a *very* antic disposition had finally reconciled me to the play. (When the production was taken to the Broadmoor high-security psychiatric hospital, an inmate said to him afterwards, 'You were really mad – take it from me, I should know, I'm a loony.') How could such consummate Shakespearean actors not see that only an actor could have written the plays? I liked the idea of a secret mission to blow the anti-Stratfordians out of the water.

I was living near Stratford-upon-Avon at the time, so had local atmosphere ready to hand. I began my draft on the train home to Warwickshire. I finished it in three weeks and sent it to Simon. He telephoned. 'I'm in a hotel room in Istanbul, writing about Orson. I've devoured your script. It's gorgeous. I could do it tomorrow. I wouldn't want to change a single word.' Eighteen comprehensive rewrites later, we finally reached the stage, touring England and playing the Edinburgh Festival Fringe.

Working on the play in the rehearsal room was my best Shakespearean education since school. I saw things I had not fully seen before. How every line of Henry V's exhortation to his men uses the actor's body as much as his words:

Stiffen the sinews, summon up the blood,
Disguise fair nature with *hard-favoured* rage,
Then *lend the eye* a terrible aspect:
Let it pry through *the portage of the head*
Like the brass cannon, *let the brow o'erwhelm* it
As fearfully as doth a gallèd rock
O'erhang and jutty his confounded base,
Swilled with the wild and wasteful ocean.
Now *set the teeth* and *stretch the nostril* wide,
Hold hard the breath and *bend up every spirit*
To his full height.

How the plays, *A Midsummer Night's Dream* most exquisitely, were grounded in Warwickshire fields and steeped in the magic of country lore, showing that Shakespeare truly was the Man from Stratford. What would an aristocrat have known of *the nine-men's morris filled up with mud* or elves that *Creep into acorn cups and hide them there* or the brownie that performs household chores at night?

Now it is the time of night
That the graves all gaping wide,
Every one lets forth his sprite,
In the church-way paths to glide.

And we fairies that do run
By the triple Hecate's team,
From the presence of the sun,
Following darkness like a dream,
Now are frolic; not a mouse
Shall disturb this hallowed house.
I am sent with broom before,
To sweep the dust behind the door.

And yes, how, for all his vaunted impersonality, it was possible to track the journey of his life and the growth of his mind through his plays. The split between family in the country and work in the city, between Stratford and London. A grammar-school education – Simon brought the house down every night when he played the exchange between cheeky schoolboy William and the Welsh schoolmaster, with his *focative* case and *horum, harum, horum*. A precocious and varied love life. The direct experience of witnessing recruiting officers mustering for the militia in rural Warwickshire and Gloucestershire. Some basic legal language learned from a life of litigation. Above all, a constant awareness that all the world's a stage, all the men and women merely players. Jaques's seven ages of man in *As You Like It* are at one and the same time the seven ages of Everyman and of that unique genius named William Shakespeare.

I also learned, as Shakespeare himself may have done, that not every idea poured out on paper will work in the theatre. My drafts included several comic set pieces – Malvolio's letter scene, Lance and his remote-controlled, battery-operated dog Crab – which either disappeared in the rehearsal room or fell away as the play metamorphosed through its five years of performance on dozens of stages, from a world premiere in

Plymouth by the clifftop where Sir Francis Drake (allegedly) played bowls as he waited for the Spanish Armada, via regional theatres large and small, on to a sell-out in the cavernous Assembly Rooms during the Edinburgh Fringe Festival, and away to distant outposts in Chicago and Trieste. But I trusted Simon and his director, Tom Cairns, on this: they were the ones who would win the plaudits or take the flak.

Only once did we have 'artistic differences'. Late in the rehearsal process, I discovered that the scene in which the rude mechanicals rehearse their play in *A Midsummer Night's Dream* had been removed. Bottom wants to play all the parts: *let me play Thisbe too . . . Let me play the lion too*. Plays within plays and images of life as *a walking shadow, a poor player / That struts and frets his hour upon the stage* – academics call it 'metatheatre', theatre about theatre – why, this was the very heart of Shakespeare, so at the heart of our play the audience should see the correspondence. Like Bottom, Simon was playing all the parts, from Juliet to Falstaff to Macbeth to Lear to Prospero.

For the first and only time in my life, I threw a hissy fit.

'If Bottom goes, I go.'

Bottom was duly restored, in a bravura sequence in which Simon played him simultaneously with Peter Quince, Francis Flute and the rest of the company. The show was ready to go on the road.

It began with Simon as Prospero storming on to the stage in the midst of a high-tech hurricane. As it evolved, we simplified both the staging and the delivery. For its three West End runs and an excursion to New York's Brooklyn Academy of Music, the polemical title *The Man from Stratford* was replaced with the more inward *Being Shakespeare*. Now Simon just wandered on and started to tell the story, quietly, conversationally: *Just before he embarked on* Hamlet, *Shakespeare wrote his great romantic comedy* As You Like It, *in which the melancholy Jaques says, 'All the world's a stage . . .'.*

We never wavered from our conviction that there are moments in the plays that go to the very heart of the Man from Stratford. Of the many reviews, the most gratifying was the one which said *conspiracy theorists look away.* Another suggested that the show might *seal the pro-Shakespeare anti-Edward-de-Vere-and-others debate.* It didn't. As Nabokov knew, no one ever will. But of the privilege of learning from such an energetic performer as Simon Callow during the seven-year life of the play, I could say with Bottom, *I have had a most rare vision.*

Simon Callow being Shakespeare, the Man from Stratford

12.

Shakespeare's Sister

To do well in our final school exams, we were again and again told, it would be important to support every argument with apt quotations. These would have to be learned by heart. I found that the best method was to recite them out loud while walking at dusk in the park, which I could enter through a wicket gate half a mile from home. Preparing myself for an *Antony and Cleopatra* question about Enobarbus, the conscience of the play, I addressed the deer in the bracken and the hooting owl in the old oak:

> I will go seek
> Some ditch wherein to die: the foul'st best fits
> My latter part of life.

'Are you all right, mate?' asked a surprised dogwalker.

Whether or not Sevenoaks really was the school mentioned by Jack Cade in *Henry VI*, the town was well known in

Shakespeare's day. It was the location of one of the greatest houses in England. At the time of his execution, Lord Saye and Sele held the manor of Knole, where he was building himself a country pile. His heir sold the property to the Archbishop of Canterbury, who completed it as a palace for himself, which was occupied by his successors down to the time of Thomas Cranmer in the reign of Henry VIII, at which point the king took it over. Queen Elizabeth gave it to her favourite, Robert Dudley, but he handed it back and it eventually passed into the hands of her cousin, Thomas Sackville, co-author of the tragedy of *Gorboduc*, the first English play in blank verse. He embarked on a huge rebuilding project, creating a home with 365 rooms, fifty-two staircases, twelve entrances and seven courtyards. The Sackvilles have lived there ever since, though since the Second World War confined to a single wing, with the main house and the deer park maintained by the National Trust.

Unfounded family tradition has it that Shakespeare paid a visit. A woman brought up in the house reminisced about her

wild dreams that some light might be thrown on the Shakespearean problem by a discovery of letters or documents at Knole. What more fascinating or chimerical a speculation for a literary-minded child breathing and absorbing the atmosphere of that house? I used to tell myself stories of finding Shakespeare's manuscripts up in the attics, perhaps hidden away under the flooring somewhere.

This was Vita Sackville-West in her family history, *Knole and the Sackvilles*, a copy of which was on our family bookcase below the row of New Temple Shakespeares. When Virginia

Woolf visited Vita at Knole in 1924, she looked with reverence on *chairs that Shakespeare might have sat on*.

Knole and the Sackvilles were given new notoriety in the 1970s because of a mildly scandalous book called *Portrait of a Marriage*, by Vita's son Nigel Nicolson. It unravelled a family history that I found a little confusing. Vita's grandfather, a Victorian called Lionel Sackville-West, who became Envoy Extraordinary and Minister Plenipotentiary to the United States, had seven illegitimate children by a Spanish dancer called Pepita. Upon his death, one of these children claimed that he was the rightful heir to Knole, alleging that Lionel had secretly married Pepita. When the case came to court, it was revealed that Pepita already had a husband, so the claim was dismissed and the estate passed to a nephew, also called Lionel. He had married one of his uncle Lionel's illegitimate daughters, Victoria Josefa Dolores Catalina Sackville-West, known as Lolo. These cousins were Vita's parents. They both had many affairs, leaving their only child free to roam around Knole and indulge her passion for writing. She completed eight novels and a batch of plays by the age of eighteen. But, being a girl, she could not inherit the house she loved. This was a source of lifelong resentment, for all that she found solace in her marriage to Harold Nicolson, her lover Violet Trefusis, and the garden she created at Sissinghurst. Much of Nigel Nicolson's book was given over to Vita's own account, unpublishable in her lifetime, of her lesbian affairs.

The curse of male primogeniture and genetic chance continued to affect the Sackvilles. Sevenoaks School admitted girls to the sixth form shortly before I left: one of the first was Sarah, fifth and last child, all daughters, of the current Lord Sackville. Which meant that when he died, Knole passed once again to a nephew.

There weren't any Shakespeare manuscripts in the attics, but in a display case in the Great Hall you can see the original manuscript of a novel by Virginia Woolf called *Orlando*. Written with the lightness of gossamer, it masquerades as a biography. Like a real biography, it includes a long set of acknowledgements to friends of the subject, scholars, librarians and archivists, but, unusually, the list begins with the author's debt to the dead, in the form of *Defoe, Sir Thomas Browne, Sterne, Sir Walter Scott, Lord Macaulay, Emily Brontë, De Quincey, and Walter Pater.* That is because the book is a love letter not only to Vita, but also to English literature. I read it shortly before going up to university and it was the ideal preparation for three years' total immersion in the subject.

Orlando was the book that made me think of Virginia Woolf as Shakespeare's sister.

★

If there was a deficiency in the range of works we studied after choosing English Literature for the last two years at school, it was the lack of women authors. There was one notable exception. 'Some people think that Jane Austen is trivial,' said the other JA, Mr Adams. He paused, then added 'and some people think that Mozart tinkles.'

Austen was accordingly given pride of place on the reading list as we began our advanced-level course. The paper on 'Literature since 1785' (i.e. since the death of Dr Johnson) involved submission of a portfolio of essays instead of an exam. The requirement was to make comparisons between any two novelists, any two poets and any two dramatists, from any country in the world. It was up to each student to make their own choices, after having been introduced in class to a wide array of possibilities – Austen for the art of irony, Forster's *Howards End* for the intricacies of the British class system, *The Great Gatsby* and *Death of a Salesman* for the American Dream, V. S. Naipaul and Chinua Achebe for the legacy of empire, and so on.

Austen was another author with local associations. Every Saturday morning when I walked down to the record shop to buy a new album or single, I glanced at the elegantly proportioned Red House just beyond the school, now the offices of Knocker and Foskett, Solicitors. A brass plaque on the railings informed passers-by that Jane Austen had stayed there with her Uncle Francis. There were other links, too. Her father was born in Tonbridge, where he was educated and then taught at our rival school; her grandmother was matron of our own Sevenoaks and housekeeper to the headmaster, Elijah Fenton, who was an early Bardolater, writing a poem in 1711 that included the lines

Shakespear the Genius of our Isle, whose Mind
(The universal Mirror of Mankind)
Expressed all Images, enriched the Stage,
But sometimes stooped to please a barbarous Age.

Only connect, wrote Tonbridge pupil Forster.

We used to go to Box Hill for family picnics. Maybe that, as well as the perfection of its form and the wit of its prose, was why *Emma* was my favourite of the novels, the one that I chose for the essay in my A-Level portfolio in which I compared the ways in which Jane Austen and Henry James (in *The Portrait of a Lady*) got inside the heads of their heroines, simultaneously doting on them and exposing their faults by means of a device known to critics as 'free indirect discourse' – writing in the third person, but from the point of view of the character, thus achieving both intimacy and detachment. I saw that it was as powerful a device for the novelist as dramatic irony – the moment when an audience knows something that the character does not – was for the playwrights we were studying, Shakespeare, Ibsen and Chekhov. Was it, I wondered, a particular gift of women novelists (and maybe their hyper-sensitive and not very masculine brothers, such as Henry James)?

The dazzling technique of *Orlando* elevated Woolf into my small pantheon of women writers, beside Austen and Emily Brontë. In my first term as an undergraduate, when I should have been studying Spenser and Dryden, I read all her other novels. I squandered a disproportionate amount of my student grant on a four-volume collection of her essays, addressed to 'The Common Reader'. I devoured her *Writer's Diary*. 'The feel of genius,' I wrote in my copy of it, 'amazing insights into an artist's mind, influences, ideas – she read so much and so quickly, absorbing every detail – must read all her letters – oh time.'

Her books sent me into the echo-chamber of memory. To my own childhood summers by the sea, of course, but also to the awkwardness of adolescence. In *The Voyage Out*, her debut novel, the girl is on a bed with a boy for the first time, *rolling slightly this way and that as the embrace tightened and slackened. 'I don't like that,' said Rachel after a moment*. A buried moment of acute embarrassment flashed into my mind. The first time I stayed with Sarah Jane at her home. We were lying on her bed as soon as I entered the house. Her parents were out, so I had not yet met them. Then the bedroom door opened. It was her father: 'I don't like this,' he said as he got his first sight of his

daughter's horizontal boyfriend. *I don't like that, I don't like this.*
'Fiction is truth?' I scribbled in another margin.

I stayed up all night in my snug student room, immersed in
the recently published two-volume biography by Virginia's
nephew Quentin Bell, transfixed by its candour:

> All that summer she was mad

and

> Mr Lytton Strachey stood on the threshold. He pointed his
> finger at a stain on Vanessa's white dress.
> 'Semen?' he said.

And finally the note to her husband Leonard, placed on the
sitting-room mantelpiece at Rodmell in Sussex:

> Dearest,
> I feel certain I am going mad again. I feel we can't go through
> another of those terrible times. And I shan't recover this time.
> I begin to hear voices, and I can't concentrate. So I am doing
> what seems the best thing to do . . . Everything has gone
> from me but the certainty of your goodness. I can't go on
> spoiling your life any longer.
>
> I don't think two people could have been happier than
> we have been.
>
> V.

When on that last page she took her walking stick and made
her way across the water-meadows to the river, where she forced
a large stone into the pocket of her coat, I thought about

Ophelia, and then just for a moment the memory returned of the smell of woodsmoke that afternoon when I came back from school on the day that our neighbour – tall, thin, elegant, grey-haired, she looked a little like Woolf – built the bonfire for herself in the garden.

★

Quentin Bell guided me through the course of his aunt's career. She had found her mature 'stream of consciousness' style in *Mrs Dalloway*, a novel that she described in her diary as *a study of insanity and suicide; the world seen by the sane and the insane side by side*. Clarissa Dalloway's mantra, recurring throughout the novel, is Shakespeare's line *Fear no more the heat o' the sun*:

> Fear no more, says the heart. Fear no more, says the heart, committing its burden to some sea, which sighs collectively for all sorrows, and renews, begins, collects, lets fall.

A better name for 'the stream of consciousness' would have been 'the breaking of the waves'. It was in Woolf's next novel, *To the Lighthouse*, that they broke again and again on the shore as she magically conjured back to life the summers of her childhood. In January 1927, she returned from another visit to Vita in Sevenoaks and was greeted by Leonard, who had read the manuscript of the seaside novel while she was away. He told her it was much her best book, a masterpiece, an entirely original 'psychological poem'.

It was published in May. In June, she went to a ceremony in which Vita was presented with the Hawthornden Prize, Britain's most prestigious literary award, for her poem *The Land*. That same day, Virginia sketched in her diary an outline for a new novel, to be called *The Moths*:

> the play-poem idea; the idea of some continuous stream, not solely of human thought, but of the ship, the night etc., all flowing together: intersected by the arrival of the bright moths.

Four years and many rewrites later, it would become *The Waves*, her most poetic novel, demanding of deep readerly concentration. She decided that while it marinated, she would dash off a quick book, a mock biography. Having written a series of *serious poetic experimental books*, she needed an *escapade*. It would be *based on Vita, Violet Trefusis, Lord Lascelles, Knole, etc.*

They had begun their affair just before Christmas 1925. Virginia fell in love with Vita as she marched into a grocer's in Sevenoaks. It must have been Payne's, at the top of the London Road, where a generation later my mother shopped twice a week. Vita had, according to Woolf's diary, *a candle-lit radiance, stalking on legs like beech-trees, pink glowing, grape clustered, pearl hung*. Neither of their husbands seemed to mind. By the summer of 1926, Vita was telling Harold Nicolson, who had no shortage of gay affairs himself, that she had slept with Virginia twice but was *scared to death of arousing physical feelings in her, because of the madness*. When Virginia visited Long Barn, Vita's house in the village of Weald, rather than becoming overly sexually entangled as had happened with Violet Trefusis, they mostly sat up talking about literature deep into the night (Harold was away by this time, as Counsellor at the British Legation in Teheran). Woolf was trying to work on a history of fiction, but getting stuck. So she had the idea of writing it in the form of a novel.

Orlando was Virginia's gift to Vita in compensation for her deprivation of Knole because she was a woman. She is made instead the inheritor of the English literary tradition that began with Sir Thomas Sackville's invention of blank-verse tragedy, the crucible out of which Marlowe and Shakespeare worked their alchemy. Woolf was inspired by her reading of *Knole and the Sackvilles*, which had revealed how the house had become a literary salon in the time of Charles Sackville, the 6th Earl, who frequently entertained John Dryden, the first Poet Laureate, and numerous other writers (he also had an affair with Nell Gwyn, who called him her 'Charles the First'). So why not create a character who was Thomas Sackville, Charles Sackville and Vita all in one?

Orlando is born in the age of Shakespeare and lives until the present. When women enter the literary marketplace in the Restoration period, as they did with the plays of Aphra Behn, he undergoes a sex change. The style of the novel progresses from Renaissance exuberance to measured Johnsonian prose for the eighteenth century, cluttered Victoriana for the nineteenth, and Woolfian stream of consciousness for the present. Having begun as an aristocratic scribbler at the court of Queen Elizabeth, Orlando ends as the author of a poem called 'The Oak Tree', which stands in for Vita's prizewinning *The Land*.

When he becomes a woman, Woolf had to be careful. She was writing at the time when Radclyffe Hall's publisher was about to be prosecuted for obscenity over the explicitly lesbian *Well of Loneliness*. Woolf deflected. Immediately after the sex change, she nodded to Jane Austen: *let other pens treat of sex and sexuality; we quit such odious subjects as soon as we can.* Out of an abundance of caution, she removed an earlier passage that is in the manuscript held at Knole: Shakespeare visits Orlando and gives him a manuscript telling the true story of his relationship with Master W. H., which Orlando burns for fear of revealing a love that dared not speak its name.

Yet Shakespeare remains a presence throughout the novel. He is glimpsed in the great house that is based on Knole:

> There, sitting at the servant's dinner table with a tankard beside him and paper in front of him, sat a rather fat, rather shabby man, whose ruff was a thought dirty, and whose clothes were of hodden brown. He held a pen in his hand, but he was not writing. He seemed in the act of rolling some thought up and down, to and fro in his mind till it gathered shape or momentum to his liking. His eyes, globed and clouded like some green stone of curious texture, were fixed.

Again and again, through the centuries, this vision returns to Orlando. It is Woolf's way of saying that Shakespeare, with what she called his androgynous or 'man-womanly' mind, is the presiding spirit of the whole of subsequent English literature.

Vita was not alone in her anger at the exclusion of women from history and historic institutions. This was also Virginia's theme in the two lectures that she delivered in Cambridge to the female students of Newnham and Girton Colleges in the month of *Orlando*'s publication. They were expanded and published the following year as *A Room of One's Own*.

It was here that Woolf asked the question: what would have happened if Shakespeare had been blessed with a wonderfully gifted sister, let us say called Judith? Could she have broken into the theatre world through the sheer brilliance of her writing? Suppose that, after honing her skills scribbling secretly in a Stratford apple-loft, she made her way to London. The theatre manager would have laughed at the idea of a woman writing:

> Yet her genius was for fiction and lusted to feed abundantly upon the lives of men and women and the study of their ways. At last – for she was very young, oddly like Shakespeare the poet in her face, with the same grey eyes – at last Nick Greene the actor-manager took pity on her; she found herself with child by that gentleman and so – who shall measure the heat and violence of the poet's heart when caught and tangled in a woman's body? – killed herself one winter's night and lies buried at some crossroads where the omnibuses now stop outside the Elephant and Castle.

But all is not lost. As the imaginary Orlando was made to live via Vita Sackville-West's inheritance of the spirit of her literary ancestors Sir Thomas and Lord Charles, so, Woolf tells the female Cambridge students, Shakespeare's fictional sister will live when women writers have five hundred pounds and a room of their own, giving them the possibility of a literary career. Judith is imagined as a continuing presence, soon to be animated in the flesh: *the dead poet who was Shakespeare's sister will put on the body which she has so often laid down. Drawing her life from the lives of the unknown who were her forerunners, as her brother did before her, she will be born.*

★

To begin with, Virginia Woolf felt excluded from Shakespeare's art. As Judith was to William, so was she to her brother Thoby.

He was brilliant, he was eighteen months older than her, he was on his way to Cambridge, he was a boy. Shakespeare seemed to belong to him, not her. He had consumed the plays, possessed himself of them. They fought, *because out he would come with his sweeping assertion that everything was in Shakespeare*. She hated the way that he seemed to have it all in his grasp. She tried to argue that the plays began *with some dull speech*. To prove the point, she opened the book. The page fell at *Twelfth Night*. *If music be the food of love, play on . . .* A good beginning, she had to admit.

It was the male confidence, verging on arrogance, that she could not abide:

> I remember his pride, for it seemed like a pride he took in a friend, at Shakespeare's shuffling Falstaff off without a sign of sympathy. That large impartial sweep in Shakespeare delighted him . . . And so I felt that Shakespeare was to him his other world; the place where he got the measure of his daily world: where he took his bearings; in which he took his way freely from Shakespeare.

Cambridge, too, belonged to him, not to her. She was deprived of the experience of being *at college, where the stir and pressure of life are so extreme, where the excitement of mere living becomes daily more urgent*.

The novel I especially loved as I worked my way through Woolf's writings during my first term at college was *Jacob's Room*, her elegy for Thoby, much of it set in the Fenland city of radiant light that was becoming my new home:

They say the sky is the same everywhere . . . But above Cambridge – anyhow above the roof of King's College Chapel – there is a difference. Out at sea a great city will cast a brightness into the night. Is it fanciful to suppose the sky, washed into the crevices of King's College Chapel, lighter, thinner, more sparkling than the sky elsewhere? Does Cambridge burn not only into the night, but into the day?

Thoby Stephen died of typhoid at the age of twenty-six. Some months earlier, Virginia had pasted a bookplate into her newly acquired set of the Whitehall Edition of the Complete Works of Shakespeare: it was her own finely executed drawing of the Bard's alleged death mask, which had been 'discovered' in Germany some fifty years before. Thoby, death and Shakespeare became interlaced in her imagination. *Death is woven in with the violets*, says Louis in *The Waves*, remembering Ophelia's withered violets, *death and again death*.

For all her grief at Thoby's death, there was also liberation. Now Woolf could take possession of Shakespeare for herself. The process is remembered in *Jacob's Room*. Early in the novel, Jacob, the protagonist who is based on Thoby, can't get on with Shakespeare:

What's the use of trying to read Shakespeare, especially in one of those little thin paper editions whose pages get ruffled, or stuck together with sea-water? Although the plays of Shakespeare had frequently been praised, even quoted, and placed higher than the Greek, never since they started had Jacob managed to read one through.

His copy is symbolically washed overboard on a boat trip to the Scilly Isles. Female characters to whom he condescends are, by contrast, immersed in Shakespeare. For one, the plays, together with *Adonais*, Shelley's poem about the death of Keats, are *sovereign specifics for all disorders of the soul*; another has all Shakespeare by heart before she is in her teens. In her imagination, Woolf is inverting the pattern of her life, where her brother had early command of Shakespeare and she initially struggled.

The novel both idealizes and ironizes Jacob's – Thoby's – Cambridge. His friends there mature him into Shakespeare and his peers: *why read anything but Marlowe and Shakespeare, Jacob said, and Fielding if you must read novels?* And later, *Already he had marked the things he liked in Donne, and they were savage enough. However, you might place beside them passages of the purest poetry in Shakespeare.* He indulges in the impassioned if pretentious undergraduate talk with which I was becoming familiar. *'I'll tell you the three greatest things that were ever written in the whole of literature,'* a fellow-student bursts out,

'Hang there like fruit my soul,' he began . . .

Wine spilling from his glass, Jacob parries with an equally inventive but less romantic line: *The devil damn you black, you cream-faced loon!* We often quoted that, too.

I discovered from a letter printed in the Quentin Bell biography that this exchange of quotations in *Jacob's Room* must have been a remembrance of Woolf's correspondence with her brother when he was at Cambridge:

I read Cymbeline just to see if there mightn't be more in the great William than I supposed. And I was quite upset! Really & truly I am now let in to the company of worshippers – though I still feel a little oppressed by his – greatness I suppose . . . Imogen says – Think that you are upon a rock, & now throw me again! & Posthumous answers – Hang there like fruit, my soul, till the tree die! Now if that doesn't send a shiver down your spine, even if you are in the middle of cold grouse & coffee – you are no true Shakespearian! Oh dear oh dear – just as I feel in the mood to talk about these things, you go & plant yourself in Cambridge.

Cymbeline is another of Shakespeare's late plays of loss and recovery. In the long closing scene, Imogen, a sister who has been loved and lost while disguised as a boy, is reunited with her brothers:

> O my gentle brothers,
> Have we thus met? O, never say hereafter
> But I am truest speaker. You called me brother
> When I was but your sister: I you brothers,
> When ye were so indeed.

For Shakespeare, was the moment a fantasy, with gender roles reversed, of his two daughters being reunited with their dead brother Hamnet? Or was he also turning over in his mind his own lost little brother, Edmund, who followed him to London and became an actor, only to die of plague, along with his young son, not long before *Cymbeline* was written? It was probably William who paid for his burial in Southwark Cathedral and for the tolling of the great bell at noon. For Woolf at the time of *Jacob's Room*, the language would have conjured up an imagined restoration of brother Thoby to her and her beloved sister Vanessa.

It is in this same scene that Imogen, thought to be dead, is also reunited with her husband Posthumus. Upon her embrace, he says:

Hang there like fruit, my soul,
Till the tree die.

Virginia Woolf loved reading biographies. In singling out the image, I suspect that she was remembering not only the play itself, but also Hallam Tennyson's memoir of his father, Alfred Lord Tennyson, who considered these lines among the greatest in the whole of literature. The memoir, which Woolf knew well, not least because Hallam married one of her relatives, records that on his deathbed in 1892 the dying Poet Laureate asked for his Shakespeare. He opened it at these lines, which he said were the tenderest that Shakespeare ever wrote. He was too weak to read them aloud one last time, saying only, 'I have opened it.' His family buried him with his copy of *Cymbeline* laid on his chest, where it had been when he died.

Shakespeare remained a comfort in the face of death in Woolf's next novel, *Mrs Dalloway*. Septimus Warren Smith, the shell-shocked Great War veteran who commits suicide towards the end of the day on which the story is set, is obsessed with Shakespeare. He was one of the first to volunteer in 1914, going to France *to save an England which consisted almost entirely of Shakespeare's plays and Miss Isabel Pole in a green dress walking in a square.* But after the war, when post-traumatic stress disorder brings back the death of his beloved fellow-soldier Evans, he turns against Shakespeare:

> Here he opened Shakespeare once more. That boy's business of the intoxication of language – *Antony and Cleopatra* – had shrivelled utterly. How Shakespeare loathed humanity – the putting on of clothes, the getting of children, the sordidity of the mouth and the belly! This was now revealed to Septimus; the message hidden in the beauty of words. The secret signal which one generation passes, under disguise, to the next is loathing, hatred, despair.

Shell shock causes Septimus to project his own despair on to Shakespeare. If he can no longer love Shakespeare, life will be intolerable. He throws himself out of a window and is impaled on the railings below. When Clarissa Dalloway is told about his death at her party that evening, she retreats to a small empty room, where she sees an old woman across the road getting ready for bed. Normal life going on, as in Auden's poem about the painting of the fall of Icarus. The mantra returns to calm Mrs Dalloway:

> There! the old lady had put out her light! the whole house was dark now with this going on, she repeated, and the words came to her, Fear no more the heat of the sun.

The words have come to her from Shakespeare: first a whisper of Othello putting out the light of Desdemona's life and then the opening line of the dirge in *Cymbeline*. It occurs shortly after a stage direction that echoes the heartbreaking moment near the end of *King Lear*: *Enter Arviragus, with Imogen, dead, bearing her in his arms.* But this is late Shakespeare, not Shakespeare in the depths of tragedy. The plot of *Cymbeline* is convoluted, to say the least. Though Arviragus and his brother Guiderius do not know it, Imogen (disguised as their adored pageboy Fidele) is not dead. She has merely fainted at the sight of a headless body that she thinks is her husband's (it is actually that of her wicked stepbrother, Cloten, who had a scheme to rape her – which must have affected Virginia Woolf, who was traumatized as a girl when she was sexually assaulted by her stepbrother). Arviragus and Guiderius chant over the body of the boy-girl:

> Fear no more the heat o' th' sun,
> Nor the furious winter's rages,
> Thou thy worldly task has done,
> Home art gone, and ta'en thy wages.
> Golden lads and girls all must,
> As chimney-sweepers, come to dust . . .
>
> Quiet consummation have,
> And renownèd be thy grave.

Words, remembered from Shakespeare, counted like rosary beads. A moment of quiet consummation in both the play and the novel, and another epitaph for the lost brother, the golden lad Thoby Stephen.

All through her literary career, the words of Shakespeare came to Virginia Woolf. They wove themselves into the fabric of her writing, as when, near the climax of *The Waves*, Bernard reaches an understanding of the flow of the world through Lear's image of himself and Cordelia as birds in a cage, telling old tales and laughing at gilded butterflies: *So now, taking upon me the mystery of things, I could go like a spy without leaving this place, without stirring from my chair. I can visit the remote verges of the desert lands . . .*

She read Shakespeare when she was ill. And she read him after writing, when her mind was *agape and red-hot*. She never ceased to be astonished *how amazing his stretch and speed and word coining power is, until I felt it utterly outpace and outrace my own, seeming to start equal and then I see him draw ahead and do things I could not in my wildest tumult and utmost press of mind imagine.*

Even the lesser-known plays, she believed, were written at a speed that was quicker than anybody else's quickest. The words drop so fast that one can't pick them up. *Look at this*, she wrote, alighting on a random passage in *Titus Andronicus*:

'Upon a gathered lily almost withered' . . . Evidently the pliancy of his mind was so complete that he could furbish out any train of thought . . .Why then should anyone else attempt to write? This is not 'writing' at all. Indeed, I could say that Shakespeare surpasses literature altogether, if I knew what I meant.

She was not intimidated. She found a way of answering to his pliancy of mind and speed of composition. I copied out a passage from her diary. She was writing of her quest for a style that was *loose knit and yet not slovenly, so elastic that it will embrace anything, solemn, slight or beautiful that comes into my mind.* Imagine *some deep old desk, or capacious hold-all, in which one flings a mass of odds and ends without looking them through,* but to which one returns with the passing of the years to *find that the collection had sorted itself and refined itself and coalesced, as such deposits so mysteriously do, into a mould, transparent enough to reflect the light of our life, and yet steady, tranquil compounds with the aloofness of a work of art.*

I wasted a lot of time in my first year at college trying to write a novel in this style. I had the good sense to put it in a drawer and never look at it again. But I wondered whether it might be possible to write literary critical prose that answered to Woolf's fluency and transparency. Not to mention her commitment to a criticism that was accessible to 'The Common Reader'.

★

My first experience of a Cambridge lecture was not auspicious. 'Introduction to Medieval Studies': old professor, rambling, mildly senile, plugging his own books. He said, 'When I hear the word relevance, I reach for my umbrella.' The only compensation was that I found myself sitting next to a Newnham fresher, flushed with sensibility, called Marianne. When I visited her college, it seemed like a girls' boarding school, but I was enchanted by her attic room decorated with kilim throws, a bowl of fresh fruit from the market and postcard reproductions of paintings by Matisse.

Attendance at lectures was optional, and it was easy to discover from second- and third-year students for which ones it was worth getting out of bed. 'Prynne is a must,' someone told me. So a couple of days later, I jostled my way into a packed lecture room to hear the poet-critic J. H. Prynne – at that time unknown outside Cambridge. Wearing his trademark black-velvet jacket, white shirt and orange tie, he delivered what I described as an 'intense, hilarious, brilliant exegesis of Coleridge's prose passage about skating and its transcendence'. The following week, he provided an 'explanation of D. G. Rossetti's theory of poetic language having to carry the weight that theology once carried'. At moments such as this – and there were many of them – one sensed that although Dr Leavis had left for York, his zeal for the discipline still hung over the Faculty. English Literature mattered because it had, as Matthew Arnold predicted, inherited the mantle of religion.

In retrospect, I see that it was a moment of dusk for the Cambridge English Faculty, and indeed the entire discipline as conceived by Leavis. But to be there and to be young was very heaven. During the course of any week in term, you could hear lectures by Christopher Ricks, Raymond Williams and Frank Kermode, the world's leading practitioners of, respectively, pyrotechnic close reading, Marxist literary analysis, and the urbane fusion of traditional scholarship with new ideas imported from Paris. Alone of the three, Ricks lectured as well as wrote with panache, yet their collective presence was thrilling because my first inspirational encounters with literary criticism at school had been his *Milton's Grand Style*, along with Williams's *The Country and the City* and Kermode's *Romantic Image* and Arden Edition of *The Tempest*. Might it be possible, I wondered, to write criticism that moved nimbly between Ricks's sense of how writers speak to their admired forebears through an art of allusion, Kermode's understanding of the process whereby a work becomes a 'classic', and Williams's attunement to the social and political contexts in which literature is produced and consumed?

Our minds were stretched by a close reading of A. E. Housman one week, an intellectual workout with Roland Barthes the next. Then it all fell apart: Williams retired, while Ricks and Kermode took opposite sides in a Faculty argument about the promotion of a Young Turk who practised literary theory which became so explosive that it hit the national press, leading the *Sun* newspaper to attempt to explain structuralism to readers more accustomed to ogling page-three girls.

We used to joke that the termly lecture list resembled a well-stocked bar: there were two Beers (John and Gillian) for the Romanticists and Victorians, a Barrell (John) for those with eighteenth-century tastes, and a Brewer (Derek) for the medievalists. The wineskins were prepared by two Tanners – Michael for the philosophically inclined and Tony for aficionados of the novel. Having imbibed English literature from 1300 to the present in the first two years, we were ready for the strong liquor of Finals, where the intimidating Tragedy paper began with Poole (Adrian) plunging us into the ancient Greeks. Directing us to Ezra Pound's translation of the climactic moment in Sophocles' *Women of Trachis*, he showed how in the instant before death the tragic hero achieves *anagnorisis*, knowledge of the self and the world:

Come at it that way, my boy, what
SPLENDOUR,
    IT ALL COHERES.

There were no set texts, only the injunction to read widely and to decide with your supervisor which authors you were going to write about. Week by week, I worked my way through the centuries, churning out essays that my supervisor, Dr Paul Hartle, stripped of priggishness and rushed judgement by means of gentle marginal comments such as 'You don't seriously believe this shit, do you, Bate?' The relationship between the exams and the lecture courses was, to say the least, tangential. Dons were given free rein to ride their hobby horses. I was particularly struck by a course offered by 'Mad Mike' Long called 'Nabokov, Marvell, Arcadia, Childhood'. The twentieth-century Russian émigré novelist Vladimir Nabokov and the seventeenth-century Metaphysical Poet Andrew Marvell seemed an unlikely pairing, but Long made the conjunction work: they shared a longing for lost childhoods and lost Arcadias – Marvell's gardens, Nabokov's pre-revolutionary Russian origins, Humbert Humbert's kingdom by the sea where he loses his first love, twelve-year-old Annabel Leigh, causing him to regress into perversion and madness, fixating on girls of her age.

The comparison gave me an idea for the dissertation I needed to submit as part of my degree. Nabokov was a butterfly-hunter. His novels are full of moths, as in the very last sentences of *Bend Sinister*:

> Possibly, something of the kind may be said to occur in regard to the imprint we leave in the intimate texture of space. Twang. A good night for mothing.

Wasn't *The Waves* originally going to be called *The Moths*? And hadn't Woolf addressed her own depression, shortly before her suicide, in an essay called 'The Death of the Moth'? Didn't these two novelists – for me, the supreme English-language stylists of the twentieth century – share a technique of using moments of vision, shards of light and whispered sounds, as a way of facing up to death and living through it? Woolf in her diary seeking to catch *the light of our life*; Humbert's first phrase for Lolita, *light of my life*. The glimpse of a pair of Jacob's old shoes. The absence of Lolita's voice from the concord of children's voices heard from a hillside in Telluride, Colorado, where Humbert is listening (and Nabokov butterflying and mothing). The art that defeats time, whether it be Shakespeare's sonnets, Renaissance frescoes, or the wall-paintings depicting extinct beasts on the walls of the caves of Lascaux:

> I am thinking of aurochs and angels, the secret of durable pigments, prophetic sonnets, the refuge of art. And this is the only immortality you and I may share, my Lolita.

My dissertation, 'The Flight of the Moth: A Comparative Study of Virginia Woolf and Vladimir Nabokov', did not get a very good mark. Too impressionistic, insufficiently scholarly (and, besides, Nabokov wasn't sufficiently *English* – despite the fact that he had studied at Cambridge). But I was proud of it. I had found my voice as a writer. And writing, with reading, would be my way of enduring the slings and arrows of outrageous fortune.

Knole: inspiration for *Orlando*

Virginia Woolf's bookplate for her Shakespeare edition:
her drawing of his supposed death mask
(thought in her time to be authentic)

13.

Ariel and Cal

I woke early one Monday morning in February 1978, after a night of strange dreams. In one of them I had tried to kiss Marianne, who was now the leading lady in my production of W. B. Yeats's play about spiritualism, *The Words Upon the Window-Pane*. She had resisted, pushing me roughly away into another dream in which I was pursued by creatures out of a medieval bestiary. That was probably because it was the term when we were studying literature of the age of Chaucer and I had been reading *Sir Gawain and the Green Knight*. Yeats was my lodestar, *Sir Gawain* my newest discovery. I could have guessed that Ted Hughes, who was on my mind, was also obsessed with Yeats, but I was not yet a good enough reader of poetry to have intuited the line that ran from his own work back to the alliterative, Northern, grounded dialect of the Gawain-poet.

During the day, I walked through the streets of Cambridge three times, pulling a college porter's trolley bearing a coffin of bleached pine. I was directing a production of Shakespeare's last play, *The Two Noble Kinsmen*. The action begins in ancient Thebes with three widowed queens kneeling in supplication before the coffins of their dead husbands. A friendly local undertaker had lent us the necessary props, on condition that we transported them ourselves and brought them back undamaged. Three coffins, so three journeys. In the evening I had dinner with Marianne at a Greek restaurant called Eros.

Then we went to the Hobson Gallery, close by Christ's College. It was a dank, chill, misty evening. Typical Cambridge weather. Exactly twenty-six years earlier, another first-year undergraduate reading English – at the college over the road from mine – had written:

Sometimes I think Cambridge wonderful, at others a ditch full of clear cold water where all the frogs have died. It is a bird without feathers; a purse without money; an old dry apple, or the gutters run pure claret. There is something in the air I think which makes people very awake.

The thing that was in the air that night, keeping us sharp, was his presence. Ted Hughes was back in Cambridge.

I hand over a prized pair of tickets. Marianne and I press our way up the stairs into the little Hobson Gallery. Leonard Baskin's crow prints are on the walls and the room is packed for the poetry reading. At this time in his career, plagued by the wrath of Sylvia Plath fanatics, Ted Hughes is not making many public appearances. We have struck lucky.

Only the cliché does justice to his appearance: he is rugged. His eye is sharp, his voice commanding.

He began with 'The Thought Fox', said that it was his first poem, written after seeing a fox on a mound and combining its memory with a Swedish fox film he'd seen two weeks earlier. That was a completely different account of the poem's origin from the one that became part of literary legend: a dream in which a fox, singed and smelling of burnt hair, came into his room at Pembroke College, put its paw on an English Literature essay he had been struggling to write, left a bloody mark and said, 'You are destroying us,' so persuading Hughes to change his subject of study from English to Anthropology.

Then he read 'Thistles', 'Pike', 'Hawk Roosting': a spoken anthology of the poems that had established his unique voice and his fame. Leonard Baskin was in the room. Hughes announced that the reading was dedicated to him and that the chosen poems were all Baskin favourites. Then he went on to explain the background to *Crow*, on which poet and artist had worked so closely together. God had a nightmare about a crow dragging him around. Crow is then born. He is questioned in an examination. His answers? The word *death* is repeated, fifteen times, maybe more. Then *who is stronger than death? – Me, evidently.* At times the imagery is intensely violent or sexually charged. Of lovers: *In the morning they wear each other's faces.*

Afterwards, I say thank you to him. He nods, then he looks at Marianne – who has beauty, brains and acting ability in equal measure – and winks at me. Wishing me luck with – what? – not, I suspect, my studies or my poetic aspirations, but rather my pursuit of Marianne. His renowned sexual charisma did not transmit itself to me. 'We're just very good friends,' she said as we parted opposite Falcon Yard, where Ted Hughes had first met Sylvia Plath. She walked away into the Cambridge fog.

How would he have replied if I had had the courage to say more? Would he have recognized a kindred spirit if I had told him that I was directing Yeats's *Words Upon the Window-Pane* and Shakespeare's *Two Noble Kinsmen*? He was fascinated by Yeats's poetic 'system', by ouija boards and spirit voices. And *Kinsmen*? I had chosen it because I was convinced that the verse of the play's first and last acts was some of Shakespeare's richest, despite – or because of – its knotted texture. Would Hughes have told me of the formative poetic experience he underwent at the home of his first serious girlfriend when he was eighteen?

At their house, too, I had the next big literary shock since discovering Yeats: this mother of my girl friend owned a Shakespeare with the apocryphal plays included. I already knew all the plays pretty well, and the poems. I read them constantly. But in her book I found *The Two Noble Kinsmen*. The passages of verse in Act I of that play had an effect on me very like the effect of *Wanderings of Oisin* formerly: very brilliant and special dreams came out of it somehow. That puzzles me slightly, now – how I could have reacted so strongly to such a slight novelty in the verse. Anyway, I did. I was 18 then.

No, he would not have told me any of this. In public, he was an intensely private man. He had more reason for this than any other English poet.

'One of the great evenings of my life,' I wrote before bed, suppressing my disappointment that Marianne had not returned to my room. 'Won't forget Ted Hughes in a hurry.'

He had been my favourite when I was introduced to poetry as a teenager. My friend Jonathan gave me a copy of *Lupercal*. 'Hawk Roosting', 'The Bull Moses', 'View of a Pig', 'The Retired Colonel', 'Thrushes', 'Pike' and 'Pibroch': we discussed them for hours. We went in search of the Wodwo. Our admired

English teacher had reservations about *Crow*. We stood up for it.

★

From Cambridge, I went to Harvard. I was still putting on plays. Wanting a showcase for three extremely talented actresses I'd met, I commandeered a basement space known as Explosives B. Deep in the bowels of one of the Harvard houses – Eliot, Lowell, Adams, I forget which – it was little more than a boiler room. There I staged an intimate studio production, lit only by candles, of Barry Kyle's *Sylvia Plath: A Dramatic Portrait*, a biographical drama that skilfully interwove passages from her journals and letters with dramatized renditions of many of her best poems – 'Lesbos' performed while peeling a pan of pota- toes; 'Daddy' played as an exorcism in which the three women stamped on a swastika; Nela, the most gifted of the three, swaying her body as if riding on a horse called Ariel

> at one with the drive
> Into the red

> Eye, the cauldron of morning.

In researching the play, I immersed myself in Plath's poetry and life and her recently published *Letters Home*. This was the period when Hughes was in the eye of the feminist hurricane. It seemed to me that those who were so eager to condemn had no understanding of mental illness. The crude equation 'no errant husband, no death' was profoundly wrong. Depression killed Sylvia Plath, not Ted Hughes. Early in the play, there was a quotation from A. Alvarez's *The Savage God* that seemed to me to come much closer to the truth:

> Just as the suicide adds nothing at all to the poetry, so the myth of Sylvia as a passive victim is a total perversion of the woman she was. It misses altogether her liveliness, and harsh wit, her vehemence of feeling, her control. Above all, it misses the courage with which she was able to turn disaster into art.

It was only when I read *The Bell Jar* in my Harvard dorm, with the snow piled thick outside, that everything fell into place. I still have the tanned paperback copy, cover half torn away, in which I scribbled in pencil on page 137, *just what Mum said – so much of this book rings true*. This was above a passage in which Plath wrote:

> Then I remembered that I had never cried for my father's death.
>
> My mother hadn't cried either. She had just smiled and said what a merciful thing it was for him he had died, because if he had lived he would have been crippled and an invalid for life, and he couldn't have stood that, he would rather have died than had that happen.

Another part of the book unlocked a past I'd tried to forget. We are sitting in the garden in most of my memories of childhood visits to Top Meadow, the home of my mother's parents in the genteel town of Tenterden, where the great Victorian Shakespearean actress Ellen Terry once kissed my aunt in her perambulator and said that she had a mouth like a rosebud, meaning that she was forever known as Bud. Cousins are sometimes there, and Gran's ginger tom Marmaduke is stretched asleep on the patio or looking at the fish in the ornamental pond covered with wire mesh to keep away the herons. Once there was the music of a violin from beneath the old plum tree: Scylla Kennedy, my mother's best friend from school, had come to tea along with her six-year-old prodigy Nigel, who was about to go to the Yehudi Menuhin School. Speaking in the poshest voice I had ever heard in a child, he said that he would play a little Mozart for us. Always it was a warm English summer's day.

But there was a chill in the house. We were told not to make any noise, never to run up or down the stairs, not to speak at table unless spoken to, never to disturb Poppa when he was sleeping in his stiffly upholstered armchair after lunch. That was my grandfather, who was immensely tall, a remote and slightly forbidding figure. I'm not sure whether that was because of his temperamental hearing aid or whether he was nursing some inner demon. On the mantelpiece, there was a fragment of artillery shell on a wooden stand marked 'Gallipoli'. It had flown into his tent behind the lines where he was conducting emergency dental surgery on wounded soldiers in 1915. Did the things he had seen continue to haunt his dreams half a century later?

My grandmother was usually full of life. She made exquisite stuffed toys for all her grandchildren, arranged the flowers in the parish church and took pride in her cottage garden. But something wasn't right. There were whisperings, secrets. Then the dam burst. It was at a large family gathering – the celebration of a landmark wedding anniversary. Her four daughters had clubbed together to buy her a fridge. When it was unveiled, she broke into hysterics. She could not possibly use such a new-fangled contraption. She had always kept her food in the cold pantry. That was never going to change.

'What's wrong with Gran?' I asked in the car on the way home. This was the first time I heard the words 'nervous breakdown'. As I grew older, confidences were shared. Gran had a history of manic depression, which was periodically treated with Electroconvulsive Therapy. It was only when I read *The Bell Jar* that I gained a glimpse of what that must have been like:

Doctor Gordon was fitting two metal plates on either side of my head. He buckled them into place with a strap that dented my forehead, and gave me a wire to bite.

I shut my eyes.

There was a brief silence, like an indrawn breath.

Then something bent down and took hold of me and shook me like the end of the world. Whee-ee-ee-ee-ee, it shrilled, through an air crackling with blue light, and with each flash a great jolt drubbed me till I thought my bones would break and the sap fly out of me like a split plant.

I wondered what terrible thing it was that I had done.

When I saw my grandmother after the shock treatment, it was as if all that life had been drained out of her. Her mouth twitched. She comprehended, I think, but said no more than one word in answer to anything. The electricity had plucked from her memory the rooted sorrow, razed out the written troubles of her brain, but it had taken her character too.

★

My mother was called Sylvia, a name that Shakespeare imported into England in his *Two Gentlemen of Verona*. The family doctor in Tenterden once said to me, 'I've known your mother since she was a child – of the four sisters, I always knew that she would be the one to inherit their mother's troubles.' She seems to have inherited the lows, not the highs. I don't think she was bipolar, though all through my childhood she too had immense energy. I see her in a bright floral 1960s blouse, cigarette always in hand, mothering, cooking the Sunday roast, harvesting strawberries and raspberries at the bottom of the garden, embroidering hassocks for the church, visiting a friend who was in the last days of terminal cancer, pumping out The Beatles on the little transistor radio in the kitchen and on one occasion dashing to Knole Park because the Fab Four were filming the videos for 'Penny Lane' and 'Strawberry Fields' there. 'They rode on white horses,' she said.

Then one summer, quite suddenly, all the energy disappeared. There must have been some trigger, probably the coincidence of menopause and my brother leaving home. Whatever the cause, for years to come there would be long months when she just sat in the living room. Her fingers scraped at the fabric of her armchair until the stuffing began to come out. She suffered from a ballooning digestive disorder, which made me wonder whether there was some truth in the ancient theory that melancholy was seated in the black bile of the belly – *windy* or *flatuous melancholy*, Robert Burton labelled it, *that which the Arabians call myrachial, and is in my judgment the most grievous and frequent.*

When things became very bad, she had spells as an in-patient at a psychiatric hospital. My most painful memory of those years is of her locking herself in the downstairs toilet and screaming, 'Don't make me go back there, please, please.' But once she was there, she recovered remarkably quickly. That was partly because she was given Lithium, regarded at the time as a new wonder drug, but also because there were other patients whose condition was so much worse than hers that her natural kindness kicked in and she worked to cheer them up, to be the life of a place where the majority of the patients were silent, turned inward, exactly as in the hospital described in *The Bell Jar*:

> none of the people were moving . . . there was a uniformity to their faces, as if they had lain for a long time on a shelf, out of the sunlight, under siftings of pale, fine dust.
>
> Then I saw that some of the people were indeed moving, but with such small, birdlike gestures I had not at first discerned them.
>
> A gray-faced man was counting out a deck of cards, one, two, three, four. I thought he must be seeing if it was a full pack, but when he had finished counting, he started over again. Next to him, a fat lady played with a string of wooden beads. She drew all the beads up to one end of the string. Then click, click, click, she let them fall back on each other.

When my mother returned home after her first discharge from the hospital, she told us that she was so shocked by the tar-blackened fingers of the old-timers that she had instantly given up smoking. She never touched another cigarette. That was an incidental benefit, adding to my relief that ECT was no longer in favour.

Sylvia Plath's novel was written from the experience of being under the bell jar of depression. It made me understand why no amount of cajoling from me had ever, or could ever, make my mother get up from her chair. Only the Lithium could do that. Reading Plath, I was angry with myself for being angry with my mother for being ill. And at that moment I saw the real reason why I could not get on with Shakespeare's most famous play: like Hamlet, I was accusing my mother of letting my father down. Not by infidelity, but by getting depression. And because she had inherited the condition from her mother, I was afraid that I would inherit it myself. That I might one day become *like mad Hamlet*.

Mum only became her true, funny, bright-eyed self again in her very last days when she was dying of bowel cancer and had been taken off her psychiatric medications. Nevertheless, for more than two decades after my father died the Lithium enabled her to manage her condition. Though still sedentary, she was no longer vacant. She would read voraciously through books from the public library, new ones appearing almost every week. Sometimes, I picked them off the tottering pile on the little stool beside her chair and read them myself. We laughed together over *The Moon's a Balloon*, the funny, sad, racy, self-deprecatory memoir of her wartime crush David Niven. Most, though, were romances aimed at her demographic, not mine. Catherine Cookson, who wrote almost a hundred novels, was a particular favourite. On the back of one of them it said, *Love, fear, revenge, greed, hate and intrigue – you'll find them all in a Catherine Cookson novel*. Not so different from Shakespeare, then. The author of any book that has helped a reader *better to enjoy life, or better to endure it* may be said to have added to the sum of human happiness.

★

Like so many dimensions of human behaviour, depression and bipolar disorder can only be explained by some combination of genetic inheritance and force of circumstance. Frieda Hughes, Sylvia Plath's daughter, became a great friend when I was writing the biography of her father. It was during that time that her brother Nicholas, subject of 'Nick and the Candlestick', one of the loveliest poems we performed in the *Dramatic Portrait*, took his own life in Alaska. Frieda told me that his depression – which was obviously in the genes – was only triggered to extremity by a family dispute after their father died. Anyone with the dark inheritance must live with the fear that one day some trigger will be pressed unexpectedly.

For Sylvia, a writer of such acute self-awareness that she could track her every mood swing, the black dog first called after her father's death a few weeks after her eighth birthday. In her copy of the Complete Works of Shakespeare, which she pored over during her time as a Fulbright Scholar at Newnham College, Cambridge, she heavily underlined Ariel's song in *The Tempest*:

Full fathom five thy father lies;
  Of his bones are coral made;
Those are pearls that were his eyes:
  Nothing of him that doth fade
But doth suffer a sea-change,
Into something rich and strange.

She made pearls of poetry as beautiful and fragile as coral out of the bare bones of mourning and melancholia.

Immediately above the song, she also underlined Ferdinand's lines about how, as he sat on a bank weeping for his father's apparent death in the shipwreck that begins the play, the music of Ariel – the spirit he cannot see – crept by him upon the waters. In the margin, she wrote 'cf. T. S. Eliot <u>Wasteland</u>'. She was thinking of a passage that we read closely when trying to get to grips with Eliot in our last term at school:

> While I was fishing in the dull canal
> On a winter evening round behind the gashouse
> Musing upon the king my brother's wreck
> And on the king my father's death before him.

'Fisher king', I pencilled beside these lines in the copy of Eliot's *Collected Poems 1909–1935* that had been a somewhat unromantic gift to my mother from a boyfriend during the war. *The Waste Land*, we learned, was shaped by the Grail legend, as described in Jessie Weston's anthropological study *From Ritual to Romance*, in which a king wounded in the groin fishes in a land that has been rendered infertile by his impotence. He is the keeper of the Grail, which he will only release when a knight comes along and asks the right question. Then the land will be healed. Eliot was retreating into myth as his 'objective correlative'; it was a way of distancing himself from his own depression and childlessness, and above all from the madness of his wife Vivienne. When I looked in the school library at the facsimile of the manuscript of *The Waste Land*, with annotations by Eliot's *miglior fabbro* ('better maker') Ezra Pound, I discovered a line written by Vivienne that could equally well have been a contribution to the poem or a savage taunt: *What you get married for if you don't want to have children?*

'There isn't a right answer to the interpretation of *The Waste Land*,' Hurdy assured us, 'or of the character of Hamlet or the meaning of *King Lear*. The whole point is to ask the right question.' Chekhov said as much in a letter to his friend Alexey Suvorin:

> You confuse two things: *solving a problem* and *stating a problem correctly*. It is only the second that is obligatory for the artist. In 'Anna Karenina' and 'Eugene Onegin' not a single problem is solved, but they satisfy you completely because all the problems are correctly stated in them. It is the business of the judge to put the right questions, but the answers must be given by the jury according to their own lights.

What was the question the questing knight was supposed to ask the fisher king? *Whom does the Grail serve?* What's the question I've been asking in this book? The one that Aristotle (or a follower presumed to be Aristotle) asked in one of his *Problems*, though I'd substitute 'many' for his 'all': *Why is it that all those who have become eminent in philosophy or politics or poetry or the arts are clearly melancholics?*

Whom does the melancholy, the madness, serve? It would be foolish to pretend to have an answer, but the end of *King Lear* comes closest. No critic has summed it up better than the greatest of the Cambridge close readers, William Empson:

> The scapegoat who has collected all this wisdom for us is viewed at the end with a sort of hushed envy, not I think really because he has become wise but because the general human desire for experience has been so glutted in him; he has been through everything.

> We that are young
> Shall never see so much, nor live so long.

Christopher Ricks, Empson's truest successor as a literary critic, quoted these words when he heard of the sudden death – a heart attack at the age of just sixty, in a New York taxi in the summer of 1977 – of another poet who suffered from manic depression. Robert Lowell, who was always known as Cal.

Hurdy introduced us to this bipolar master-poet of contemporary America at school. At university, a memorable Practical Criticism class was devoted to 'Skunk Hour':

My mind's not right . . .
I myself am hell,
nobody's here –

I got to know the full range of his poems at Harvard, where the name Lowell was in the fabric of the place. Finding a copy of *Life Studies* second-hand in the basement of the Harvard Book Store, I saw how it had inaugurated a new kind of 'confessional' poetry. Lowell didn't like the term, but it was merited by his honesty in confronting his family history and his own mental illness.

If Sylvia Plath was Ariel, Lowell was indeed Cal – Caliban, or was it Caligula? He was rough and wild. He treated his wives abysmally. There were times when he really was mad: during one of his manic episodes he turned up, drugged to the eyeballs and soon drunk as well, wearing a jacket over a pyjama top that was open to the navel, to present a poetry prize to Seamus Heaney. Instead of making a short speech, he began dissecting a Heaney poem line by line until his (third) wife, Lady Caroline Blackwood, arrived with two men in white coats who carted him off to St Andrew's Hospital in Northampton, where John Clare had been confined for the last two decades of his life.

And yet Lowell was a supreme craftsman who turned his madness to art. There is no better poem about being in a psychiatric hospital than 'Waking in the Blue':

> the pinched, indigenous faces
> of these thoroughbred mental cases . . .
> each of us holds a locked razor.

The poem is both tender and funny in its evocation of his fellow-patients – 'Stanley' like a seal in his bath and 'Bobbie' horsing naked at chairs – just as my mother was in her stories about Oakwood Hospital, where she was cured as much by her personal interactions as by the drugs. And it reminds the reader that mental illness is no respecter of class or privilege: the ward is peopled by 'Mayflower screwballs', Harvard men from the New England elite, yet now they are watched over by a night attendant who is a mere sophomore at the far less prestigious Boston University on the other side of the river.

I also admired Lowell as a great public poet. During my year at Harvard, he was my guide to American history. Standing by the bronze relief sculpture on Boston Common that honours Colonel Robert Shaw and the Massachusetts 54th Regiment, I recalled his moving tribute to the Black soldiers who fought on the side of freedom in the Civil War:

> Two months after marching through Boston,
> half the regiment was dead;
> at the dedication,
> William James could almost hear the bronze Negroes
>   breathe.

In the summer of 1964, as Lowell was preparing to publish *For the Union Dead*, the volume named from this poem, he wrote to his close friend and fellow-poet Elizabeth Bishop. As so often, he was in what he called a place of 'gruelling murk'. There was only one life that could save him, that of reader and writer:

> Nothing could be more terrible than *Lear* and the *Oresteia*, both of which I have been reading. And there is no more harmless way for the elemental and black to come out than in words, paint and notes, where nothing can ever be hurt.

In his best poems, he succeeded in releasing the elemental and the black into words. It was often a struggle to do so. The first of his poems that we were given at school was the double sonnet – first half Shakespearean in form, second Petrarchan – 'Night Sweat'. It begins with the poet sitting by lamplight at his desk surrounded by books and crumpled papers, his typewriter stalled. He is suffering from writer's block. He wants to sweat his life's fitful fever out into poetry, but he can't:

> one life, one writing! But the downward glide
> and bias of existing wrings us dry –
> always inside me is the child who died,
> always inside me is his will to die –

His body is like a funeral urn, in which *the animal night sweats* of his spirit are burning. In the second sonnet, his wife comes up behind him. Elizabeth Hardwick, his second wife, an author herself. She is a muse. She brings light, absolution and release. She enables his poem, his child, to explode into life:

your lightness alters everything . . .
absolve me, help me, Dear Heart, as you bear
this world's dead weight and cycle on your back.

'Poetry is the art of showing, not telling,' said Hurdy as we puzzled over Lowell's train of thought, 'a poem's meaning isn't something to be extracted like a tooth.' Then I got it. In this poem, Lowell shows that he knew, at least in the moment, *how to work and how to love*. But that is not his 'message'; the poem itself *is* the work and the love. Out of his hurt, and thanks to his wife's love, which in life he would repay with desertion, in his art he created for her, and for us, *sounds and sweet airs that give delight and hurt not*. It was because he bore so much of the dead weight of depression in the cycle of his own life that Cal could make the music of Ariel.

★

I wasn't so convinced by his later work. I bought a copy of *The Dolphin* in the Harvard Book Store. It was written when he had moved to England, leaving Elizabeth Hardwick and their daughter Harriet behind in America, and had begun an affair with Lady Caroline Blackwood. They lived not far from my home in Kent, in a dilapidated mansion just outside Maidstone. Many of the poems in the collection included lengthy verbatim quotations from letters written by Hardwick, as Lowell was in the midst of divorcing her. This didn't seem right. Anyone who enters into a relationship with a writer knows that they run the risk of becoming fodder for plot, dialogue and character. Sometimes words exchanged in the heat of passion are too potent not to use as raw material. But surely it was the writer's duty to disguise and transform them. Maybe there was a time when Anne Hathaway berated Shakespeare in the manner of Adriana in *The Comedy of Errors*, but she wouldn't have done so in exactly the words that he crafted for the play. There was something lazy as well as cruel about these poems. They served only the writer himself, not the reader.

Just occasionally, though, the old art was there. Taking a particular personal memory and enlarging it into an understanding of the difficulty of life. There was one called 'Ivana', about a six-year-old child:

> Small-soul-pleasing, loved with condescension,
> even through the cro-magnon tirade of six,
> the last madness of child-gaiety
> before the trouble of the world shall hit.

The previous poem had ended with a line about a boiling kettle dropped on a child. It must have been her, because the lines at the white-hot core of this poem were

> Though burned, you are hopeful, experience cannot tell
>   you
> experience is what you do not want to experience.

I borrowed the recently published biography of Lowell from the library. Yes, Ivana was a child, Caroline Blackwood's daughter. And she had been badly burnt in an accident at the house near Maidstone.

She would have been taken to the nearby hospital in East Grinstead, where there was a specialist burns unit that had pioneered plastic surgery on pilots who had been shot down in the Battle of Britain. Realizing this, I was taken back to an experience that I did not want to experience.

★

August 1980, the second anniversary of my father's death. A few weeks later, I would be boarding a plane for the first time, off to begin my year at Harvard. Today, my brother was also heading for a maiden long-haul flight. His girlfriend was teaching in a school in a remote part of Nigeria, and he was going to visit her. My mother and I drove him to Gatwick. We saw him to his gate and then went up to the spectator viewpoint. I was frightened by the size, noise and frequency of the planes. One readjusted course just before landing; another crossed a jumbo's path on the taxiway. My brother's plane climbed steeply into the blue and diminished to a speck, as if it were a mark on my glasses. Then it dissolved into the clouds. I remembered Imogen's image in *Cymbeline* of watching a loved one sail away into exile:

> I would have broke mine eyestrings, cracked them,
>   but
> To look upon him, till the diminution
> Of space had pointed him sharp as my needle:
> Nay, followed him, till he had melted from
> The smallness of a gnat to air, and then
> Have turned mine eye and wept.

At that moment I realized how much I loved my only brother. Next time it would be me, carried away in the belly of the roaring sky whale.

We returned home for tea in the garden and, for the first time in those two long years, Mum broke down. 'Sometimes I wish so desperately that Daddy were here.' The words of Lear echoed in my head: *Thou'lt come no more, / Never, never, never, never, never.* 'But I mustn't be silly,' she added. It was my job to comfort her: 'It'll be the holiday of a lifetime and he'll be home soon after I leave for America.'

Three weeks later, just days before I was due to leave, Mum woke me abruptly. She was in tears again. There had been a phone call from my brother's girlfriend's parents. They had received a cable from Nigeria: 'EMB's legs moderately burnt. Returning home immediately.' Struck dumb, my mother put down the phone. I called back to try to get more details, but there were none. Later in the day, there was a call from Gatwick airport: he would be arriving the following afternoon. I was to meet the wheelchair and take him to the burns unit in East Grinstead.

When he appeared at the arrival gate, adrenalin pushed me aggressively through the crowd. On the way to the hospital, he told me what had happened: late at night, during a power cut, he had been pouring petrol from a jerrycan into the car, lit by a hurricane lamp at a safe distance of fifteen feet. A spillage on his trousers, the vapour blown by a sudden gust of wind – the lamp ignited and the flame ignited him. A six-hour journey through the bush to the nearest hospital, four days of hell before a transfer to Kano, then a cock-up over flight clearance. And so on. In East Grinstead, he screamed as they removed the bandages. Skin grafts would be needed. It would be a long journey, but he was alive.

As I left the hospital he said, 'God burned me and God will heal me and if God had wanted me to die, that is well and good.' Though burned, he was hopeful.

I was still a kind of believer, but my faith had more to do with the comfort brought by the rhythms of the liturgy in the Cranmer prayer book, with Tudor polyphony in the college chapel and the calm of mind that descended during weekly evensong. I could not share the assurance of his faith – the faith to which Hamlet comes on his return from England:

There's a special providence in the fall of a sparrow. If it be now, 'tis not to come. If it be not to come, it will be now. If it be not now, yet it will come: the readiness is all.

I thought back on the whimsical idea that every island of desolation needs a Bible and a Shakespeare. The Bible had always been my brother's guide and the faith that it brought enabled him to survive his ordeal with physical but no ostensible mental scars. But this time my guide, my Shakespeare, had let me down. I understood Hamlet's words about providence and readiness, but I could not feel them or believe them.

Cambridge student Sylvia Plath
underlines Ariel's song in *The Tempest*

The Beatles filming in Knole Park, watched by Sevenoaks School pupils
(and my mother, another Sylvia)

14.

There's My Comfort

When I was working on William Blake in my student days, I took a copy of the Oxford Edition of his complete writings on the train to York. I was off to stay with my friend Chris in a student house filled with the fumes of pot. 'Getting stoned is probably the only way you'll understand *The Four Zoas*,' he said. I saw what he meant when I encountered such lines as *Four Universes round the Mundane Egg remain Chaotic*. Mildly high, I turned to the marginalia that Blake scribbled in his copy of Spurzheim's *Observations on the Deranged Manifestations of the Mind, or Insanity*:

Cowper came to me and said: 'O that I were insane always. I will never rest. Can you not make me truly insane? I will never rest till I am so. O that in the bosom of God I was hid. You retain health and yet are as mad as any of us all – over us all – mad as a refuge from unbelief – from Bacon, Newton and Locke.'

For Blake, William Cowper, a depressive poet of extreme 'sensibility', stood as an intermediary between the Age of Reason, epitomized by the empirical science and philosophy of Bacon, Newton and Locke, and a new way of thinking that revelled in the counter-reality of imagination. We call it Romanticism.

The late eighteenth and early nineteenth centuries. For Dickens, *it was the age of wisdom, it was the age of foolishness, it was the epoch of belief, it was the epoch of incredulity, it was the season of Light, it was the season of Darkness, it was the spring of hope, it was the winter of despair.* It certainly seems to have been a time when you had to be at least a little bit mad to be a poet. There wasn't any money in poetry, as opposed to novel-writing, unless you became a celebrity like Lord Byron or Walter Scott. And you did your best work when you weren't entirely in your right mind. Wasn't that the problem with William Wordsworth? When he was young and in love, intoxicated by the French Revolution, or when he was wandering and homeless, depressed and alone, he created poetry of unprecedented freshness and feeling, but when he settled down to happily married life and a government sinecure as Distributor of Stamps for the County of Westmorland, his muse left him and he started writing verse of unremitting tedium, while revising *The Prelude*, his glorious poetic autobiography, for the worse.

At school, our first introduction to Romanticism was Samuel Taylor Coleridge's opium dream of 'Kubla Khan', interrupted by the knock of a person from Porlock. In a French class, we read and translated the sonnet 'El Desdichado', written in a Paris mental hospital by Gérard de Nerval, who had taken to perambulating through the gardens of the Palais-Royal with his pet lobster Thibault on a blue-silk lead:

There's My Comfort

Je suis le Ténébreux . . .
  et mon luth constellé
Porte le soleil noir de la Mélancolie.

'I am the twilight and my star-studded lute wears the black sun of depression.'

I didn't study German, but it was the subject of my housemaster, Ian Huish, and he introduced me to the beautiful but baffling poetry of Rainer Maria Rilke, for whom love and art were the only bulwarks against depression within and a crumbling world without – the Great War, the end of Habsburg Europe, the chaos of modernity. From Ian, I learned of how the headless torso of an ancient statue of Apollo in the Louvre made Rilke think about what is broken and what endures and how that thought made him say to himself and to us, *Du mußt dein Leben ändern, You must change your life*. I learned, too, of his idea of the angel, which seemed like a symbol of inspiration but which I did not really understand until I found a beautiful poem called 'Der Geist Ariel' that Rilke wrote after reading *The Tempest*: Ariel was Prospero's angel, the instrument of the magical power of art, which to be truly loved had to be renounced. It was the same with memory: because it is all that we have of those we have lost, we must cherish it but also let it go. Rilke imagines Prospero

  Weeping too, perhaps,
when you remember how he loved and yet
wished to leave you: always both, at once.

Then there was another of my second-hand bookshop finds: a slender Faber paperback selection by Ted Hughes of the poems of Emily Dickinson. His Introduction spoke of *the tranced suspense and deliberation in her punctuation of dashes, and the riddling, oblique artistic strategies, the Shakespearian texture of the language, solid with metaphor.*

> Much Madness is divinest Sense –
> To a discerning Eye –
> Much Sense – the starkest Madness –
> 'Tis the Majority
> In this, as All, prevail –
> Assent – and you are sane –
> Demur – you're straightway dangerous –
> And handled with a Chain –

In sixth-form General Studies we had learned about the theory of the 'anti-psychiatrist' R. D. Laing that we all have a 'divided self', and that schizophrenia is not so much an illness as an extreme manifestation of this. A hundred years before this very 1960s idea, Dickinson was suggesting that madness and sanity are not so much biological facts as socially determined conventions: it is the *Majority* who decide on the labels 'mad' and 'sane'. Was the role of the poet, I wondered, to be *a discerning Eye* that questions the majority opinion?

Our French teacher, David Vann, prescribed Albert Camus' *La Chute* as an A-Level set text. A self-proclaimed existentialist, he took me and Chris under his wing for some extra tutorials, tracing the ideas of Camus and Jean-Paul Sartre back to Kierkegaard and Nietzsche. I was particularly struck by a passage in *Twilight of the Idols* where Nietzsche set out to explain 'the psychology of the artist':

For art to exist, for any sort of aesthetic activity or perception to exist, a certain physiological precondition is indispensable: intoxication. Intoxication must first have heightened the excitability of the entire machine: no art results before that happens. All kinds of intoxication, however different their origin, have the power to do this: above all, the intoxication of sexual excitement, the oldest and most primitive form of intoxication.

Save for occasional forays to the pub with my friends, there was very little intoxication in my own life at this time, so I found it vicariously in the Romantic poets. While Chris wrestled with Sartre's *pour soi* and *en soi*, I thrilled to Richard Holmes's biography *Shelley: The Pursuit*. Gradually, though, I began to question the idea that great art emerges from a state of mania or drug-induced or sex-inspired intoxication. I witnessed an episode of schizophrenia at first hand – someone dear to me hearing voices coming from the wall. This was no condition in which to produce enduring insights into the way of the world. As for what we were learning to call 'affective bipolar disorder', I could see that the manic phase might well produce elated creativity, but didn't the (usually far more sustained) periods of depression yield only blackness and torpor? I read about how John Clare would write poetry manically, compulsively, addictively, for a few weeks, then for months barely be able to get himself out of bed, let alone pick up his pen and compose. And in Virginia Woolf's diary I found that when she was in phases of depression, the most she could achieve in the way of writing was the occasional book review. She could do nothing with her novels.

John Dryden, the Poet Laureate who visited Knole in the late seventeenth century, wrote a much-quoted rhyming couplet:

Great Wits are sure to Madness near allied,
And thin Partitions do their Bounds divide.

Creativity may well reside somewhere close to that thin parti-
tion, but once the boundary is crossed there is only silence or
the nightmare of what Clare called his 'blue devils', or the
terrifying cacophony of disordered voices that is experienced
in schizophrenia.

★

The 'special subject' I chose for my final undergraduate year
was a newly designed course called 'Shakespeare and the
Development of English Literature'. Its particular focus was his
influence on the Romantic movement. This was perfect: my
two literary passions yoked, not by violence, together. I immersed
myself in the lectures on Shakespeare that Coleridge and William
Hazlitt delivered in Regency London, fascinated to find that
while the former focused on the poetic language and what he
called a 'psycho-analysis' of the characters, the latter was more
interested in the politics of the plays and the charisma of the
actor Edmund Kean.

It was then that I read Charles Lamb's essay on how
Shakespeare's tragedies are too great for the stage. It was written
before Kean made his debut. Prompted by Hazlitt, Lamb changed
his mind: yes, Kean had done justice to Hamlet and Macbeth,
Richard III and Shylock, Othello and Iago. Not, however, to
King Lear. No actor, he maintained, could truly get inside the
head of Lear in the way that a reader can.

In another essay, entitled 'Sanity of True Genius', Lamb
suggested that Shakespeare could only portray Lear's madness

so convincingly because he was supremely sane himself. The essay begins by taking issue with Dryden's famous couplet:

So far from the position holding true, that great wit (or genius, in our modern way of speaking), has a necessary alliance with insanity, the greatest wits, on the contrary, will ever be found to be the sanest writers. It is impossible for the mind to conceive of a mad Shakespeare. The greatness of wit, by which the poetic talent is here chiefly to be understood, manifests itself in the admirable balance of all the faculties. Madness is the disproportionate straining or excess of any one of them . . . The ground of the mistake is, that men, finding in the raptures of the higher poetry a condition of exaltation, to which they have no parallel in their own experience, besides the spurious resemblance of it in dreams and fevers, impute a state of dreaminess and fever to the poet. But the true poet dreams being awake. He is not possessed by his subject, but has dominion over it . . . Or if, abandoning himself to that severer chaos of a 'human mind untuned,' he is content awhile to be mad with Lear, or to hate mankind (a sort of madness) with Timon, neither is that madness, nor this misanthropy, so unchecked, but that, – never letting the reins of reason wholly go, while most he seems to do so, – he has his better genius still whispering at his ear, with the good servant Kent suggesting saner counsels, or with the honest steward Flavius recommending kindlier resolutions.

To enter the territory associated with mental extremity, but to resist intoxication: that is the mark of the true artist, Lamb was arguing, in sharp distinction from Nietzsche. *It is impossible for the mind to conceive of a mad Shakespeare* because Shakespeare is always so supremely in control of his material, so flexible in his capacity to inhabit the diverse voices of all his characters. Lamb seemed to me absolutely correct that whenever Shakespeare introduced a 'mad' character, he accompanied him with *saner counsels*: not only the wise and kind words of Kent in *Lear* and the good servant Flavius in *Timon of Athens*, but also Camillo seeking to calm Leontes' fevered mind in *The Winter's Tale*, Horatio with Hamlet, and a dozen more.

There have been attempts to conceive of a depressed, if not an actually mad, Shakespeare. The Victorian Anglo-Irish critic Edward Dowden suggested that the dramatist's turn in the first years of the seventeenth century towards tragedy and dark tragi-comedy (*Hamlet, Measure for Measure, Troilus and Cressida*, eventually *King Lear*) was bound up with some deep personal trauma. This was Shakespeare 'in the depths', as opposed to the Shakespeare of the serene last plays, where he was back 'on the heights'. There is, however, no evidence for speculations of this kind: they represent a back-projection of nineteenth-century Romantic conceptions of creativity on to the Renaissance.

The intriguing thing about Lamb's essay on the sanity of true genius was that he had experience of deep personal trauma.

★

On Friday afternoon the Coroner and Jury sat on the body *[i.e. the case]* of a Lady, in the neighbourhood of Holborn, who died in consequence of a wound from her daughter the previous day.

There's My Comfort

So began a report in the London *Times* on a September morning in 1796:

It appeared by the evidence adduced, that while the family were preparing for dinner, the young lady seized a case-knife laying on the table, and in a menacing manner pursued a little girl, her apprentice, round the room. On the calls of her infirm mother to forbear, she renounced her first object, and with loud shrieks approached her parent. The child, by her cries, quickly brought up the landlord of the house, but too late. The dreadful scene presented to him the mother lifeless, pierced to the heart, on a chair, her daughter yet wildly standing over her with the fatal knife, and the old man her father weeping by her side, himself bleeding at the forehead from the effect of a severe blow he received from one of the forks she had been madly hurling about the room.

The diligent court reporter went on to explain that for a few days prior to this the family had observed some symptoms of insanity in the young lady. By the Wednesday night, they were worried. Early on the Thursday morning her brother went to the well-respected family doctor. But he wasn't at home.

It seems the young lady had been once before deranged, the report concluded, with the result that *The Jury of course brought in their verdict, LUNACY*. Her name was Mary Lamb.

Charles, her brother, wrote to his best friend from school, Samuel Taylor Coleridge:

Some of my friends or the public papers by this time may have informed you of the terrible calamities that have fallen on our family. I will only give you the outlines. My poor dear dearest sister in a fit of insanity has been the death of her own mother. I was at hand only time enough to snatch the knife out of her grasp. She is at present in a mad house, from whence I fear she must be moved to an hospital. God has preserved to me my senses, – I eat and drink and sleep, and have my judgment I believe very sound. My poor father was slightly wounded, and I am left to take care of him and my aunt . . . thank God I am very calm and composed, and able to do the best that remains to do. Write, – as religious a letter as possible – but no mention of what is gone and done with. – With me 'the former things are passed away,' and I have something more to do than to feel –

God almighty have us all in his keeping. –

C. Lamb.

Mention nothing of poetry. I have destroyed every vestige of past vanities of that kind. Do as you please, but if you publish, publish mine (I give free leave) without name or initial, and never send me a book, I charge you.

The two friends had been planning to publish a joint collection of poetry. Lamb, though claiming to be *very calm and composed*, was clearly in a state of extreme shock. His first reaction to the trauma of what he had witnessed was to renounce poetry altogether. He dismisses as a 'vanity' the expression of emotion that was, in his view and Coleridge's, the purpose of poetry. *I have something more to do than to feel*: his task now, he says, is only to care for his wounded father and his aunt and to pray for his sister. Religious faith will be his only comfort; poetry, at least in the immediate aftermath of crisis, was of no use to him.

Was it any wonder, then, that Lamb believed in the sanity of true genius? For him, madness meant the psychotic behaviour manifested in his sister's violent act. It did not mean the divine fury of writing poetry.

Under the surprisingly liberal mental-health regime of the age, after a short period of confinement in the Islington madhouse, Mary Lamb was released back into the community on the condition that her brother served as surety for her good behaviour. A poet and dreamer by nature, Charles reined himself in to a prosaic life in the service of his sister, maintaining a tedious but secure post as a clerk in the offices of the East India Company and banishing all thought of marriage or of giving up the day job for the risk of a full-time writing career. He survived with the help of his sense of humour (he was an obsessive punster), his circle of friends such as Coleridge, and daily doses of wine and brandy.

There were times when Mary had further manic episodes and was returned to the asylum. There were times when Charles sank into depression and he too was temporarily consigned to the madhouse. But they endured, and one of their tools of endurance was writing. Charles gradually returned to literature. He became one of the leading essayists of the age and Mary one of the leading children's authors. Their most successful work was one on which they collaborated, though only the name of Charles appeared on the title page. *Tales from Shakespear designed for the use of Young Persons* became, for more than a hundred years, the standard work that introduced children to the plays. Mary turned the comedies into prose narratives, Charles the tragedies.

The book was designed, according to its Preface, *to teach courtesy, benignity, generosity, humanity*. To spare the blushes of parents reading the stories to their children, it glossed over many more adult details in the plays. So, for example, in *The Winter's*

Tale Mary omitted the fact that the seed of Leontes' jealousy is his belief that Hermione and Polixenes are having sex. Even when Paulina brings on the baby, the text does not explain that Leontes banishes the child because he believes that her father is Polixenes.

Of all Mary's stories, the most effective is her version of *Twelfth Night*. A play about the bond of brother and sister, it pierced to the heart of the Lambs. Mary's narrative version runs directly from the parting of Viola and Sebastian to Olivia's mourning for her dead brother. *Viola, who was herself in such a sad affliction for her brother's loss, wished she could live with this lady, who so tenderly mourned a brother's death.* Mary thus highlights the parallel between the two women who have each lost a brother. Then the sea captain explains that the grieving Olivia will not admit anyone into her household, leading Viola to go instead to serve Duke Orsino in disguise. In Mary's telling, the bond between sister and brother matters more than the marriage plot: *wedded on the same day, the storm and shipwreck, which had separated them, being the means of bringing to pass their high and mighty fortunes.*

Sister and brother, Mary and Charles are Viola and Sebastian through the looking glass, reading and talking Shakespeare, writing together in order to assuage their trauma. In a letter, Mary conjured up their love, manifested in their collaboration:

> You would like to see us, as we often sit writing on one table (but not on one cushion sitting), like Hermia and Helena in the Midsummer Night's Dream; or, rather, like an old literary Darby and Joan: I taking snuff, and he groaning all the while and saying he can make nothing of it, which he always says till he has finished.

There's My Comfort

Shakespeare, words, bonds, writing: their comfort.

★

Many of the other graduate students in the English Department were unhappy during the year I was at Harvard. They thought the place was old-fashioned and wished they had gone to Yale, which was the epicentre of a new phenomenon called Deconstruction. The 'Yale Mafia' – five high-profile professors – had just published a manifesto, which they said wasn't a manifesto, called *Deconstruction and Criticism*. It included a head-spinning essay by their French Visiting Professor Jacques Derrida – an essay with a single footnote that spidered its way through a hundred pages. Derrida was the father of Deconstruction. His proposition was that since all texts are made of language and all interpretations are made of language, there is nothing outside the text. Meaning is always indeterminate, always deferred, and in every text there is self-contradiction that sends the interpreter into an abyss of uncertainty. Literary theory was becoming very superior, as clever critics began to chide hapless creators for falling into the heffalump trap of lucidity or letting slip politically incorrect sentiments.

Then there was an essay by Harold Bloom that began with the claim that the word 'meaning' is closely related to the word 'moaning' and that all poetry is therefore a form of moaning in which the poet wrestles with the Oedipal influence of a poetic father, because 'the truest sources' of inspiration are to be found 'in the powers of poems *already written*, or rather, *already read*'. All truly original writing, Bloom had argued a few years earlier in his one-man manifesto *The Anxiety of Influence*, is a form of 'strong misreading'. And he set out to prove his

245

case by looking at the way in which the Romantic poets had been inhibited by the epic achievement of their alleged 'father', John Milton. 'I have given up *Hyperion*', wrote John Keats of his own attempt at an epic, because 'there were too many Miltonic inversions in it . . . Life to him would be death to me.'

This was all very original, and at least Bloom's prose was less impenetrable than that of his colleagues, but it didn't seem to me quite right. In my undergraduate course on the Romantics as readers of Shakespeare, I had discovered that they failed disastrously when they tried writing plays in his style, but they didn't seem especially anxious about this. They knew they could never be as good as Shakespeare, but they didn't regard him as an oppressive influence. On the contrary, they rejoiced in his genius and treated him as a talisman. Keats's *own intensity of thought and expression visibly strengthened with the study of his idol*, according to his close friend Charles Cowden Clarke.

When Keats was feeling lonely and unwell in rented accommodation on the Isle of Wight, he was delighted to find an engraved portrait of Shakespeare in the hallway. His landlady kindly let him take it away when he left. You can just make it out on the wall of his Hampstead home in his friend Joseph Severn's portrait of the poet reading, with the door to the garden ajar, as if to let in the song of the nightingale. I am sure that he is imagined to be reading Shakespeare.

One of Keats's close friends was the manic-depressive painter Benjamin Robert Haydon, who eventually committed suicide, ending his diary with the lines from *King Lear* about being stretched no longer on the rack of this tough world ('longer' – such a brilliant, painful pun). It was to Haydon that Keats wrote from the Isle of Wight:

I remember your saying that you had notions of a good Genius presiding over you. I have of late had the same thought, for things which I do half at Random are afterwards confirmed by my judgment in a dozen features of Propriety. Is it too daring to fancy Shakspeare this Presider?

Bloom may have been right that Milton was the great Inhibitor for the Romantics. But Shakespeare was the benign Presider. Keats went on to hope that the landlady giving him the portrait of Shakespeare was a good omen. Then he dipped into gloom: *I am glad you say every man of great views is at times tormented as I am*. But Shakespeare was his solace in such times of torment. A little earlier, he had written to his brothers: *I felt rather lonely this Morning at breakfast so I went and unbox'd a Shakspeare – 'there's my Comfort'*. The quotation is from Caliban in *The Tempest*; that character's comfort was alcohol, whereas for Keats it was Shakespeare.

One day I went into the Houghton Library at Harvard and unboxed the very Shakespeare to which Keats was referring. His own copy of a multi-volume pocket edition, printed in Chiswick in 1814. I traced my hand over his underlinings and marginal annotations. I especially liked the last page of the text of *A Midsummer Night's Dream*. *Fie*, he had written, as he inked out Dr Johnson's lukewarm comment on the play. And, echoing and inverting the closing line of Theseus' speech on the lunatic, the lover and the poet, *Such tricks hath weak imagination*. At that moment, I saw what the theme of my doctoral dissertation should be: a riposte to Harold Bloom's 'anxiety of influence', with the working title 'Strong Imagination: The Consolation of Influence in Romantic Shakespeare'.

Back in England the following year, I went on a wintry day

to Keats's house in Hampstead. I put on the white gloves provided by the curator and opened Keats's other copy of Shakespeare. Harvard had the boxed edition, but this was a greater prize: John Keats's facsimile of the First Folio itself. There was a blank half-page at the end of *Hamlet*, opposite the beginning of *King Lear*. He had filled it with a poem called 'On Sitting Down to Read King Lear Once Again'. I understood the idea of a compulsion to *re*-read Shakespeare's darkest play. For Keats, life was indeed, as he wrote in the poem, a *fierce dispute betwixt Damnation and impassion'd clay*. *Bitter-sweet* as the *Shakspearean fruit* of Lear's descent into madness inevitably was, the experience of re-reading the play gave him comfort. It turned the embers of his own sorrows to new fire, new creativity, new hope:

Give me new Phoenix Wings to fly at my desire.

★

For some of the Romantics, though, there was no comfort. 'I am glad you can amuse yourself by writing,' said a well-meaning visitor to the poet who had been in the Northampton General Lunatic Asylum for nearly twenty years. John Clare replied,

I can't do it – they pick my brains out. Why, they have cut off my head and picked out all the letters in the alphabet – all the vowels and consonants and brought them out through my ears; and they want me to write poetry! I can't do it . . . I liked hard work best, I was happy then. Literature has destroyed my head and brought me here.

When I began researching the life of Clare, I took for granted the view of the poet's first biographer that one of the villains in his story was his doctor, Fenwick Skrimshire, who allegedly committed him to the asylum on the grounds that he had been driven mad by, as the asylum admission papers put it, *years addicted to poetical prosing*. According to that first biographer, Frederick Martin, writing in the immediate aftermath of the poet's death in the asylum at the age of seventy, Clare was incarcerated for the mere fact of being a poet.

But I discovered that, far from being the country ignoramus supposed by Martin, Skrimshire was an educated and cultivated doctor with particular expertise in the area of mental illness. The remark about Clare's addiction to poetry was not the grounds for admission to the asylum, but the answer to a question on the admission papers that was intended to provide assistance in diagnosis and treatment: has the insanity been 'preceded by any severe or long continued mental emotion or exertion'? Skrimshire had been treating his patient for two decades: he knew that the addictive writing of poetry was indeed a long-continued mental emotion and exertion for Clare. Maybe literature really was what destroyed his head and drove him to the asylum.

When I gave talks about my biography of Clare at literary festivals, the question was sometimes asked: 'How would he have been treated if he were alive today?' My answer was that he would be diagnosed with bipolar disorder ('manic depression') and treated with Prozac or Lithium to even out his highs and lows. But if his creativity was intimately bound to his cyclical journey, if the writing was the fruit of his 'up' or 'manic' times, then would the administration of a drug such as Lithium have killed his muse? Would he have achieved stability in his everyday life at the cost of his poetry? As human beings, we would not wish for poets – for a John Clare, an Emily Dickinson, a Robert Lowell – to suffer mentally, but as lovers of literature we would not wish to be without the poems that enable us better to enjoy life and better to endure it. Is the true role of poets to be, as William Empson suggested of King Lear, scapegoats who take upon themselves the mental fight of their readers?

FINIS.

On sitting down to read King Lear once again.

O Golden-tongued Romance, with serene lute!
  Fair plumed Syren, Queen of far-away!
  Leave melodizing on this wintry day,
Shut up thine olden Pages, and be mute.
Adieu! for, once again, the fierce dispute,
  Betwixt Damnation and impassion'd clay
  Must I burn through; once more humbly assay
The bitter-sweet of this Shakesperean fruit.
Chief Poet! and ye Clouds of Albion,
  Begetters of our deep eternal theme!
When through the old oak forest I am gone,
  Let me not wander in a barren dream:
But, when I am consumed in the fire,
Give me new Phoenix wings to fly at my desire.
      Jan. 22. 1818

John Keats writes out his sonnet
as he sits down to re-read *King Lear*

15.

Voyage to Illyria

I had a row with my father a few days before he died. Something that hardly ever happened, so why did it have to happen *then*? I should have said sorry, but never got round to it. This piece of unfinished business has been a regret which still irks me more than forty years on.

The argument was the usual teenage thing: I wanted the family car for the evening. I had tickets for the theatre. I was supposed to be picking up my friend Karim. My parents had taken the car out for the afternoon and were back later than I had expected. My father apologized, explaining that they had gone for a drive and a walk in the countryside because it was such a lovely afternoon, and they were so happy that my mother was feeling so well after those years of depression. I should have rejoiced in this, instead of grabbing the keys and driving off at breakneck speed. We made it to the theatre just in time.

The Royal Victoria Hall in Southborough, just outside Tunbridge Wells, was commissioned in 1897 in celebration of the Queen's Diamond Jubilee. It was the oldest municipally funded theatre in Britain, though the building costs were generously subsidized by Sir David Lionel Goldsmid-Stern-Salomons, a local barrister who made a fortune by creating some of the earliest electric cookers and alarms, and even an electrically operated butter churn. Elegantly designed to Sir David's personal specification, the theatre opened in January 1900 with a patriotic concert in aid of the Transvaal War Fund. In 2017, the local council demolished it, unable, they said, to afford the necessary repairs. The revels there are ended, the insubstantial pageant faded. But that night in the summer of 1978, the Royal Shakespeare Company was in town with a stellar cast led by Ian McKellen as Sir Toby Belch (the largest part) in a glorious double act with skinny Roger Rees's sad Sir Andrew Aguecheek, baiting Bob Peck's grumpy Yorkshire Malvolio.

The stage was bare, raking gently away from the auditorium. A floor-length mirror gleamed against the rear wall, upstage centre. The musical food of love was accompanied by the sound of swishing waves. The Duke and his Edwardian flunkies entered downstage. And there at the back was Viola, in a white nightshift that wetly hugged her body. She held her hand against the mirror as she gazed into the dream world. Then we saw that the mirror was an illusion, a trick of light: we are seeing not her reflection but her double, an aged clown, Feste, crouching low, gazing back at her.

What country, friends, is this?

With these words, Viola steps into Illyria. A dukedom by the sea, a place of illusion, a topsy-turvy carnival where all the people seem to be mad. *Twelfth Night; or, What You Will* is a play that invites us to share the experience of going through the looking glass, to the other side of the world where all expectations are upended.

It can't be a coincidence that it is about brother-sister twins and that Shakespeare had twins, his son Hamnet and daughter Judith. For all the lessons I learned at school and university about Shakespeare's impersonality, about drama not being self-expression, and about the fallacy of biographical interpretation, I am convinced that *Twelfth Night* was shadowed by the death of Shakespeare's only son, young Hamnet – who was named after a Stratford neighbour, Hamnet Sadler, who in Shakespeare's will was spelled *Hamlet* Sadler. I think of the play as a gift for Judith.

Judith and Hamnet were born in February 1585. Their father's fascination with the dramatic possibilities of double selves is apparent from his early *Comedy of Errors*. Then, in the summer of 1596, the eleven-year-old Hamnet died. Shakespeare had lost his only son and Judith would be forever bereft of her second self. There is an inescapable poignancy to the images of loss in *Twelfth Night*: when Feste sings of sad cypress (*Come away, death*) or Viola alludes to *Patience on a monument, smiling at grief*, I can only think of Shakespeare's own lost boy. Olivia mourns a brother, while Viola assumes that hers, Sebastian, has been drowned. When she takes a male disguise and 'becomes' Cesario, it is as if she impersonates her own opposite-sex twin:

I am all the daughters of my father's house
And all the brothers too.

The principal source of *Twelfth Night*'s tale of siblings lost and found, and of a cross-dressed servant sent to woo on behalf of a master whom she herself loves, was a short Elizabethan novel called *Apolonius and Silla*. There the brother and sister who are the originals for Viola and Sebastian are not twins, but *the one of them was so like the other in countenance and favour that there was no man able to discern the one from the other by their faces, saving by their apparel, the one being a man, the other a woman*. Critics sometimes express puzzlement that Shakespeare makes so much of the resemblance between Viola and Sebastian, given his presumed personal knowledge that boy-girl twins are not identical. But this passage in the source-novel reveals the absurdity of such a criticism: siblings don't even have to be twins to look remarkably alike.

One of the greatest challenges for a writer is to imagine what it would be like to be a member of the opposite sex. The particular demand faced by Shakespeare and the boy actors who played his women's parts was to get beyond the age's conventions of proper female behaviour, which commended silence and submissiveness in public settings. 'Cesario' is partly a device to give Viola an active voice, to enable her to break the shackles of passivity. But the lovely combination of quick-witted facility, wonder and vulnerability with which she slots into her impersonation is something more than a reaction to social convention or codes of propriety. In terms of the play's imaginary world, Viola plays Cesario so effectively because of her prior knowledge and love of Sebastian – this is what allows the otherwise implausible conceit of Olivia marrying Sebastian in the belief that he is Cesario. Was the germ sown by Shakespeare's observation of the intuitive understanding between his twins as they learned to speak and to play together?

Shakespearean comedy often imagines a journey from the secure womb of the family to a world of shipwreck and isolation, and thence to the bond of marriage. The characters lose themselves to find themselves. Broken families are restored in the same instant that new families are anticipated through the pronouncement of love vows. The climax of *Twelfth Night* is one of the great reunion scenes, as the parted twins are joined:

> ORSINO One face, one voice, one habit, and two persons,
> A natural perspective, that is and is not . . .
> ANTONIO How have you made division of yourself?
> An apple cleft in two is not more twin
> Than these two creatures.

The language is richly suggestive of one made two and two made one, and of the workings of nature combined with the trick of art (a 'perspective' was a distorting glass that created the optical illusion of one picture appearing as two). In a single action, brother and sister find both each other and their object of desire.

And yet. The peculiar poignancy of *Twelfth Night* comes from the sense that there are many losses even in this moment of wonder. Antonio, who has been like a brother and even a lover to Sebastian, is left alone. Malvolio has been humiliated just a little too far (*Ah'll be revenged on t'whole pack o' yer*, scowled Bob Peck). The union of Sir Toby and Maria leaves Sir Andrew isolated – he was adored once, too, but we cannot imagine that he will be again. And Feste is there to sing another sad song of time and change. Above all, Cesario is no more: Orsino closes the dialogue by addressing Viola by her boy-name one final time before she assumes her female garb and becomes his *fancy's queen*. But *fancy's queen* is the very language of that shallow courtly love with which Orsino had tried to woo Olivia: the language that Cesario cast off when (s)he began speaking in his/her own voice. In the closing moments of the play, Viola does seem to revert to silence and passivity; Shakespeare had an intuitive understanding of what we now call gender fluidity, but his age was not ready to accept that idea save in the play-time of the theatre.

What is going through the imaginary heart of the character as the play comes to an end? When Sebastian is found, Cesario is lost. Could Viola be saying goodbye to the feigned twin into which she has made herself? The name Cesario suggests untimely birth – as in 'Caesarean section', a baby *from his mother's womb untimely ripped* – but Viola's boy-persona undergoes an untimely death. A few months before starting the comedy of *Twelfth Night*, Shakespeare completed *Hamlet*. There are unfathomable cross-currents at work here: in creating and destroying Cesario, perhaps Shakespeare was saying a goodbye to his own Hamnet. Viola is diminished when bereaved of her invented second self. Was this Shakespeare's delayed response to poor Judith's desolation on the loss of her twin?

In preparing to direct the play for the Royal Shakespeare Company in 2009, Gregory Doran, himself a twin, noticed a coincidence neglected by the legion of Shakespeare's biographers and critics. Hamnet and Judith Shakespeare were baptized on 2 February, the feast of Candlemas (which celebrates the presentation of the baby Jesus in the Temple in Jerusalem – a fitting moment for the baptism of a treasured first son). And it was on that very same festival day seventeen years later, 2 February, Candlemas, that *Twelfth Night* received its earliest recorded performance, before the law students of the Middle Temple in 1602. Malvolio describes Cesario/Viola as:

Not yet old enough for a man, nor young enough for a boy.
As a squash is before 'tis a peascod, or a codling when 'tis
almost an apple: 'tis with him in standing water, between boy
and man.

On 2 February 1602, Judith was in standing water between girl
and woman. By allowing Sebastian to return from the devouring
sea of death, Shakespeare allowed himself the consoling fantasy
of a seventeenth-birthday reunion for his own separated twins.

★

I think that *Twelfth Night* is special for me because it is set
beside the sea.

If life has a base that it stands upon, if it is a bowl that one
fills and fills and fills – then my bowl without a doubt stands
upon this memory. It is of lying half asleep, half awake, in
the nursery at St Ives. It is of hearing the waves breaking,
one, two, one, two, and sending a splash of water over the
beach . . . and feeling, it is almost impossible that I should
be here; of feeling the purest ecstasy I can conceive.

Virginia Woolf also spoke to me because, like her family, mine
spent our summer holidays by the sea. Those days are my
happiest memory of childhood. She had the whole summer in
a big house in St Ives; for us, it was a mere week in Broadstairs.
But no less magical. The excitement of the night before we
left home. The fear that my cricket bat would be left behind.
Then the journey itself, the family Mini packed to the gunwales.
Games of I-spy and eager glances at the road signs counting

down the miles to the coast. Swinging into West Cliff Road and touching the stone lions that guarded the front door of our grandmother's house. The scent of China tea. Gulls screeching overhead as my brother and I settled for the night in narrow twin beds. Then in the morning, the laughter of bathers in the chilly outdoor pool of the Grand Hotel at the bottom of the road and the crash of waves below. And down the stone steps into Viking Bay, from where we looked across to the bleak house on the clifftop where Charles Dickens spent his summer holidays. Batting and bowling with my father in the Victoria Gardens by the bandstand; more elaborate games of beach cricket with uncle, aunt and cousin. The special treat of fish and chips wrapped in newspaper on the last night before home.

When John Keats – who came for sea air to Margate, just along the cliffs from Broadstairs – first looked into the Elizabethan translation of Homer's *Odyssey*, the first great sea poem of the Western world, his eye fell on the line *The sea had soaked his heart through*. That, he thought, was true poetry.

Because of those holidays, the sea had soaked my heart through. And Shakespeare? We don't know how often he saw the sea. Probably only a few times. In late July 1597, the London theatres were closed by order of the Privy Council. Ben Jonson and Tom Nashe had written a play called *The Isle of Dogs*, full of lewdness and slanderous matter that greatly offended the royal court. Shakespeare's acting company, the Lord Chamberlain's Men, left town for a tour that took them to the south-eastern coast. They played at Rye in late August, and the following week were paid thirteen shillings and fourpence for their performance at Dover. Did the salt spray in the air lodge the idea for *Twelfth Night*?

Shakespeare must have seen the white cliffs. His acting company, now with the upgraded title of the King's Men, or His Majesty's Players, revisited Dover in 1606, during another period when the London theatres were closed, this time due to plague. In *King Lear*, written that very year, the blinded Earl of Gloucester asks Edgar/Mad Tom, *Dost thou know Dover?* He demands to be taken to

> a cliff whose high and bending head
> Looks fearfully in the confinèd deep.

He wants to jump off it, in order to end his misery. Edgar leads him there – or rather, pretends to lead him there – and then conjures it into the imagination of both his sightless father and the listening theatre audience:

> Come on, sir, here's the place: stand still. How
>   fearful
> And dizzy 'tis to cast one's eyes so low!
> The crows and choughs that wing the midway air
> Show scarce so gross as beetles: halfway down
> Hangs one that gathers samphire, dreadful trade!
> Methinks he seems no bigger than his head.
> The fishermen that walk upon the beach
> Appear like mice, and yond tall anchoring bark
> Diminished to her cock, her cock a buoy
> Almost too small for sight. The murmuring surge,
> That on th'unnumbered idle pebble chafes,
> Cannot be heard so high. I'll look no more,
> Lest my brain turn and the deficient sight
> Topple down headlong.

No writer has ever evoked the giddiness of a cliff edge so vividly. No wonder Gloucester really believes he is there. Yet when he jumps, he falls flat on his face. His pratfall takes him beyond the urge to suicide, tricks him into acceptance of all the horrors that life has thrown at him:

> henceforth I'll bear
> Affliction till it do cry out itself
> 'Enough, enough' and die.

We must endure our afflictions; it is not for us to choose the moment of our death. It will come when it will come, as Hamlet also learns to see. Until then, *Let it be* (words that imprinted themselves on Paul McCartney's memory when he was studying *Hamlet* at school).

When Lear awakens from his madness, assisted by the ministrations of a doctor and music in one of the early texts, of Cordelia in the other, he thinks that he has died and is in hell looking up to heaven:

> You do me wrong to take me out o' th' grave:
> Thou art a soul in bliss, but I am bound
> Upon a wheel of fire, that mine own tears
> Do scald like molten lead.

When he finally realizes that he is speaking not to a spirit but to the living Cordelia, he asks for her forgiveness. She has great cause to resent her father, but she says *No cause, no cause.*

It was because this reunion is so short-lived, the ensuing murder of Cordelia so cruel and unexpected, that Dr Johnson could not bear to re-read the play until he had to do so as an editor. A year or two later, Shakespeare wrote a version of the father–daughter scene again, but this time without the tragic turn that follows it in *Lear*. Once again, his thoughts went down to the sea. The play was called *Pericles* – it would be excluded from the Folio, probably because Shakespeare wrote only the second half of it.

After losing his daughter, who is named Marina because she was born at sea, Pericles wanders the Mediterranean for year upon year until his ship fetches up at the port of Mytilene on the island of Lesbos. A young woman renowned for medicinal and almost magical arts is brought aboard. Pericles asks her to tell the story of her endurance, comparing it to his own. She looks, he says, in an echo of Viola's line in *Twelfth Night* about the monument,

> Like Patience, gazing on kings' graves and smiling
> Extremity out of act.

She is, of course, Marina. The love of a daughter for her father has the power to smile extremity – suffering, grief – out of existence, if only for a moment. Few other thoughts in Shakespeare have affected me so deeply.

My first acquaintance with *Pericles* came when, together with a few friends, I stayed on at school for an extra term after A-Levels in order to take the Oxbridge entrance exam (a hurdle rightly abolished a few years later, since it inevitably favoured the schools – mostly private – that had the resources to offer the extra term). To raise our game, JA and Hurdy introduced us to some challenging texts. It was then that we read *King Lear*. We were also put through our paces with the archetypal 'difficult' poet: T. S. Eliot. I liked J. Alfred Prufrock measuring out his life with coffee spoons and admitting that he was *not Prince Hamlet, nor was meant to be*, but I was baffled by the polyphonic voices of *The Waste Land*, with its dense jungle of literary quotations and allusions, none of which I grasped other than the parodic rewriting of Shakespeare's description of Cleopatra on her barge. The Eliot poem that did speak to me, and that I began to recite to myself when walking in Knole Park, was 'Marina', one of a group of so-called 'Ariel Poems'. I liked it because it smelled of the sea:

> What seas what shores what grey rocks and what islands
> What water lapping the bow
> And scent of pine and the woodthrush singing through
>   the fog
> What images return
> O my daughter.

Hurdy explained that the poem was a response to the reunion of father and daughter in *Pericles*. It was written soon after Eliot became a committed Christian, which led him, with some justification, to read Shakespeare's last plays as allegories of death and resurrection – Hermione returning to life in *The Winter's Tale* and, earlier in *Pericles*, a scene where Marina's mother Thaisa is revived after apparently dying in childbirth and being cast overboard. And this, the reawakening of a father by his daughter. The staging of hope:

> This form, this face, this life
> Living to live in a world of time beyond me; let me
> Resign my life for this life, my speech for that unspoken,
> The awakened, lips parted, the hope, the new ships.

★

At the end of the performance of *Twelfth Night* in the Royal Victoria Hall, the paired-off lovers, their bags packed for a new journey, were framed by the mirror that was now turned round to face the audience. They jumped off the stage and into the audience, as if to invite us on our own journeys into Illyria and out of it. But Feste, the old clown, is left alone and melancholy on stage. He sings, as the Fool in *Lear* will also sing, of how *The rain it raineth every day*. And earlier he has sung of the uncertainty of life:

What's to come is still unsure.

And

Youth's a stuff will not endure.

Shakespeare's plays are full of surprises, both happy and sad. They give a constant reminder that *what's to come is still unsure*. They don't give you answers when things that you think will endure turn out not to endure. But at least they prepare you for the uncertainty.

★

Summer 2005. You can tempt fate once, but not twice. Twice and the gods will have you.

'Life doesn't get any better than this,' says Paula as she lies on a blue and white striped *matelas* looking out over the sun-sparkled Mediterranean, a glass of chilled birthday champagne in her hand. Her presents are beside her: a booking slip for an afternoon appointment with the bronzed beach masseur and a compact lime-green iPod, quite the latest thing in the dawn of the digital age. Her favourite music was clandestinely preloaded before the drive through France. Tom, aged six, and Ellie, five, sun-kissed, laughing, are building a sand wall against the gentle waves. Brother and sister are a year apart, but they look and behave as if they were twins.

Usually we lay our towels on the public beach, but today's birthday treat is the paying enclave with mattress, parasol, waiter bringing drinks on demand and a table for lunch. It's fun to watch the boats of the millionaires at anchor in the gulf, but you do so in the knowledge that happiness is not conferred by wealth. Happiness is here: your family, the sun, the few weeks of distance from the pressure of work. And your health – but you don't think about that, you take it for granted. It's been a few years since you saw and smelled the inside of a hospital.

Over the coming week, Ellie is not herself. She complains of tiredness and does not want to swim. Fortunately, Tom finds a friend, Rufus, a slightly older boy. They spend hours and hours in vigorous pool games – races, jumps, bombs. The older boy has guts: one of his legs is swollen along its full length and hard to manoeuvre, but he does not let it impair him. Some rare condition. His mother tells us its name and the history of his symptoms. We listen with interest and sympathy, but also that tiny element of *Schadenfreude* that is always present when the parents of healthy children converse with those less fortunate than themselves. The striking thing is that Rufus's condition seems to cause his mother and her husband no anxiety: all their worries are directed at their younger boy, who is physically in the best of health but socially maladjusted, short-tempered, babyish for his years. A 'difficult' child. We talk about the *spectrum* of autistic and quasi-autistic conditions, agreeing that mental health is so much more difficult to manage than physical.

Has Ellie picked up a bug from the water? Whatever she's got, it's dragging on, but isn't severe enough to merit a trip to the doctor and the effort of explaining the symptoms via the medium of dimly remembered A-Level French. She is uncharacteristically irritable. She complains perpetually of aching legs, demanding to be carried every time we come back up the hill from the pool. This annoys us: 'You're not a baby, we can't carry you everywhere.' On the beach and at the Crazy Golf she becomes her impish self again, but then she flops and doesn't want to eat. If it wasn't for whatever it is she has, we would stay an extra day or two – the return ferry ticket is open. 'She's still not right,' says Paula. 'It's been a great holiday but I want to get home now.'

We leave in the late afternoon and make good time: we're halfway through France by one in the morning, when we break for a few hours' sleep in an American-style motel. Ellie is very, very tired, but that makes the journey easier. Fewer repetitions of 'Are we nearly there?' In the morning we take a more leisurely pace. A bright and breezy Channel crossing: the ferry is slower than the tunnel, but for Tom and Ellie a sea voyage is always an adventure.

If you get your route and your timing right, and throw in a slice of luck, you can drive the whole way from the Riviera to Calais without encountering a single traffic jam. But the inevitable comes at three o'clock on a humid mid-August afternoon when you find yourself on the M25 near Heathrow. You are stuck and your five-year-old is desperate for a wee. We sing songs to take her mind off her bladder. KT Tunstall's *Eye to the Telescope* has been the soundtrack of our summer. Ellie sings along with perfect pitch. Over and again we play it: *You are*, her little voice soars, *the other side of the world to me*. The traffic breaks, we swing left on to the M40 towards Oxford and the relief of the service station, where we pile out of the car, cheering for KT and congratulating Ellie on her bladder control. I swoop her up and carry her into a cubicle in the gents. Nothing comes out.

We're angry: 'How can you say you're so desperate and then not do a wee? What are we going to do now? Are we going to have to stop at the next service station as well?' Maybe it's psychological: she got so wrought up holding it in that now she can't let it out. 'She's always doing this on long journeys,' Paula says, 'nagging that she needs to go when she doesn't, it's maddening.' We'll give the kids half an hour in the play area, then get her to try again. She does, and still there's nothing. Oh well, maybe because it's such a hot day she's just sweated it off.

We don't give it another thought. We are home in a couple of hours. The final forty minutes, along a quiet road in the green of north Oxfordshire and south Warwickshire on a perfect summer's evening, remind us how lucky we are. Reunion with rooms, toys, guinea pigs puts other things out of mind and we all settle for an early night.

First thing in the morning, Paula takes Ellie to the GP's surgery in Stratford-upon-Avon, a stone's throw from the house where Shakespeare's twins were born. 'Just to get her checked over and to set my mind at rest.' They're back within half an hour.

'She's fine – chest clear, no problems.'

'Which doctor was it?' I ask.

'That good-looking woman who's a mum at the school – I can't remember her name.'

Though we haven't registered the fact, she is actually the nurse-practitioner, not a doctor. Streamlining and financial controls within the primary care trusts of the National Health Service mean that nurse practitioners, who are trained more fully than regular GP practice nurses but not to the level of doctors, are the first port of call for many routine visits.

Through the blazing afternoon, Tom, Ellie and some of the other village children play on the green and bounce on the trampoline in the garden. I start attacking weeds and Paula lies on our own *matelas* and talks to her mother on the phone. 'Yes, it was a great holiday. But I've come to a decision. I'm not going to have any more babies. I've got what I want – two beautiful, happy, healthy children, a boy and a girl. That's enough, our life is perfect. Now I'm going to focus on my career.'

Twice and the gods will have you. *As flies to wanton boys.*

★

Just before six o'clock, Ellie comes in from the garden, complaining that she is tired. Thinking that she has overheated, Paula puts her in a cool bath. 'What do you want to do now?' she asks afterwards. 'Settle down with some quiet telly or go straight to bed?'

'I don't care,' says Ellie.

Mothers are hard-wired with alarm bells. Ellie is not the sort of child who says, 'I don't care.' Every choice she makes, every moment of every day, is made with heart and soul.

Paula comes into the garden, her voice and face stretched with anxiety. 'Something's not right with Ellie, I'm convinced of it.' She has phoned the surgery. We are lucky in our timing. They are just about to close for the evening, but Dr Fitchford is running late and if we come immediately, he could have a quick look at her. As at most practices, there is a panel of doctors and you get used to seeing whichever one happens to be on. By good fortune, Fitchford is the one we know best and trust most.

I am wearing an old T-shirt and shorts, I have mud on my knees and sandals. I'm not so worried – wasn't Ellie given the all-clear by the doctor this morning? But Paula's mind must be set at rest, so I agree to drive her straight into town. The kids have been playing all afternoon with two older girls, Grace and Maddie – Tom will be fine with them, we'll only be half an hour. They promise to tell their mums what is going on.

It's in the car that I get worried for the first time. Ellie had looked all right when she had that bath half an hour ago, but suddenly she seems very weak. She's falling asleep. Is she just dog-tired or is she close to fainting?

We're at the surgery in less than ten minutes. She's asleep as I carry her in my arms. The building is almost empty. A receptionist, in the midst of closing up, gestures us to go straight into Dr Fitchford's room. Ellie wakes as he checks heart and pulse. He's concentrating. You try to decipher every flicker of expression. Is he grave? If anything, he seems puzzled. Three times he takes her blood pressure. It's a traditional machine, where he holds the little bulb in his fist, pumps gently and watches the ball of mercury rise in the tube. 'I can't seem to get a reading,' he says, 'I wonder if it's a problem with the machine.' But he *is* getting a reading: the ball is high in the tube, close to two hundred. If it's high in the tube, does that mean her blood pressure is high? What does it mean for a child to have high blood pressure? That's a condition I associate with older people, like Paula's dad, who has to take some pills for it.

Now Fitchford is making a phone call. 'I have a little girl in here who I'd like you to take a look at.' He mentions a couple of numbers, but we're not really attending. We're looking at each other and at her. He's phoning the hospital: this must be serious. What gets me is that he doesn't seem to know what's wrong. I'm not used to that. I'm used to doctors saying, 'It's a virus, get some rest and take plenty of fluids. If it hasn't gone in a few days, come back and I'll give you antibiotics.'

'I'd like you to drive her over to Warwick,' he says. 'Now. Go straight to A and E. They'll be expecting you.'

'Is she going to be all right, doctor?' asks Paula, voice choking and pupils dilated.

'I think we need to get her checked over as soon as possible,' he replies.

'Should we be calling an ambulance?' I ask.

'No, you can drive her, but go now.'

'Ought we to keep her awake in the car?'

'It's OK to let her sleep, if that's what she wants.'

We've lived in the area for two years, but have never been over to Warwick Hospital. It takes about twenty minutes to get there, and it is easy enough to find.

In the car, Paula has held Ellie, who is drifting in and out of sleep – or do I mean of consciousness? I pull in where it says Accident and Emergency, saying, 'Go in, I'll park up and follow you.' After passing through the barrier into the car park, it occurs to me that I don't have any money on me. Just my gardening clothes and mud on my knees.

I'm ushered through to a small room where Ellie is already on a bed covered with a paper sheet. A blood-pressure cuff is on her arm, connected to a digital machine. A doctor is examining her and asking questions about her symptoms.

'Is she weeing?'

I am not attuned to his accent. The w sounds like a v. I look completely blank.

'Wee,' he says, 'I need to know that she has been weeing.'

Still blank – I am so dazed by the speed of developments that I have no idea what he is talking about.

'You know, going to the toilet,' he says in frustration at my stupidity.

'Yes, I think so,' I say, completely forgetting the M25, KT Tunstall's 'Other Side of the World' and the service-station wee that wasn't. Completely forgetting that more than once while we were on holiday, I had taken Ellie to the loo by the pool and she had come out saying, 'That's funny, I didn't need one after all.' Completely forgetting that just once, the day before we left France, I went to the toilet after she had not flushed the chain and there was no sign of urine in the bowl, just a tiny dark drop at the bottom that I thought for a moment might have been blood, but then dismissed the thought.

The junior doctor is by now looking very baffled. He summons the on-call paediatric consultant, Dr Davies, a some- what shambling but very amiable figure, reeking of cigarette smoke. He takes charge as Ellie is hooked to one of those vital-signs monitors you see in films, where there always comes a point when the green ziggy line goes flat and the beep-beep-beep is replaced by a shrill monotone resembling the sound that televisions used to make when being turned off. He orders an emergency chest X-ray, which sounds very ominous, and says that he will give her a diuretic.

'That's to make her wee, isn't it?' asks Paula. I can't understand why the wee is so important. And what it's got to do with the chest.

Every development now seems to take place in double time, simultaneously lasting an instant and an eternity. The result of the chest X-ray is back. The sort of thing that in normal NHS circumstances takes several days, if not weeks.

Dr Davies explains that Ellie's heart is struggling. I've noticed the monitor reading the beat at 160, but don't have any sense of what that means. He's holding up the X-ray, which is showing marked swelling of the ventricles on one side.

'This is a condition called myocardosis,' he says. 'In non-technical terms, we would call it heart failure.'

Ah, right, I think, my five-year-old daughter is in heart failure. Images flash into your mind. Newspaper headlines that speak of 'miracle surgery performed on baby born with hole in the heart'. Or my father's pallid body as he lay dead from his massive coronary – but that sort of thing happens to men in their sixties, not little girls aged five. Doesn't it?

He's clarifying now. We're not talking about a heart attack, it's rather that the heart has been struggling to do its work of pumping the blood around the body. The X-ray shows that because of all that work, the muscles have become distended. The diuretic ought to help. It should have its effect soon. Here's the plan: we'll get her a bed on McGregor ward, that's the children's ward, continue to monitor her through the night and do some more tests in the morning. Davies explains that he is a general all-round paediatrician: tomorrow we'll get a specialist cardiologist to take a look.

Meanwhile, he says, he'll just make a quick call to a colleague in Birmingham who has special expertise in this area. He might be able to offer some further advice.

We have been going up the chain of command. From GP to junior hospital doctor to consultant and now to some kind of super-consultant. From local surgery to local hospital to big city unit, home of the heavyweights. This is not good.

It's around eight o'clock. We need to do something about Tom. Ellie's going to be taken down to the ward and nothing else will happen tonight. Paula can stay with her. I can go back, explain the situation to Tom and get some bits and pieces for them for the night.

I tell the security office about how the doctor told us to rush here, which meant that I have no money to get my car out, but that I'll be back in an hour. Can I pay then? With the look of a man who's had his fill of unconvincing excuses, he writes down my name and registration number, and gives me an exit ticket.

When I get home, I'm expecting an empty house. Tom will be at Maddie's or Grace's. I burst in, intending to have a quick shower and get changed before going round to ask if he could stay for another hour while I take some nightwear and a tooth-brush over to Warwick.

But the house isn't empty. Maddie's mum, Gill, is there, with Caitlin, her older daughter. They are looking serious.

'Where's Tom?' I ask, thinking for an insane moment that the problem is with him (tree, fall? bike, car?).

'He's fine – he's having supper over at ours. Paula just phoned to say that soon after you left, Ellie took a bit of a turn for the worse. They're moving her up to Birmingham tonight. Paula's gone with them in the ambulance. There's no hurry, because it'll take them a while to get there, but when you've got what you need, you must drive to the Children's Hospital.'

The car is only a few months old and is fitted with SatNav. I've established that the Birmingham Children's Hospital is located on Steelhouse Lane and the calm-voiced digital lady is taking me there by the 'quick' route of the motorway as opposed to the 'short' one cross-country. She does a good job until we reach the centre of Birmingham itself, where it becomes apparent that the one-way system has completely changed since the navigation system was programmed. After going round twice in a circle, I'm finally on Steelhouse Lane. The parking spaces outside the hospital are all vacant. I check the meter, noting that there will be no charge until eight in the morning, but that a lot of coins will be required thereafter. With a bit of luck, Ellie will be sorted by then, allowing me to head home and explain everything to Tom.

The hospital doors are locked, the whole place seemingly deserted. My first instinct is to hammer on the glass. At last I see the buzzer and the explanatory notice that are staring me in the face. 'After 8 p.m. ring here for Security.' I do so. They tell me to go round the side, where there is a separate entrance. I find Accident and Emergency. I give Ellie's name to the receptionist. She ushers me through without having to look at her computer. I think I detect pity on her face, but I'm probably being paranoid.

I am shown into an observation room that is bristling with equipment, crowded with doctors and nurses. Fear is etched on Paula's face as I hold her. 'She's not going to die, is she?' she keeps asking. The medical staff do not know enough about what is happening to be able to say anything, either reassuring or not. All they can do is monitor, stabilize, then think about testing and investigating. They make it clear that stabilization is the priority. The ambulance had arrived with the siren going. The driver had said that it was only because there was rather a lot of traffic on the motorway, even at that time of night. But what parent would believe that that was the only reason?

Paula brought me up to date. Almost as soon as I had left, Dr Davies, the Warwick consultant, had said, 'I'm a fool, I've got it the wrong way round.' The powerful diuretic had done nothing: that meant it wasn't heart failure causing kidney failure but kidney failure causing heart failure. The kidneys had stopped working, so fluid had filled the lungs and the heart in turn was now struggling. The advance phone call from hospital to hospital, booking the emergency admission to the Birmingham Children's, had been made while the diagnosis was still heart failure, so Ellie had been admitted into the care of a cardiologist. He was young, but seemed to be in command. As each new doctor or nurse came into the little room, he briefed them. I heard terms like 'pulmonary oedema', 'platelets' and 'possible HUS or maybe even FSGS'.

They watched, they talked, they seemed uncertain what to do. I could only have been in the room a few minutes and yet it was obvious even to me that Ellie was deteriorating before our eyes. There was a failed attempt to lift her up and persuade her to get some urine out. The heartbeat and blood-pressure numbers were going up and up. Purple bruises were appearing all over her body, on the legs especially. They hadn't been there when I arrived. It was as if her whole body was shutting down, organ by organ.

She keeps losing and regaining consciousness. She is very weak.

I ask the young cardiologist what he can tell me. Just that they are working hard to stabilize her. So what are HUS and FSGS, then? 'You're going to hear a lot of technical terms being bandied about over the coming days, don't worry yourself about them for now.'

Then another doctor takes charge. He's tall, curly-haired, good-looking. Incongruously but somehow comfortingly, he is wearing Doc Marten boots, like the no-nonsense Cordelia in the Kaboodle production of *King Lear* which so affected me. I do not let myself think about how it ended for her. 'Right, let's stop messing around,' he says, 'we'll get her up to Intensive Care, sedate her and start draining her off.'

Before we know it, we have ascended in a lift and followed her bed along a corridor. We are in the cool, dimly lit haven of the Intensive Care Unit. The only noise is the bleep of the monitors above some half-dozen beds.

The booted doctor who has taken charge now introduces himself. He is Simon and he is the consultant looking after the unit for that night. He takes us through some admissions forms and parental consent documents. He explains what will happen: the first thing is to get the heart rate down. 'She's very distressed.' This clearly refers to her body state, not her emotions. Though there is no doubting that she is also very distressed in the conventional sense.

The consent form that we are signing is for them to sedate her. This will help the heart to slow. He is obliged to tell us of the risks before we sign. With sedation there is always a slight risk that the patient will not come round or that there will be some reaction or damage. But this is very rare. She really needs to be sedated. In your head, you imagine the prospect of her remaining in a persistent vegetative state, but you say nothing. You sign. You will sign anything to keep her alive.

Once she is sedated, Simon continues, they will connect her to another machine that will start drawing off the excess fluid that has filled her lungs. She is going to be connected up to a lot of lines and tubes, including a catheter, and we won't want to see them doing this, so we should see her now for a moment and then they will draw the curtain across.

She has already been stripped naked in readiness. An array of machinery is being gathered around the bed. You have a picture of it all from episodes of *ER*, but you have never imagined that you will know the reality. The farewell before she goes under is unbearable. You hold on to the hope. Of course she will come round. Of course this is not *that* goodbye. But nothing is certain any more.

When we see her again, she is serene. Very, very still. You mustn't make the comparison, but you do: like a corpse. A ventilator is doing her breathing for her. The draining machine is beginning its work. Wires trail from her every extremity. A drip is nourishing her with saline. It lets out a ping every few minutes, scaring us until a nurse explains that it is just a faulty alarm. The good news is that the monitor is already showing a steadier heart and pulse. For the first time, there is some sense of stability as opposed to panic. The spontaneous bruising, which was the most terrifying thing, seems to have eased. The catastrophe has been averted, or at least suspended. It is the best that can be hoped for. Two nurses are assigned to watch. Vital signs to be checked every five minutes.

Now someone else has arrived. Another young consultant, a woman this time. She is smartly dressed in what is obviously not a work outfit. She has been on call, come in from some social event. She introduces herself as Catherine, a consultant paediatric nephrologist. That is to say, a children's kidney expert. Simon has briefed her, towering above her in those Doc Martens. She sits us down for a chat. For a moment, this feels good: it must be serious for her to have been called in, but she is obviously the woman with the answers. She will tell us what is wrong and how they will fix it.

Catherine begins by asking us what we do for a living. What's that got to do with it? Paula realizes, though I do not, that it is in order to gauge her language. The protocol must be to establish a level of education and to adapt accordingly. Is there some scale they learn in their training, an equation which gives people with university degrees the full truth, those who leave school at sixteen a simplified version? This is Birmingham, where there is a babel of languages among the anxious parents in A & E. Are there on-call translators as well as on-call consultants?

What she says next does not require any level of educational attainment: 'I wish I could tell you for sure that your little girl will come through this, but I can't.' These are words to which there is no reply.

There is not yet much to get technical about. Ellie is clearly in massive kidney failure. The cause is unknown. Catherine is honest: it is an unusual presentation and one that has them puzzled. Usually there is a history. Gradual degeneration. Complaints of tiredness for a period of months, even years. Diminution of urine output. We have said that she has no prior medical history. We can confirm this? Yes, we confirm it. She was born five weeks premature and initially had some breathing problems, but that all cleared up. No history of urine infections or anything of that kind. She did have what seems to have been a rather persistent tummy bug when we were on holiday – we explain about the two trips to the doctor earlier in the day. Can it really be the same day? No, it's just past midnight now.

There are sudden viral infections that can attack the kidneys. This is a possibility that will have to be looked at. A battery of blood tests is already under way in the lab. The obvious question: 'If it's a virus, does that mean she'll get better fairly quickly, like with a normal virus?' It must be a good thing if it's *just a virus*, not a congenital condition. Mustn't it? Well, no, Catherine explains, it's not that simple. We really can't tell at the moment what the longer-term outlook is. We just need to concentrate on getting her through the night.

Do we have any other questions? We have a hundred, but are too tired and too scared to ask them.

'So what you're saying,' I hazard, 'is that you really don't know what's wrong with her, apart from that it's kidneys?'

She nods.

'That's rather scary, isn't it?' She cannot disagree.

'Yes, it is,' she said, 'but it can only be a good thing for you to talk about your feelings.'

She tells us a little more about how important the kidneys are. Paula just wants the prognosis, however bad. I want detail, as much in the way of technicalities as I can take in. Information is a defence. It becomes clear that kidneys are very remarkable, very important, multi-purpose organs. The sky-high blood pressure, for example: I had no idea that kidneys had a role in regulating blood pressure.

What did I know of kidneys? Nothing, except that we have two of them and they are something to do with the production of urine. And that they were the first organs to be transplanted successfully. Their key function, Catherine is explaining, is to expel not only fluid but also toxins. The problem with kidney failure is not just the fluid overload that is causing the lungs to fill and the heart to struggle. It is also the toxins. But that is enough for now. She encourages us to get some rest. A long night and long days are ahead of us. We will not want to leave Ellie's side, but if we can bear to, we should take turns to try to sleep a little in the parents' room. They can't provide a proper bed tonight, but on subsequent nights arrangements will be made.

Paula will not retreat to the parents' room. She will watch her daughter's motionless body all night, stroke her hair and talk to her. She only leaves the bedside once, to phone her own mother soon after Catherine departs. I advise against: it's one in the morning, there's nothing Ellie's Nan can do, and once she knows what's happened she'll be awake all night, sick with anxiety. But for Paula there is no question. Her mother has to know. The phone call is the only time in the long night when she allows herself to cry.

After the call, I stay in the parents' room for a while, trying to grab some sleep on a hard, insufficiently long sofa. Pulling a blanket over me, I pray – not something I do habitually, but the thing almost all of us do at such a time. Why a five-year-old child, why not me? Let it be me instead. If she recovers, I will do anything. If she survives, I will do anything. Please, Lord, if you are there, prove it now. Then the fatigue, the emotion and the fear well up and I weep, I howl uncontrollably. I am at a personal ground zero. There is a terror, a raw pain. I have seen my father's body and was there at the moment my mother died – peacefully, gracefully. That was part of the cycle of things. This is something else. A child should not die.

After the tears, I go back into the ICU. Nothing has changed. The doctors are gathering around another bed. Paula sees that I have been crying. My weakness adds to her strength. At the same time, she knows that there will be times when it will be the other way round. That is how we will get through it together. It will bring us closer than ever. We will get through it together. As long as Ellie comes through it. The long night will end. I will do anything to make it end.

A kidney can be transplanted. There is hope. Perhaps my kidney will be a match. What a gift that would be. And as I toss and turn on the sofa in the parents' room, the words come to me just before dawn, bringing some modest comfort. Not Shakespeare's words, but Eliot's, inspired by Shakespeare:

> This form, this face, this life
> Living to live in a world of time beyond me; let me
> Resign my life for this life.

★

Just before eight in the morning, I remember the parking meter. I go down to put some coins in. But there is already a yellow ticket on the windscreen. How can this be? The notice said that parking was free until eight o'clock. Some mistake, surely.

When I decipher the citation, I discover that the offence is that I am 'incorrectly parked in bay'. My wheels are indeed a metre or so outside the marking. Hardly a hanging offence, considering the state I was in when I arrived the previous night. Suddenly the anguish, the fear and the tiredness turn to anger. Two policemen happen to be chatting on the other side of the road. I will complain.

I march over and begin my speech. They cut me off and tell me that I must take up the matter with the officer who issued the ticket. I should ask inside the police station, which happens to be right there opposite the Children's Hospital. I go in and demand to speak to officer M365. The desk sergeant reluctantly agrees to establish whether said officer is still on shift. Time passes. Then M365 arrives. He is about to knock off. I hand him the ticket. The speech again: I followed an ambulance in, late the previous night, my five-year-old daughter was being brought in with suspected heart failure. I have spent the whole night in Intensive Care. Then made a point of going down to put money in the meter before the charging period began at eight o'clock. Granted, I am not strictly inside the parking bay, but my wheels are only out by a couple of feet.

The officer looks at me as if I am mildly deranged. He judges, though, that at such a time in the morning this is unlikely to be a fabricated excuse, of which he has heard so many. He opens a large handwritten ledger, like something out of Dickens. After scrutinizing it for an interminable period, he rears himself up to his full height and dignity and says, 'In the circumstances, sir, I will *re-sin* this ticket.' He pauses, satisfied with that word *re-sin*. Then his voice modulates out of police-speak. 'And I *do* hope your daughter pulls through, sir.'

I cross the road to my car and notice for the first time that it is a one-way street. Thanks to the inadequacies of SatNav lady, I have driven down it the wrong way. The reason I am 'incorrectly parked in bay' is not some mild infraction of two feet but the fact that I am facing in the direction which makes it quite clear that I have driven in illegally. I contrive to reverse into the hospital entrance, turn the car round, park in another bay and put my money in before receiving a second ticket. Or do I mean re-sinning?

There are difficult phone calls to make. But I pause for a moment and smile. That policeman, with his glorious mala-propism of *re-sin* for *rescind*. He is Dogberry, the most lovable of Shakespeare's clowns. *Much Ado About Nothing* is another of those plays about getting a second chance, losing someone and getting them back. The scheming villain's plot is unwittingly exposed by the bumbling Constable and his watchmen. Dogberry, who gets his words wrong but is the embodiment of innocence and kindness:

Our watch, sir, have indeed comprehended two auspicious persons, and we would have them this morning examined before your worship . . . Marry, sir, they have committed false report; moreover, they have spoken untruths; secondarily, they are slanders; sixth and lastly, they have belied a lady; thirdly, they have verified unjust things; and, to conclude, they are lying knaves.

All will end well, Shakespeare seems to say, because there are Dogberrys in this world. And because there are Dogberrys, the weight of sad times may be lifted in a moment of laughter. I remember Dr Johnson reminding us that Shakespeare's plays are never all tragedy, never all comedy, but rather that they are like the real world, in which *joy and sorrow* are *mingled* and *in which, at the same time, the reveller is hasting to his wine, and the mourner burying his friend; in which the malignity of one is sometimes defeated by the frolick of another; and many mischiefs and many benefits are done and hindered without design.*

★

It's often assumed that Hamnet Shakespeare died of bubonic plague. That is possible, though there is no record of an epidemic in Stratford-upon-Avon in the summer of 1596. It is more likely that there was some other cause. Child mortality was very common. It could just as well have been kidney failure. There was no dialysis then, let alone transplantation.

What we can say for sure is that there is no surviving work in which Shakespeare writes directly about the death of his first and only son. Biographers sometimes suggest that he shrouded his grief in some beautiful lines in *King John*, spoken by Queen

Constance. Her son Arthur has been imprisoned and she is so wracked with grief that she seems to be mad – though she insists that she is not. *If I were mad, I should forget my son*, she says. She *feels the plague* of her calamity all too well:

> Grief fills the room up of my absent child:
> Lies in his bed, walks up and down with me,
> Puts on his pretty looks, repeats his words,
> Remembers me of all his gracious parts,
> Stuffs out his vacant garments with his form.

What do you do with the clothes of a dead child? Can you even bear to clear out the closet? For a moment, the imagery makes you believe that Shakespeare must have known grief like Constance's, but then you recall that his gift of putting feelings into words extended to a universe of things he could not possibly have experienced himself. Besides, the date of *King John* is fiercely contested by scholars: it is not at all certain that he wrote it after Hamnet's death.

Ben Jonson was more willing to scratch at his own wounded self. In 1603, as London was engulfed with plague, he decamped to the home of a wealthy patron in the country, leaving his family behind in the city. One night he dreamed – fearfully, guiltily – that his seven-year-old son appeared to him in the semblance of a man *with the Marke of a bloodie crosse on his fore-head as if it had been cutted with a sword*. In London, whenever someone in a household contracted the plague, the family would be locked in for forty days' quarantine, a red cross marking the door and a man keeping watch. The day after the night of the dream, a letter arrived from Jonson's wife: the boy was dead.

At the core of the Cambridge degree in English was the

discipline of Practical Criticism, as pioneered in the 1920s by a tutor called I. A. Richards. It required the attentive line-by-line reading of a poem, without prior knowledge of its authorship or historical context. We went for our 'Prat Crit' classes to a narrow house in a narrow lane called Portugal Place, where we would be welcomed by the smiling figure of Dr Glen Cavaliero, a poet himself, who would hand out dog-eared carbon-copy pages on which he had typed out that week's poems or passages of prose. We squeezed into his front parlour, where there was barely room to move between the grand piano, the guttering gas fire and the floor-to-ceiling bookshelves. It was there that I encountered Jonson's 'On my First Son':

> Farewell, thou child of my right hand, and joy;
> My sin was too much hope of thee, lov'd boy,
> Seven years thou wert lent to me, and I thee pay,
> Exacted by thy fate, on the just day.
> O, could I lose all father now! For why
> Will man lament the state he should envy?
> To have so soon scap'd world's and flesh's rage,
> And, if no other misery, yet age?
> Rest in soft peace, and, ask'd, say, 'Here doth lie
> *Ben Jonson* his best piece of poetry.'
> For whose sake henceforth all his vows be such,
> As what he loves may never like too much.

Probing beneath the seemingly simple surface, Glen helped us to discover how the poem was packed with as much thought as emotion. He explained that 'Benjamin' in Hebrew means 'son of the right hand' and that the Greek word *poiesis* means 'making', so that a child is a poem and a poem is a child. We explored the idea that children are only *lent* to their parents, who will be fined (*exacted*) by time or fate if they take them for granted. We argued over whether it might be a relief not to live the aches of old age. We worked out how the rhetoric of the poem built to the conclusion that if you lose someone you love with all your heart, then you may make yourself vow that you will hold some part of yourself back from all your future loves, because if you love them *too much* you will only have to go through this grief again. And so we came to see that in each line there was complexity and reality and struggle.

Glen was another of my teachers who was mad about literature. An only child, he was a compulsive reader from an early age. Like Forster, about whom he wrote an excellent book, he went to Tonbridge School. Shortly after he graduated from university, on a singular day that he would never forget, his father's business was declared bankrupt and his mother dropped dead without any prior medical history. His response was to become ordained in the Church of England. But then he had a crisis of faith, closely related to his sexuality, so he took refuge in the kingdom of literature instead.

He taught me that every great literary work is a voyage to Illyria. You step ashore in a world that is and is not like your own. You turn your head to the sea and are opened to a distant horizon. Venturing in, you find solace, stimulation, surprise and companionship in moments of recognition and of unexpected revelation. The power of an author, Glen believed, in the spirit of Dr Johnson, was to make new things familiar and familiar things new. The writer's way of doing that, he told us, quoting Coleridge, was to choose the best words and to combine *a more than usual state of emotion with more than usual order; judgement ever awake and steady self-possession with enthusiasm and feeling profound or vehement.* As painters have traditionally learned their craft by imitating the Old Masters, so there was no better preparation for a life of writing than the close reading of passages in which these gifts were made manifest.

The epitaph and the elegy, poems in remembrance of the dead, he reminded us, are among the most ancient and enduring forms of writing. The last line of Jonson's poem in memory of his *best piece of poetry* is in fact a translation of the closing line of an epigram by the Roman poet Martial about a beautiful dead enslaved boy:

> *Quidquid amas, cupias non placuisse nimis*
> Whatever you love, pray that it may not please you too
> much.

Martial, dead for fifteen hundred years, gave Jonson the words to express his own feelings. So Jonson and Shakespeare can give us words when we need them.

★

After the draining weeks, first in Intensive Care and then on the nephrology ward, we are sent home, trained in the art of delivering nightly peritoneal dialysis. An elaborate hand-washing routine for the avoidance of infection, a dressing removed every night and renewed every morning, a machine plugged into a child's body. Her cries of pain each hour on the hour as the extraction cycle begins. 'Just one last thing,' Catherine says as we leave, thanking her and all the NHS team for saving our daughter, 'it's not the time to make any big decisions in your lives.' We look at each other knowingly: we have already made a decision. We are going to have another baby. We do not want the home to be dominated by illness; we want Ellie to have something to look forward to. As soon as Harry is born, she becomes a carer instead of a cared-for.

Just over a year later, they are ready to begin the work-up towards transplant. Blood tests reveal that my kidney is a match. Disappointingly, though, they do not want to use it. The surgeon is casual: 'The virus might still be in her body – it could attack the new kidney and we'd lose it within weeks. We don't want to waste your good kidney. First time round, we'll throw one in from a cadaver and wait to see what happens. If it takes, she could get a good few years out of it and then we'll have yours ready and waiting. So you must stay fit.'

To begin with, every time the phone rings you think it is going to be *the call*. In the early months we are so diligent that wherever we go, we check the five little bars on the mobile to make sure that there is a signal. I am paranoid about missing the call. Gradually, though, I relax my guard, then I become careless. Every now and then I forget to charge the phone or leave it turned off in a meeting. We stop checking the messages the instant we return home from the school run or the shops. We travel a little further from the hospital, spend a few more hours out of contact.

We are popular with the community nursing team because we do not ask for too much. We regard our lives as easy in comparison to those of parents whose children have special needs of other kinds – autism, behavioural disorders, rare conditions affecting brain development. Dialysis has become part of our nightly routine. It dominates our lives, but the performance of evening set-up, nightly alarm correction and morning disconnection has become a steadying ritual. For the team, a child with no kidneys is a rarity. Day in, day out, we are required to create sterile conditions and initiate a complex medical procedure which lasts for eleven hours a night, without which our six-year-old daughter would die. Most of the time, the work of a community nurse must be routine, even dull, in comparison to that on an acute hospital ward. Home dialysis offers them a touch of the cutting edge. So they are queuing up to learn how to operate the machine. Instead of getting respite once a month, it will now be once a week. They have the joyful bonus of baby Harry rolling on the floor, smiling and gurgling. Our adult life is beginning to return. We talk eagerly of movies, theatre trips, meals out, half knowing that our appetite for such things is only so great because we have been deprived of them – chances are, when we can go out, we won't want to.

We have been told that the normal pattern is for surgery to take place in the afternoon. First the surgeon will deal with that day's emergencies, then he (all the surgeons, it seems, are 'he') will perform the transplant. My mental picture of a midnight traffic accident, a kidney plucked still warm from the wreckage and rushed to a ready operating theatre is all wrong.

What will happen is quieter, sadder, planned. In a hospital somewhere, brain-stem death will be established. Consents will be obtained. A family will say goodbye. A heart will go on beating, courtesy of a ventilator. The donor, now legally dead, will be wheeled into theatre and anaesthetized (troubling, that) prior to the removal of the organs. That will happen in the morning and Ellie will receive her kidney in the afternoon.

At monthly clinic, Catherine says she is a little surprised that Ellie has not yet had 'an offer'. Children get priority, the match score is first-rate, she's been on the list for six months. After a year, the matchability criteria will be reduced: at the moment, the computer is rejecting all incoming kidneys with fewer than four out of six matching antigens. Just before Christmas that will go down to three.

Paula tells her mother some things that she doesn't tell me. For instance, that she is convinced *the call* will come in May. Time and again, she has demonstrated her quasi-psychic powers. She is a mother, so she knows. We fathers do what we can, blundering in with practical help, but there is a whole other dimension – the stuff of instinct – where we flounder. Our attempts to organize, to manage, are ultimately counterproductive. We do the best we can, but we often say the wrong thing. With our focus on questions such as whether or not the phone is charged, we are simple creatures. There are encounter groups for carers, but there is no one out there to train men in the art of saying the right thing at the right time to a mother who is living day and night with a child's acute medical needs. Mothers and fathers do have different ways of coping, and that's one of the reasons why drift and strain break apart so many couples who live with chronically ill or special needs children.

Whitsun half-term arrives, and Paula tells her mum that she is surprised because she always thought it would be in May. 'May's not over yet,' says her mum.

For a couple of weeks now, I haven't given it a thought. But then a news story breaks. A Dutch television channel is to broadcast a new reality show, produced by the makers of *Big Brother*. It is to be called *The Big Donor Show*. A woman who is dying of cancer will donate a kidney to one of three contestants. Viewers will help her to make up her mind by texting in votes for the candidate who makes the best case for their need. Dutch government and British press are in a state of moral panic. This is a new low for reality TV. The programme must be banned.

To anyone who knows anything about the procedure – which means us, but apparently not the media – it doesn't make sense. Something is fishy. Would organs really be accepted from a terminal cancer patient? Surely not even in the Netherlands do dying donors *decide* who is to receive their organs? Besides, shouldn't there be two winners, one for each of the poor woman's kidneys? And what about the matchability criteria? Someone is on the radio, saying that it should be doctors and not the tele-vision-viewing public who make such decisions. But that is wrong: it is not doctors who decide, it is the computer. The organ goes to the patient on the list with the best match, because that is what gives the organ the best chance of long-term survival. The advance publicity for the programme has said nothing about the role of tissue-matching in the selection of the contestants. Still, the controversy has put the question of organ donation on to the front pages and the top of the news bulletins across Europe. That can only be a good thing. Eventually, the whole charade is revealed to be a hoax contrived for precisely that purpose.

The day after the story breaks, Paula takes Tom and Ellie to visit their cousins in London. I look after Harry. I try calling in the late afternoon, but her phone is turned off. They get home late, having been caught on the M25 in rain and traffic of equal heaviness. Ellie is shattered. I carry her up to bed. The dialysis machine is set for the usual eleven hours' treatment. Because it is half-term, she can stay connected in the morning, so it does not matter that the drain-and-fill cycle is beginning at half past nine instead of the usual eight o'clock.

Paula is equally exhausted from the day and the drive. She falls into a deep sleep.

At a quarter past midnight the phone rings. My first thought is that someone, probably drunk, has misdialled – our number is one digit away from that of Othello Taxis. But the woman's voice says my name. My heart is now racing. For most people, the unexpected call in the night means an illness or death in the family. Not for us. This must be it. *The call.*

All I say is 'Yes. That's good. We'll be there.'

Paula leaps out of bed. 'Give me the phone.' She calls back. She and the nurse laugh at the maleness of my (lack of) reaction. 'I did wonder whether he really understood,' says the nurse, 'People usually scream or cry.'

We must be at the hospital at six in the morning for prep. The operation will be in the afternoon. We should let Ellie sleep. She will have a long day and many weeks of recuperation. Paula phones her parents. She and her mother were right about May: it is the morning of the thirty-first. Her dad says, 'Tonight is not about you, not even about Ellie. Tonight we all pray for the person who has died, and their family.'

Of course we are curious. When we ask, they are not initially supposed to tell us. But someone in the hospital says, 'Don't be surprised if she wakes up with a craving for a curry and a beer.' Apparently there really are cases where the recipient of a transplant develops the tastes of the donor. Motorcycle accidents are the source of an exceptionally high proportion of organs. Bikers are generous. But we are apprehensive at the prospect of our skinny little daughter walking around with the kidney of a burly rider. She makes a joke of it. Riding, after all, is her passion. When we wake her to tell her that the kidney is in, all she says is, 'How long will it be before I can be back on my pony?'

We wait while she is in theatre. As on the night in Intensive

Care, there is nothing to read. *Time travels in divers paces with divers persons*, says Rosalind in *As You Like It*. These are the longest four hours. We go to the Bullring and buy nightwear for Ellie, not knowing how long she will have to remain in hospital. Initially she will be in isolation to guard her from infection. My mobile rings: 'They've nearly finished, you'd better come back now.'

As soon as we see the surgeon and his team walking down the corridor, we know from the spring in their step that it has gone well. 'Sorry it took so long, it was quite a big one, and she's very small – bit of a struggle to fit it in. But she started urinating all over the table the moment we plugged it in, and that's a very good sign.' Not a drop for two years and now an instant flood. Some lines from a Shakespeare play about a doctor's daughter came to my mind: *They say miracles are past . . .* But they are not: Helen has cured the King of his fistula. *All's Well That Ends Well*.

It is not the end of the battle for Ellie. The immunosuppression regime will require her to take eighty pills a week, and the transplanted kidney will not last for ever. It is a beginning. *The awakened, lips parted, the hope, the new ships*.

Since the transplant has been successful, she is given the opportunity to write to the unnamed family of the donor, via the hospital. They might reply, we are told, but many families do not. We learn that it was not a biker after all. There was some mix-up. It was the kidney of a twenty-one-year-old girl who had died of a brain tumour. We ache for her family, but there is nothing we can offer other than words.

A transplant is not a miracle. It is modern medicine of a kind that not even Shakespeare could dream. Later, we ask ourselves what we can give back. The work of editing Shakespeare has been my survival tool through the two years of dialysis and the wait for the call, but the teaching of literature has come to seem an indulgence. Literary criticism, cultural theory, deconstruction – what was the point when the only thing that matters is health?

Then Paula recalls the long night in the ICU. The parents' room where there was nothing to read but dog-eared copies of *Hello* magazine. As if it would help anyone at such a time to be invited into the gaudy home of some Z-list celebrity. She had taken comfort instead from a prayer card, given to her by a friend, that happened to be at the bottom of her bag. The revelation of Julian of Norwich that T. S. Eliot had quoted in 'Little Gidding': *all shall be well, and all shall be well, and all manner of thing shall be well.* She had recited the words over and over.

'Why don't we put together an anthology of stress-relieving poems and give it to hospital waiting rooms and doctors' surgeries? Maybe hospices and prisons and mental-health units, too. A sort of Gideon Bible for people of any faith or none.' And that is what we did. When we received a letter from a reader that began, 'Your book has literally saved my life', I wished that Dr Johnson had been alive to nod his approval.

*

There is a tide in the affairs of men. Every life ebbs and flows like the tide, the waves leaving high and low watermarks.

Virginia Woolf, haunted by the childhood memory of the waves breaking on the beach at St Ives, saw this and saw that writing is one way of tracking the tide, marking the pattern, revealing some order, making sense of a life. There are what she called *Moments of Being* when, with splendour, everything seems to cohere. Strangely, such moments may come with peculiar force in reaction to a shock, a blow, a pain. Literature is a way of staying these moments:

> The shock-receiving capacity is what makes me a writer. I hazard the explanation that a shock is at once in my case followed by the desire to explain it. I feel that I have had a blow; but it is not, as I thought as a child, simply a blow from an enemy hidden behind the cotton wool of daily life; it is or will become a revelation of some order; it is a token of some real thing behind appearances; and I make it real by putting it into words. It is only by putting it into words that I make it whole; this wholeness means that it has lost its power to hurt me; it gives me, perhaps because by doing so I take away the pain, a great delight to put the severed parts together.

★

June 2016. For nine years now the new kidney has been functioning well. Ellie has grown into a teenager, taller than her peers, no longer stunted by the dialysis. She is a fearless rider at country horse shows. She has persuaded us to buy a puppy and I have agreed, on condition that it has a part in the production of *Twelfth Night* that the students are staging in our Oxford garden to mark the four-hundredth anniversary of Shakespeare's death.

From the moment that I moved into the house, with its gravel walk in front of a row of impeccably clipped yew trees, I have known that this will be the perfect stage for the Malvolio letter scene. He is, of course, overheard by Sir Toby and Sir Andrew, but I've never known what to do with Fabian, the straight man in the scene. It has to be one of the most boring little parts in Shakespeare. We couldn't ask a student to give up their time for that, so we decide to keep Maria together with the two roistering knights hiding behind the hedge, to redistribute Fabian's lines between the three of them, and to cast Coco Chanel the Havanese puppy as 'Fabian, the Lady Olivia's loyal servant'. She is trained to love Olivia and Sir Toby, but to resist when Malvolio tries to take her for a walk. Not even canine Fabian likes the man in black, who will soon turn yellow.

Thanks to Ellie's skill as dog wrangler and some strategically placed Parma ham in Sir Toby's doublet, the trick has worked a treat. The weather has held all through the week of the performances and word has spread that this will be a production to remember, that it will earn its place in the annals of outdoor student Shakespeare, even be spoken of in the same breath as the fabled *Tempest* which ended with Ariel running to freedom across the surface of the college lake.

Now, on the last night, clouds are gathering. The reunion of brother and sister, walking towards each other across the grass stage in mirror motion, pricks tears into my eyes. I wonder what my father, who was so close to his sister Joan, thought of this scene when he saw Peggy Ashcroft play Viola a few months before the beginning of the war; and I remember Virginia Woolf's memory of this moment when she saw the play at the Old Vic in 1933, still mourning, nearly thirty years on, the loss of her brother Thoby:

Perhaps the most impressive effect in the play is achieved by the long pause which Sebastian and Viola make as they stand looking at each other in a silent ecstasy of recognition. The reader's eye may have slipped over that moment entirely. Here we are made to pause and think about it; and are reminded that Shakespeare wrote for the body and for the mind simultaneously.

And then, in the soft summer evening, the cast move to the back of the audience and they hum in time to the words sung by Feste, who sits on the stone balustrade of the steps that lead up to the house, leaning against the golden Cotswold stone, picked out in a solitary spotlight:

When that I was and a little tiny boy,
With hey, ho, the wind and the rain,
A foolish thing was but a toy,
For the rain it raineth every day . . .

A great while ago the world begun,
With hey, ho, the wind and the rain,
But that's all one, our play is done,
And we'll strive to please you every day.

At this moment, as the audience rise in applause, the skies open. The crew rush to move the lighting rig indoors and the crowd scatters for home, laughing at the divine stage effect. I look to the far end of the lawn, where Ellie is letting Coco run free as a reward for her patient performance. And Ellie herself is running, barefoot in the rain, her tread as light as it had ever been on the Mediterranean sand in the days before her illness.

And for me, it is a Moment of Being:

Voyage to Illyria

From this I reach what I might call a philosophy; at any rate it is a constant idea of mine; that behind the cotton wool is hidden a pattern; that we – I mean all human beings – are connected with this; that the whole world is a work of art; that we are parts of the work of art. *Hamlet* or a Beethoven quartet is the truth about this vast mass that we call the world. But there is no Shakespeare, there is no Beethoven . . . we are the words; we are the music; we are the thing itself.

But that's all one, our play is done:
Indyana Schneider as Feste in *Twelfth Night*
(Worcester College, Oxford, June 2016)

Acknowledgements

I told my wonderful editor Arabella Pike at William Collins that I wanted to write a memoir about my life with Shakespeare and a book about the effect of mental illness on some writers I have loved, including Samuel Johnson, Edward Thomas, Virginia Woolf and Sylvia Plath. She saw, as I had not, that by yoking the two themes into a single book I might alleviate some of the self-absorption that is inevitable in a memoir and test the proposition that literature in general, and Shakespeare in particular, may bring solace in the face of adversity. Whether or not I have succeeded is for the reader to decide, but I am deeply grateful to Arabella for giving me the opportunity to try.

My account of different actors' approach to *King Lear* was given a trial run in *The Lancet*, where I also wrote about Burton's *Anatomy of Melancholy*; my memory of Cheek by Jowl's *As You Like It* draws on a more detailed account that I contributed to a book in honour of Stanley Wells, my guiding light in writing about Shakespeare in the theatre and for the common reader.

Stephen Pickles read a draft with a friendly but very sharp eye and ear, and much has changed as a result: my thanks. Philip Davis encouraged me to go on when I nearly stopped after the first two chapters. I am grateful to my copy-editor, Linden Lawson, and to Iain Hunt and Jo Thompson at William Collins. Ernest Michael Bate, Richard Bate, Jon Campbell, Ian Huish and Christopher Ridgway helped me to remember my past. Paula Byrne has been my present joy for more than twenty-five years. Tom, Ellie and Harry Bate are my future, and Ellie especially has been kind in letting me write about things that are painful to recall and record. Ian McKellen, Simon Russell Beale and Simon Callow generously allowed me to report private conversations.

The book is an elegy for a lost age of youthful reading and a tribute to my teachers in both the classroom and the theatre. If it reignites a passion for Shakespeare (or indeed for literature more generally) in just a few teachers burdened by the bureaucracy and constraints of today's assessment regimes, it will have done its work.

★

Shakespearean quotations are from *The RSC Shakespeare: Complete Works*, edited by Jonathan Bate and Eric Rasmussen (Macmillan, London, and The Modern Library, New York, 2007).

For purposes of criticism, the book includes insubstantial quotations from the following works that remain in copyright: A. Alvarez, *The Savage God* (Weidenfeld & Nicolson, 1971); W. H. Auden, *Another Time* (Faber and Faber, 1940); *The Diary of 85 (Essex) Medium Battery Royal Artillery 1943–1945*, edited by Monty Bate (W. J. Parrett, 1947); Peter Brook, *The Empty Space* (McGibbon and Kee, 1968, repr. Penguin, 1972); T. S. Eliot, *Collected Poems 1909–1935* (Faber and Faber, 1936) and *Four Quartets* (Faber and Faber, 1944, repr. 1959); William Empson, *The Structure of Complex Words* (Chatto & Windus, 1951); L. P. Hartley, *The Go-Between* (Hamish Hamilton, 1953, repr. Penguin, 1958); Ted Hughes, Introduction to *A Choice of*

Acknowledgements

Emily Dickinson's Verse (Faber and Faber, 1968) and *The Letters of Ted Hughes*, selected and edited by Christopher Reid (Faber and Faber, 2007); Robert Lowell, *Robert Lowell's Poems: A Selection* (Faber and Faber, 1974), *The Dolphin* (Farrar, Straus and Giroux, 1973) and *The Letters of Robert Lowell*, edited by Saskia Hamilton (Farrar, Straus and Giroux, 2005); Charles Marowitz, *'A Macbeth': Freely Adapted from Shakespeare's Tragedy* (Calder and Boyars, 1971); Vladimir Nabokov, *Bend Sinister* (Henry Holt, 1947, repr. Penguin, 1974); Sylvia Plath, *Ariel* (Faber and Faber, 1965) and *The Bell Jar* (Harper and Row, 1971); Vita Sackville-West, *Knole and the Sackvilles* (Ernest Benn, 1969); C. H. Sisson, *In the Trojan Ditch: Collected Poems and Selected Translations* (Carcanet, 1975); L. C. ('Kim') Taylor, Introduction to *Experiments in Education at Sevenoaks* (Constable, 1965); Helen Thomas, *As It Was and World Without End* (William Heinemann, 1935, repr. Faber and Faber, 1972).

The poetry anthology mentioned in the final chapter is *Stressed Unstressed: Classic Poems to Ease the Mind* (William Collins, 2016), all royalties from which support the work of the ReLit Foundation for reading and well-being (relitfoundation.org).

Picture Credits

Chapter 1: © Ernest Bate

Chapter 2: © Bill Boaden (Creative Commons License)

Chapter 4: © Shutterstock

Chapter 5: © Tristram Kenton / Lebrecht Music and Arts / Granger (*Antony and Cleopatra*)

Chapter 6: © Edward Thomas Archive, Special Collections, Cardiff University

Chapter 9: © Joe Cocks, The Shakespeare Centre, Stratford-upon-Avon

Chapter 12: © dreamstime.com (Knole); © the Library of Leonard and Virginia Woolf at Manuscripts, Archives, and Special Collections, Washington State University Libraries (Woolf bookplate)

Chapter 13: © Peter K. Steinberg (Sylvia Plath's Shakespeare, with the kind permission of Mortimer Rare Book Collection, Smith College, and the Estate of Sylvia Plath); © Tracksimages.com / Alamy Stock Photo (Beatles)

Chapter 15: © original photography by Daniel Kim

Other photographs are public domain images from the author's collection.